Lalita A. Manrai, PhD
Ajay K. Manrai, PhD
Editors

# Global Perspectives in Cross-Cultural and Cross-National Consumer Research

*Pre-Publication
REVIEWS,
COMMENTARIES,
EVALUATIONS...*

"*Global Perspectives in Cross-Cultural and Cross-National Research* provides a much needed collection of readings, each of which links specific consumer behavior concepts to the study of International Marketing. The authors explicitly take cultural factors into account while discussing and developing new theories of Consumer Behavior. Some of the chapters provide empirical evidence which attempts to validate existing Consumer Behavior theories, using a diverse set of cross-cultural comparisons and contrasts, extending to contexts such as Europe, Japan, Poland, Romania, and Germany, among others. In addition, methodological issues, such as scale validation and measurement techniques, are evaluated in terms of cultural differences.

For those who are involved in the study and research of international mar-

*More pre-publication*
*REVIEWS, COMMENTARIES, EVALUATIONS...*

kets, this book is an important addition to their library. It integrates the complexity of culture with cutting-edge issues in international marketing, and links them clearly with the study of Consumer Research.

The chapters have clear extensions to existing Consumer Research, through an array provided by the editors, which depicts each chapter by cultures and nations studied, the cultural components involved, the constructs and processes which are considered, and the specific concepts drawn from Consumer Behavior. The chapters provide a wealth of integrating charts, cross-disciplinary linkages, and excellent comprehensive references, which should be welcomed heartily by international scholars.

*Global Perspectives* is a welcome departure from studies which simply apply traditional theories in cross-cultural contexts, without directly asking first whether those concepts and theories are relevant, applicable, and stable when used in other cultures. Instead, the authors challenge us to critically examine Consumer Research methods, before delving into cross-cultural studies. They set an important high standard for future research."

**Carol Felker Kaufman, PhD**
*Associate Professor of Marketing*
*Rutgers University School of Business*

"*Global Perspectives in Cross-Cultural and Cross-National Consumer Research*, edited by Lalita Manrai and Ajay Manrai, offers a collection of ten papers encompassing various aspects of cross-cultural consumer research. Almost all parts of the world receive attention from the authors who originate themselves from a large variety of countries: North America, Western and Eastern Europe, Asia. Unlike most reading-books, this one provides a strong introductory chapter in which the contributions of the various articles are identified and cast into a general framework. The papers are well balanced between conceptual and empirical contributions. They refer to various cultural environments, cultural componants and consequences, and consumer behavior concepts.

This set of readings is a must for any person interested in the study of the cultural aspects of international consumer behavior, and especially for researchers in the field."

**René Y. Darmon, PhD**
*Associate Dean, Research,*
*ESSEC, Paris-Cergy, France*

# Global Perspectives in Cross-Cultural and Cross-National Consumer Research

ALL INTERNATIONAL BUSINESS PRESS
BOOKS AND JOURNALS ARE PRINTED
ON CERTIFIED ACID-FREE PAPER

# Global Perspectives in Cross-Cultural and Cross-National Consumer Research

Lalita A. Manrai, PhD
Ajay K. Manrai, PhD
Editors

International Business Press
An Imprint of
The Haworth Press, Inc.
New York • London

Published by

International Business Press, 10 Alice Street, Binghamton, NY 13904-1580 USA

International Business Press is an imprint of The Haworth Press, Inc., 10 Alice Street, Binghamton, NY 13904-1580.

*Global Perspectives in Cross-Cultural and Cross-National Consumer Research* has also been published as *Journal of International Consumer Marketing*, Volume 8, Numbers 3/4 1996.

©1996 by The Haworth Press, Inc. All rights reserved. No part of this work may be reproduced or utilized in any form or by any means, electronic or mechanical, including photocopying, microfilm and recording, or by any information storage and retrieval system, without permission in writing from the publisher. Printed in the United States of America.

The development, preparation, and publication of this work has been undertaken with great care. However, the publisher, employees, editors, and agents of The Haworth Press and all imprints of The Haworth Press, Inc., including The Haworth Medical Press and Pharmaceutical Products Press, are not responsible for any errors contained herein or for consequences that may ensue from use of materials or information contained in this work. Opinions expressed by the author(s) are not necessarily those of The Haworth Press, Inc.

### Library of Congress Cataloging-in-Publication Data

Global perspectives in cross-cultural and cross-national consumer research / Lalita A. Manrai, Ajay K. Manrai, editors.
    p. cm.
    "Has also been published as Journal of international consumer marketing, volume 8, numbers 3/4, 1996"–T.p. verso.
    Includes bibliographical references and index.
    ISBN 1-56024-737-1 (alk. paper)
    1. Consumers–Research–Cross-cultural studies. I. Manrai, Lalita A. II. Manrai, Ajay K.
HF5415.32.G55 1996
658.8′34–dc20                                                              95-47013
                                                                                                                CIP

# INDEXING & ABSTRACTING

Contributions to this publication are selectively indexed or abstracted in print, electronic, online, or CD-ROM version(s) of the reference tools and information services listed below. This list is current as of the copyright date of this publication. See the end of this section for additional notes.

- *ABI/INFORM Global (broad-coverage indexing & abstracting service that includes numerous English-language titles outside the USA available from University Microfilms International (UMI), 300 North Zeeb Road, P.O. Box 1346, Ann Arbor, MI 48106-1346)*, UMI Data Courier, Attn: Library Services, Box 34660, Louisville, KY 40232

- *ABSCAN, Inc.*, P.O. Box 2384, Monroe, LA 71207-2384

- *AGRICOLA Database*, National Agricultural Library, 10301 Baltimore Boulevard, Room 002, Beltsville, MD 20705

- *Business Education Index, The*, Eastern Illinois University, Department of Business Education and Administration Information Systems, Charleston, IL 61920

- *Cabell's Directory of Publishing Opportunities in Business & Economics (comprehensive & descriptive bibliographic listing with editorial criteria and publication production data for selected business & economics journals)*, Cabell Publishing Company, Box 5428, Tobe Hahn Station, Beaumont, TX 77726-5428

- *CNPIEC Reference Guide: Chinese National Directory of Foreign Periodicals*, P.O. Box 88, Beijing, People's Republic of China

- *Communication Abstracts*, Temple University, 303 Annenberg Hall, Philadelphia, PA 19122

- *Contents Pages in Management*, University of Manchester Business School, Booth Street West, Manchester M15 6PB, England

(continued)

- *Food Science and Technology Abstracts (FSTA) Scanned, abstracted and indexed by the International Food Information Service (IFIS) for inclusion in Food Science and Technology Abstracts (FSTA)*, International Food Information Service, Lane End House, Shinfield, Reading RG2 9BB, England

- *Foods Adlibra*, Foods Adlibra Publications, 9000 Plymouth Avenue North, Minneapolis, MN 55427

- *INTERNET ACCESS (& additional networks) Bulletin Board for Libraries ("BUBL"), coverage of information resources on INTERNET, JANET, and other networks.*
  - JANET X.29: UK.AC.BATH.BUBL or 00006012101300
  - TELNET: BUBL.BATH.AC.UK or 138.38.32.45 login 'bubl'
  - Gopher: BUBL.BATH.AC.UK (138.32.32.45). Port 7070
  - World Wide Web: http://www.bubl.bath.ac.uk./BUBL/home.html
  - NISSWAIS: telnetniss.ac.uk (for the NISS gateway)
  
  The Andersonian Library, Curran Building, 101 St. James Road, Glasgow G4 ONS, Scotland

- *Journal of Health Care Marketing (abstracts section)*, Georgia Tech-School of Management, Ivan Allen College-225 North Avenue NW, Atlanta, GA 30332

- *Management & Marketing Abstracts*, Pira International, Randalls Road, Leatherhead, Surrey KT22 7RU, England

- *Marketing Executive Report*, American Marketing Association, 250 South Wacker Drive, Chicago, IL 60606

- *Market Research Abstracts*, The Market Research Society, 17 Kenelm Close, Harrow HA1 3TE, England

- *Social Planning/Policy & Development Abstracts (SOPODA)*, Sociological Abstracts, Inc., P.O. Box 22206, San Diego, CA 92192-0206

- *Sociological Abstracts (SA)*, Sociological Abstracts, Inc., P.O. Box 22206, San Diego, CA 92192-0206

- *Textile Technology Digest*, Institute of Textile Technology, 2551 Ivy Road, Charlottesville, VA 22903-4614

(continued)

# SPECIAL BIBLIOGRAPHIC NOTES

*related to special journal issues (separates)
and indexing/abstracting*

- [ ] indexing/abstracting services in this list will also cover material in any "separate" that is co-published simultaneously with Haworth's special thematic journal issue or DocuSerial. Indexing/abstracting usually covers material at the article/chapter level.

- [ ] monographic co-editions are intended for either non-subscribers or libraries which intend to purchase a second copy for their circulating collections.

- [ ] monographic co-editions are reported to all jobbers/wholesalers/approval plans. The source journal is listed as the "series" to assist the prevention of duplicate purchasing in the same manner utilized for books-in-series.

- [ ] to facilitate user/access services all indexing/abstracting services are encouraged to utilize the co-indexing entry note indicated at the bottom of the first page of each article/chapter/contribution.

- [ ] this is intended to assist a library user of any reference tool (whether print, electronic, online, or CD-ROM) to locate the monographic version if the library has purchased this version but not a subscription to the source journal.

- [ ] individual articles/chapters in any Haworth publication are also available through the Haworth Document Delivery Services (HDDS).

# ABOUT THE EDITORS

**Lalita A. Manrai, PhD, MBA,** is Associate Professor of Marketing in the Department of Business Administration at the University of Delaware, Newark, where she teaches graduate and undergraduate classes in International Marketing Management. Her research interests deal with international/cross-cultural consumer behavior issues relating to consumer perceptions, preference and choice, consumer satisfaction/dissatisfaction, and consumer responses to marketing communications. Dr. Manrai has published widely in professional journals and in proceedings of the American Marketing Association, European Marketing Academy, Association for Consumer Research, and Academy of Marketing Science, and has presented several research papers at conferences held in the U.S. and abroad. In addition, Dr. Manrai is Book Review Editor for the *Journal of Global Marketing* and serves on the editorial board of the *Journal of Transnational Management Development.*

**Ajay K. Manrai, PhD, MBA,** is Associate Professor of Marketing in the Department of Business Administration at the University of Delaware, Newark. Dr. Manrai is a recipient of the prestigious University-wide Excellence in Teaching Award at the University of Delaware and is the only faculty in his college to receive this distinguished award for teaching at the graduate level. He has also received the Outstanding MBA Teacher Award of the College of Business and Economics. He has published extensively and has presented numerous papers at leading U.S. and international conferences. Dr. Manrai is the recipient of several awards and grants for his theoretical and empirical research in the areas of brand choice models, perceptual mapping and multidimensional scaling, and optimal product design and positioning. He is Associate Editor of the *Journal of Transnational Management Development* and serves on the editorial boards of several other professional journals.

# Global Perspectives in Cross-Cultural and Cross-National Consumer Research

## CONTENTS

| | |
|---|---|
| Introduction<br>*Erdener Kaynak* | 1 |
| Current Issues in the Cross-Cultural and Cross-National Consumer Research<br>*Lalita A. Manrai*<br>*Ajay K. Manrai* | 9 |
| Hyperreality and Globalization: Culture in the Age of Ronald McDonald<br>*Russell W. Belk* | 23 |
| The Key to Successful Euromarketing: Standardization or Customization?<br>*Berend Wierenga*<br>*Ad Pruyn*<br>*Eric Waarts* | 39 |
| Collectivism, Individualism and In-Group Membership: Implications for Consumer Complaining Behaviors in Multicultural Contexts<br>*Harry S. Watkins*<br>*Raymond Liu* | 69 |
| An Investigation of Construct Validity and Generalizability of the Self-Concept: Self-Consciousness in Japan and the United States<br>*Shuzo Abe*<br>*Richard P. Bagozzi*<br>*Pradip Sadarangani* | 97 |

German and American Consumer Orientations
   to Information Technologies: Implications for Marketing
   and Public Policy     125
        *Norbert Mundorf*
        *Ruby Roy Dholakia*
        *Nikhilesh Dholakia*
        *Stuart Westin*

Value Differences Between Polish and Romanian
   Consumers: A Caution Against Using a Regiocentric
   Marketing Orientation in Eastern Europe     145
        *Dana-Nicoleta Lascu*
        *Lalita A. Manrai*
        *Ajay K. Manrai*

Measuring Values in International Settings:
   Are Respondents Thinking "Real" Life
   or "Ideal" Life?     169
        *Suzanne C. Grunert*
        *Thomas E. Muller*

The Search for Universal Symbols: The Case of Right
   and Left     187
        *Judy Cohen*

Consumer Advertising in Germany and the United States:
   A Study of Sexual Explicitness and Cross-Gender
   Contact     211
        *Francis Piron*
        *Murray Young*

Reviewers     229

Index     231

# Introduction

## Erdener Kaynak

Professors Lalita Manrai and Ajay Manrai are to be congratulated for developing such an excellent special volume as *Global Perspectives in Cross-Cultural and Cross-National Consumer Research*. The topic is very timely indeed and the contributors to this volume are the movers and shakers of the field. I think our readers are in for a real treat with this collection.

The multinationalization of world business, increased introduction of satellites into world communication and similar other trends seems to have reduced the world to one large economic order, yet cultural differences persist and many multinational companies have made marketing blunders that have cost them millions of dollars. Although there appears to be attractive cost savings that successful globalization may yield, it is extremely important when globalization is likely to work and when it could result in an expensive mistake.

The first paper titled "Current Issues in the Cross-Cultural and Cross-National Consumer Research" by Manrai and Manrai provides the conceptual framework that is used in this publication. It also develops a model effects of culture on consumer behavior by focusing on social, personal, and psychological components/consequences of culture and the effects these components have on consumer behavior. The co-editors also summarize the nine other papers included in this book and discuss the managerial implications of the same. In order to facilitate reading of the special volume, a super-summary of all the papers is presented in Table 1 (p. 15).

Much has been heard recently of the rise of global consumer culture, especially since the 1989 collapse of Communism in the former Soviet Union and Eastern Europe. The desire for consumer goods and lifestyles

---

[Haworth indexing entry note]: "Introduction." Kaynak, Erdener. Published in *Global Perspectives in Cross-Cultural and Cross-National Consumer Research* (ed: Lalita A. Manrai and Ajay K. Manrai) International Business Press, an imprint of The Haworth Press, Inc., 1996, pp. 1-8. Single or multiple copies of this article are available from The Haworth Document Delivery Service [1-800-342-9678, 9:00 a.m. - 5:00 p.m. (EST)].

© 1996 by The Haworth Press, Inc. All rights reserved.

from the West had at least as much to do with Communism's collapse as the desire for democracy did. Transnational consumer goods and services corporations including McDonald's, Disney, and Coca-Cola are becoming increasingly prominent throughout the world. With faster and more affordable transportation, international tourists increasingly populate ever more remote regions of the world. Stars of music, world cuisine, and world fashions are becoming increasingly prevalent. All of these factors suggest the dawn of a global consumer culture in which universal homogeneity of consumption seems to be the ultimate inevitable outcome.

Yet the paper by Russell W. Belk argues this forecast is premature and mistaken. Local cultures are found to resist globalization through adapting universal commercial icons to meet unique local, national, ethnic and other cultural or subcultural needs. Because we tend to define who we are by contrasting ourselves to the "other" rather than view products and services associated with other cultures as just like our own, we tend to exaggerate and stylize the differences between us and them. Thus, rather than obliterate cultural differences, global trends in consumer culture tend to polarize them. This tendency is discussed in terms of hyperreality of the sort we have come to expect in theme parks. The hyperreal version of the world is safe, clean, and innocuous, but it is also banal, nostalgic, and potentially stifling. The paper concludes with some hopeful trends in consumer actions to stop the advance of global hyperreality.

For companies marketing their products in different countries, especially manufacturers to branded goods, there are major advantages in following a standardized marketing policy. This means that the same products with the same brand names and the same price, advertising and distribution policies are offered in different countries. For such standardized marketing policies it is required that consumers in the different countries are similar in their income levels and preferences and also that the marketing infrastructures in the different countries are sufficiently similar so that the same marketing mix can be applied everywhere.

In the paper by Wierenga et al. it was examined to what extent these conditions are met in the countries of the European Union (EU). It turned out that there are tremendous differences in income levels, income spending patterns and consumption levels of individual products in the different countries. Also factors such as values and lifestyles which are important for consumer decision processes differ considerably over the various countries. Moreover, it appears that the differences in marketing infrastructure (e.g., retailing systems) among the EU countries are large. Also, if a cultural homogenization process among the EU member countries takes place at all, it is likely that such a process is slow. These findings imply that at this moment it is very difficult to think of many product classes for which one Eurowide standardized marketing strategy can be recommended unconditionally.

Nevertheless, the many measures that had been taken by the European Union to harmonize the business conditions in the various countries offer opportunities for the development of European strategies. A gradual development, with a clear recognition of the existing differences can ultimately lead to 'European Consumers.' It is expected that the suppliers of products and services will play a more important role here than the autonomous cultural homogenization process in Europe. Of course the message is different for suppliers of different types of products. Industrial products are much easier marketed at an international scale than consumer products, for example. Within the category consumer products, non-foods are more for standardized marketing policies than food products (the latter usually have a higher cultural content). The European Union is far from a homogeneous market and caution is necessary for too enthusiastic Euromarketers. If ever the right timing of strategies is important, this definitely applies to Euromarketing strategies.

The effective management of customer satisfaction and responses to dissatisfaction are increasingly recognized by managers as critical aspects of maintaining successfully long term relationships with customers. However, customers from different cultures (e.g., Japan, China) or different subcultures within the United States (e.g., Hispanics) will respond differently to dissatisfying consumption experiences. Complaining behaviors have been traditionally divided up into three categories; voice (complaining to the supplier), negative word-of-mouth (telling friends or colleagues about the problem), and exit (switching to another brand or supplier). Management's objective when customers experience post-purchase problems with products or services should be to encourage voice (so that the customer's problem can be resolved) and to discourage negative word-of-mouth and exit.

This is difficult enough in the United States (where consumer voice rates for problems with nondurables are often less than 20%). However, this paper suggests that efforts to encourage voice and discourage negative word-of-mouth will eventually be even more difficult in many other parts of the world. In contrast to U.S. consumers who are relatively individualistic, consumers in much of the rest of the world (Asia, South America, Africa, the Mid East, and Southern Europe) are relatively collectivist. Collectivists depend heavily on "in-groups" of family members, friends, co-workers, etc., for their identity, their purpose, and for guidance as to how to interact with the world. The models proposed by Watkins and Liu suggest that collectivist consumers are, in general, even less likely than individualist consumers to communicate with suppliers about post-purchase problems. In contrast, they are more likely to engage in negative word-of-mouth to in-group members, and these negative communications are more likely to be attended to by other members of their in-group(s). Attitudes and feelings concerning the supplier and complaining behaviors among collectivist consumers will be strongly affected by whether management can cause the firm and its products to become identified by customers as a member of a relevant "in-group," i.e., perceived as trustworthy, and intimately concerned with each particular customer's well-being. The implication is that effective relationship management in collectivist cultures is both especially demanding and particularly critical to long term business success.

The purpose of the article by Abe et al. is to examine aspects of the self-concept as reflected in the self-consciousness scale (Fenigstein, Scheier, & Buss, 1975). This scale has been used in consumer research before but in rather limited ways. For example, consumer researchers have treated the self-consciousness scale as either a unidimensional construct or else have taken components of it, where the components are operationalized as the sums of selected items. If the scale is not unidimensional and all items are summed together, the existence of underlying dimensions will be obscured and predictions based on the total summation will be weighted average of the dimensions and difficult to interpret. If sums of selected items are used in an investigation, the omission of items corresponding to other dimensions may lead to omitted variable biases to the extent that the true dimensions are intercorrelated. Clearly, neither the common practice of summing all items in the self-consciousness scale nor the recent practice of using subsets of items are desirable when the scale is multidimensional.

In the present study, the authors considered the validity of a three-dimensional representation of self-consciousness that was originally suggested by psychologists and supported by exploratory factor analyses. They use confirmatory factor analysis (CFA) instead of exploratory factor analysis because it provides more elaborate and precise ways of testing hypotheses. Another limitation of consumer research with the self-consciousness scale has been its exclusive reliance on a within-culture focus. The authors outline a theory of the self-concept for independent–versus interdependent–self cultures and test implications on the self-consciousness scale and its relationship to attention to social comparison information (ATSCI) and action control (AC), two scales also recently used by consumer researchers. Consumers from Japan and the United States are surveyed to test the hypotheses.

The paper also develops the theoretical foundation for the self-concept and relates it to research on self-consciousness. Hypotheses are developed with respect to effect of independent–versus interdependent–self-concepts on the (a) mean levels of the dimensions of self-consciousness, (b) relations among dimensions, and (c) relations between the dimensions and ATSCI and AC. The section following this introduces the methodology. Then the results are presented, and finally, an interpretation of findings is considered.

As information technologies break down national and industry boundaries, concern for the use of these technologies for global competitive and advantage can be increasingly heard in the corridors of corporations and public policy making institutions. The results by the Mundorf et al. study suggest that there is a general techno-optimist attitude among the U.S. population that will support continuation of policies that favor high-tech industries. Germans, on the other hand, seem to express lower familiarity with technologies as well as greater skepticism towards newer technologies. This is likely to create greater challenges in the development of policies in Germany where there are two conflicting concerns regarding the proliferation of technologies that could potentially diminish the quality of life and development of technologies that provide global competitive advantage.

Eastern Europe presents many opportunities to transnational companies. Firms have already established themselves in the region and many more are contemplating a presence there, necessitating a full understanding of this market. One aspect of the market that must not be overlooked in the process is its heterogeneity. The article by Lascu et al. recommends against a regiocentric philosophy (assuming a culturally-similar market and using standardized appeals) when targeting consumers in Eastern Europe. It focuses on Poland and Romania and notes differences in the relationship between cultural values and demographics in the two countries. While Poland and Romania share a Communist past, they differ in region, language, and development under Communism (Poland had more freedom, access to the West, and higher development than Romania). Thus, Romanians are thought to be more collectivistic in the Hofstede (1980) sense, while Poles, more individualistic due to greater Western influence. These traits were explored in a study of the relationship between values and demographics.

The study found consistently with its hypotheses, that age leads to higher rating of terminal and instrumental values for Polish consumers, since age solidifies values. For Romanians, values were less likely to be related to age since they mirrored community values. Educated Poles rated both values lower than less educated Poles, since, in Poland, material achievement was no longer linked to education after Communism; Romanians' values were not affected by education, since their values mirror societal values. Lastly, high-income Poles rated both values highly compared to low-income Poles, since they had attained success by working in the system. Income had less impact on the importance ascribed to values for Romanians, since values there are collectively determined.

Companies planning to do business in these countries should not target, in the short-term, segments of similar age, education, and income under the assumption that consumer demographics bear a similar relationship to individuals' values. However, in the long-term, as Romania advances, the relationship between demographics and values there will become more similar to the equivalent relationship in Poland, rendering a regiocentric strategy in this market more appropriate. Measuring personal values has become widespread practice among international market researchers who subscribe to lifestyle segmentation strategies and who want to get a vivid, workable description of their target market. However, most studies use questionnaires asking consumers to rank and/or rate the importance of a set of personal or social values. The value items used in these orientation inventories are well grounded in theory. However, researchers typically do not assess how the respondents, themselves, understand and evaluate the stimuli presented to them as "values." This means that marketers cannot be quite sure what the value questionnaires are actually measuring. Are consumers ranking the values under some imagined "ideal" life situation, or are they giving their responses for "real" life conditions where they take into account their present situations, roles, and the expectations of others? The study by Grunert and Muller conducted in Canada and Denmark, aimed at a better understanding of respondents' reactions to value items. The main idea was to test alternate approaches to measuring people's value priorities. This differentiation was achieved by explicitly distinguishing between respondents' day-to-day ("real") life and their "ideal" life. In order to assess the predictive power of both value types, the concept of product involvement was also employed. Results from both countries reveal a number of significant differences between "real" and "ideal" life values which were interpreted in terms of deficit and surplus achievement, respectively. Both value types were to some extent related to product involvement. This study highlights the need for greater attention to the method used for obtaining value data, especially in cross-national marketing research.

According to Judy Cohen international advertisers must be concerned with the issue of whether, given differences in cultures, advertising can be standardized globally. Because standardization offers benefits such as costs savings, it would be useful to find symbols which are universal. Right/left symbolism appears to be universal to all cultures. This is no doubt based on the fact that most people are right-handed, which appears to be physiologically based.

On the most general level, "right" is associated with "good" and "left" is associated with "bad." To the extent that this is true in a culture, the "good" (i.e., advertised) product or situation (i.e., results of use of the advertised product) should be placed to the right in advertisements; the "bad" (i.e., competitors) product or situation (i.e., nonuse or preuse of the advertised product) should be placed to the left. Another association with "right" is male and "left" is female. It is therefore proposed that male models, and products meant for males, should be positioned on the right; the opposite is true for females. The general rule of "right"-"good" or "male"/"left"-"bad" or "female" placement in an advertisement may be confounded when the product is positioned with respect to a model, because certain audiences may use the model's right and left as a reference point, while others may not. "Right" is also associated with rational thinking and science, while "left" is associated with emotional thinking and nature. It is proposed that with rational appeals, the product should be placed on the right; with emotional appeals, the product should be placed on the left. In addition, products associated with culture should be positioned to the right, while products associated with nature should be positioned on the left. Cultures vary with respect to the strength of right/left associations. Research should be done in specific cultures to determine the effects of the right/left positioning in those cultures.

Prior research indicates sexually explicit messages may hinder advertising effectiveness. None the less, use of models in provocative attire or posture and suggestive cross-gender contact are common in advertising. This may be particularly so in media where advertisements for product categories such as fashion wear and personal care products are common.

A study of seven sexual advertising elements in select German and U.S. magazines targeting upscale female readers was conducted by Piron and Young. According to the study results, from 1986 to 1992:

a. American magazines carried higher levels of "sexy" advertising, though, overall, the rate was low in both countries on the basis of total magazine pages published. This may be related to increased sensitivity by some advertisers to social issues such as pornography and the spread of sexually transmitted diseases.

b. A trend toward less frequent use of more explicit stimuli was observed. Advertisements showing cross-gender contact were relatively few, and those depicting intimate contact were very rare. This may signal attempts by some advertising agencies and clients to avoid visual elements that could be construed as antifeminist. Similarly, use of partially clad or nude models decreased and use of more subdued appeals (i.e., the use of suggestively clad models) increased. Such changes may indicate a response to criticism that advertising too frequently depicts women as alluring sexual objects rather than as real people.

The methodology described can, and should, be used to study the phenomena in other media and countries. Such research might reveal a "maturing" in both advertising philosophy and execution, at least in that portion targeting upscale, female consumers. If so, such efforts to appeal to a higher order of personal needs and advanced cultural norms are to be encouraged.

# Current Issues in the Cross-Cultural and Cross-National Consumer Research

Lalita A. Manrai
Ajay K. Manrai

**SUMMARY.** A conceptual model of effects of culture on consumer behavior is developed in this paper. The model focuses on the social, personal, and psychological components/consequences of culture and identifies intermediary variables and processes associated with each of these three components. A summary of the other nine papers included in this special volume is provided and a super-summary is presented in Table 1 that classifies the various papers on the following five dimensions: (i) nature of a paper, e.g., conceptual, empirical, or methodological; (ii) cultures and/or nation compared and samples; (iii) cultural component/consequence; (iv) construct: intermediary/process/others; and (v) type of consumer behavior that is studied, e.g., complaining behavior, response to information technology, product involvement, and response to advertising. *[Article copies available from The Haworth Document Delivery Service: 1-800-342-9678.]*

## INTRODUCTION

The importance of cross-cultural and cross-national consumer research in international marketing has been amply recognized by researchers for

---

Lalita A. Manrai is Associate Professor of Marketing and Ajay K. Manrai is Associate Professor of Marketing at the College of Business and Economics, University of Delaware, Newark, DE 19716. Bitnet: HKG32760@UDELVM.UDEL.EDU.

Address all correspondence to Lalita A. Manrai.

[Haworth co-indexing entry note]: "Current Issues in the Cross-Cultural and Cross-National Consumer Research." Manrai, Lalita A., and Ajay K. Manrai. Co-published simultaneously in *Journal of International Consumer Marketing* (International Business Press, an imprint of The Haworth Press, Inc.) Vol. 8, No. 3/4, 1996, pp. 9-22; and: *Global Perspectives in Cross-Cultural and Cross-National Consumer Research* (ed: Lalita A. Manrai, and Ajay K. Manrai) International Business Press, an imprint of The Haworth Press, Inc., 1996, pp. 9-22. Single or multiple copies of this article are available from The Haworth Document Delivery Service: [1-800-342-9678, 9:00 a.m - 5:00 p.m. (EST)].

© 1996 by The Haworth Press, Inc. All rights reserved.

several decades (Domzal and Unger 1987; Dunn 1976; Hampton and Van Gent 1984; Plummer 1977; Winick 1961). Today this need for understanding cross-cultural consumer behavior is even more acute. While multinationalization of world business, satellitazation of world communication and similar other trends seem to have reduced the world to one large economic order, cultural differences persist and textbooks are full of marketing blunders that have cost multinational companies millions of dollars (Assael 1992, p. 377; Cateora 1993, p. 139; Engel, Blackwell and Miniard 1993, p. 61; Solomon 1992, p. 478). Attracted by the cost savings that successful globalization can yield, multinational companies have attempted to globalize the elements of their marketing mix and have often found that they were better off adapting their marketing mix to take into account the cultural differences. It is thus extremely important to understand when globalization is likely to be successful and when it is not.

## DEFINITIONAL ASPECTS OF CULTURE AND ITS INFLUENCE

Despite the importance of this topic, the extant research on cross-cultural and cross-national consumer behavior is rather limited (McCarty 1989; McCort and Malhotra 1993). The basic reason for this seems to be the complexity of the concept of culture which makes it extremely difficult to define culture and the nature of its influence on consumer behavior. Such a lack of definition in turn interferes with the advancement of the theory of cross-cultural and cross-national consumer research. Three basic issues related to the definitional aspect of culture and its influence that need to be understood are: (1) the unit of analysis or the level at which culture is to be defined, i.e., nation or otherwise, (2) the meaning of culture or what all it includes, and (3) the nature of cultural influence or the ways in which culture affects consumer behavior.

The title of this special volume clarifies the scope of studies included in this collection in terms of the first point, i.e., the unit of analysis. The title deliberately specifies both the terms "Cross-Cultural" and "Cross-National" thereby acknowledging that the unit of analysis for cross-cultural comparison can be other than the "nation," i.e., as in subcultural research or the comparison of different cultural groups within a nation. However, the title of the special volume, at the same time, also specifies that the perspective has to be international or global thereby conveying that subcultural research is not included in this special collection and comparisons are made only at the level of country or a group of countries, i.e., as in comparison of ethnic groups, i.e., Hispanic countries versus non-Hispanic countries or as in comparison of geographic groups, i.e., Eastern European countries versus Central European countries, etc. Considering that many multinational companies are actively seeking globalization, such groupings of countries in segmentation and positioning strategies is quite common and of strategic interest to international marketers.

The second issue concerns the meaning of culture or what all it includes. Culture is an extremely complex concept and several definitions of culture have been offered. An early definition by Kluckhorn (1951) defines culture as "the distinctive way of life of a group of people, their complete design for living." Another early definition by Murdock (1945) includes as many as 73 items as cultural universals. This complexity of culture continues to fascinate the social science researchers as is reflected in a recent definition by Ferraro (1990, p. 18) who defines culture as "Everything that people have, think and do as members of their society." Kroeber and Kluckhorn (1985) analyzed more than 160 definitions of culture and concluded that in general there was agreement that culture is learned, shared and passed on from generation to generation and is reinforced through social institutions. Culture, therefore, is a dynamic force resulting from the interaction of humans with their environment such that both humans and their environment influence each other. Not surprisingly, therefore, it is an extremely interesting but complex concept to comprehend and deal with.

While acknowledging the complexity and vastness of its scope, researchers have also attempted to come up with more manageable definitions of the concept of culture by classifying these large numbers of cultural universals into sets of items that go together. Herskovitz (1948, p. 348) defines culture as the "man-made part of the human environment" and classifies the cultural components into five groups, i.e., material culture, social institutions, humans and the universe, aesthetics, and language. Classifications similar to this have been advocated in most international marketing textbooks (Czinkota and Ronkainen 1990, p. 133; Jeannet and Hennessey 1988, p. 67; Terpstra and Sarathy 1991, p. 97).

Narrowing this classification further, two basic components of culture commonly cited are: the "Material Elements" which include such items as clothes, books, tools, art, etc., and the "Abstract Elements" which include values, customs, shared system of attitudes and behaviors, norms, ideas, etc. (Engel, Blackwell and Miniard 1993, p. 63). Support for this dichotomization of culture can be found in a variety of disciplines dealing with human behavior. In the Marxist tradition, culture was dichotomized as "base" (material base) and "superstructure." Early views propagated that the material base of culture determines its values and ideology and not vice versa. The current thinking on Marxist philosophy (Williams 1977, p. 79-80) views these two components to be interactive. Wuthrow (1992) in his revised version of Marxist sociology of culture calls these two components "Infrastructure" and "Superstructure" acknowledging similar interactions.

Sociologists have also acknowledged similar divisions of culture. Winston (1933, p. 25-26) defines culture as "the totality of material and nonmaterial traits, together with their associated behavior patterns, plus the language which a society possesses." Winston (1933) further submits that material culture includes such tangible things as tools and houses and non-material culture includes such non-tangible things as religion and family.

Psychologists view non-material elements as those capturing the dynamics of the meaning of human life and experiences and material elements as the physical objects that are used to convey such meanings. Triandis (1972, p. 4) further elaborates on Herskovitz's (1948, p. 348) conceptualization of culture and defines "Subjective Culture" as "a cultural group's characteristic way of perceiving the man-made part of its environment." His definition of subjective culture includes: associations, attitudes, beliefs, concepts, evaluations, expectations, memories, opinions, perceptions, role perceptions, stereotypes, and values (Triandis 1972, p. 10).

In the field of consumer behavior, researchers dealing with topics such as materialism and semiotics view products as cultural artifacts or physical objects that are used for conveying the cultural meaning (Belk 1985, 1990; Holbrook 1989). In contrast to subjective component, therefore, this part of culture can be viewed as the physical component.

The above discussion suggests that the two components of culture, i.e., the material elements or the physical component and the abstract elements or the subjective component are interrelated and interactive. Accordingly, two basic approaches to the study of relationship between culture and behavior are: (1) the "interpretive" approach where the researchers interpret the cultural meaning by placing themselves in the culture or its artifacts thereby "soaking up" the meaning and (2) the "predictive" approach whereby consumers' behavior including their acquisition, creation and consumption of artifacts is predicted by studying the influence of abstract elements such as values and norms. The research utilizing each of these two different approaches is represented in this special volume.

The third cross-cultural issue that we need to deal with concerns the nature of cultural influence or the ways in which culture affects consumer behavior. Harris and Moran (1987) identify the following ten attitudes and behaviors to be influenced by culture: sense of self and space, communication and language, dress and appearance, food and feeding habits, time and time consciousness, relationships (family, organizations, government, etc.), values and norms, beliefs and attitudes, mental processes and learning, work habits and practices. An examination of this list reveals the clear confounding that exists between the meaning of culture itself and its consequences as identified above. Many of the items identified in this list as consequences are also included in the definition of the culture either as artifacts, i.e., food, dress or as abstract elements, i.e., values and norms. In order to clearly understand the effect of culture on consumer behavior, this confounding in the components/consequences of culture needs to be acknowledged so that consumer behavior consequences of culture can be specified *beyond* other types of behaviors that are implicitly included in the definition of culture itself. Secondly, a distinction also needs to be made between the "intermediary variables" such as values and "processes" such as perception motivation and learning, both of which (intermediary variables and processes) explain the effect of culture on consumer behavior.

Using the framework suggested by Triandis (1984), McCort and Malhotra (1993) have classified selected cross-cultural studies into those dealing with processes such as perception, perceptual categorization, perceptual influence, information processing strategies and intermediary variables such as values and self-concepts. This framework provides a useful starting point for organization of cross-cultural research. However, there is a need for a much expanded model in which the consumer behavior domains need to be identified separately from the components/consequences of culture. Also, the cultural influences need to be specified in terms of both the intermediary variables and processes and their ultimate effect on specific consumer behavior issues needs to be examined.

## EFFECT OF CULTURE ON CONSUMER BEHAVIOR: A CONCEPTUAL MODEL

A basic model of consumer behavior suggested by Kotler (1994, p. 174) identifies cultural, social, personal and psychological factors as the four types of influences shaping consumer behavior, cultural influence being the "broadest and deepest" (Kotler 1994). These influences in turn are interrelated with a broader influence effecting the narrower ones. For example, family (an item included under social factors) is likely to affect life style (an item under personal factors, which is a narrower influence than social factors). Comparing the items suggested by Kotler (1994) under social, personal and psychological factors with the components/consequences of culture discussed in the current research on culture's effect on consumer behavior, it can be said that the components/consequences of culture can be classified into these three categories, i.e., social, personal and psychological. Further, each of these three categories can be divided into intermediary variables and processes affecting consumer behavior. For example, the items motivation, perception and learning identified by Kotler (1994) under psychological factors are "processes" whereas the fourth item, beliefs and attitudes, also identified under psychological factors, is an intermediary variable. Similar lists, separated by social and personal factors that divide them into intermediary variables and processes are developed. Other variables (besides intermediaries and processes) that affect culture are also identified. A conceptual model capturing the above discussion is given in Figure 1.

## *SCOPE OF ARTICLES INCLUDED IN THIS SPECIAL VOLUME*

Next, we discuss how the articles included in this special volume provide coverage of many of the issues related to cross-cultural and cross-national consumer research which have been identified and discussed above. A summary of all the articles is provided in Table 1 covering the following: the nature of the paper (i.e., conceptual, empirical, methodological), cultures and/or nations compared, type of cultural component/consequence (i.e., social, personal, psychological), specification of the nature of the cultural component/consequence in terms of the specific constructs as identified in Figure 1 under the intermediary/process/others category, specific consumer behavior studied, sample details and the research instrument/methodology.

Out of the nine other papers included in this special collection in addition to this paper, two papers discuss the issue related to globalization/standardization. Out of the seven remaining papers, two are conceptual pieces which develop propositions drawing upon multicultural contexts and examples and five papers are empirical/methodological studies conducted in specific pairs of countries as summarized in Table 1. The two papers dealing with the overall issue of globalization/standardization versus adaptation/customization are given first. The remaining seven papers are arranged in the order of the model presented in Figure 1, i.e., in the order of social, personal and psychological aspects.

The second paper in this special volume, by Belk, entitled "Hyperreality and Globalization: Culture in the Age of Ronald McDonald" discusses the course of and effects of globalized hyperreality created by multinationalization. Belk examines the possible threat that world cultures may lose their identity into a "global commercial culture." His analysis indicates that this threat of obliteration of culture is premature and mistaken. The cultures are resilient and globalization is likely to polarize them rather than obliterate them. At the same time we need to be concerned about the

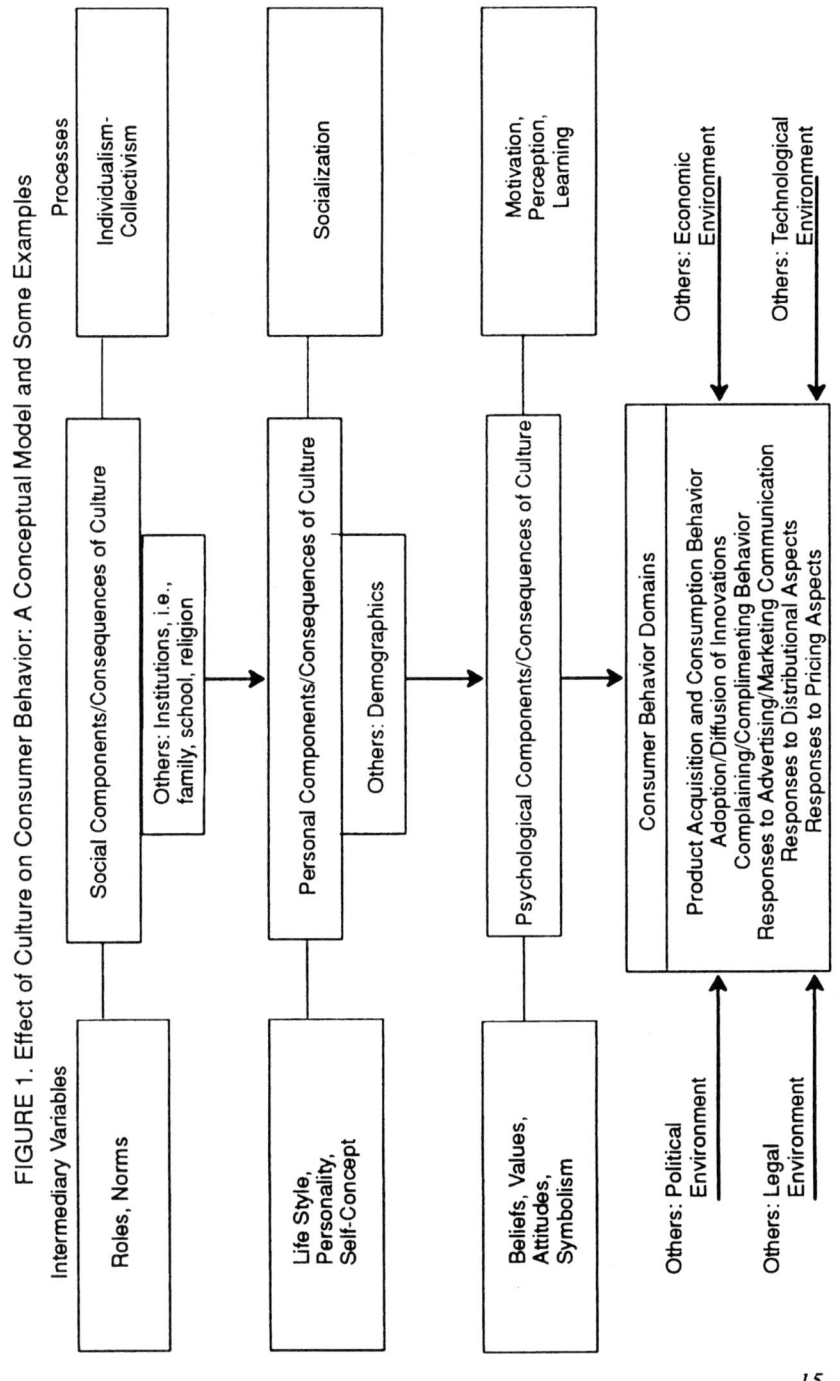

FIGURE 1. Effect of Culture on Consumer Behavior: A Conceptual Model and Some Examples

TABLE 1. Cross-Cultural and Cross-National Consumer Research: Summary of Articles Included in This Special Volume

| | Authors | Nature of the Paper | Cultures and/or Nations Compared and Samples | Cultural Component/ Consequence | Construct: Intermediary/ Process/Others | Consumer Behavior |
|---|---|---|---|---|---|---|
| 1. | Manrai & Manrai | Development of a Conceptual Model of Effect of Culture on Consumer Behavior and Summary of Articles 2 through 9 below. | | | | |
| 2. | Belk | Discussion of Globalized Hyperreality: Its Course, Effects and Ways to Resist the Trends | | | | |
| 3. | Wierenga, Pruyn & Waarts | Discussion of Standardization versus Customization Strategies in the Context of Europe '92 | | | | |
| 4. | Watkins & Liu | Conceptual | Multiple Cultures | Social | Individualism-Collectivism | Complaining Behavior |
| 5. | Abe, Bagozzi & Sadarangani | Empirical/ Methodological | USA: 246 (students) Japan: 419 (students) | Social | Interdependent-Independent Cultures Self-Concept | |
| 6. | Mundorf, Dholakia, Dholakia & Westin | Empirical | USA: 212 (students) 244 (field) Germany: 84 (students) 50 (field) | Socio-Political Personal | Party Philosophy Age, Gender | Responses to Information Technology |
| 7. | Lascu, Manrai & Manrai | Empirical | Poland: 117 (field) Romania: 123 (field) | Psychological Social | Values (Rokeach) Individualism-Collectivism | |
| 8. | Grunert & Muller | Empirical/ Methodological Conceptual | Canada: 351 (field) Denmark: 220 (field) Multiple Cultures | Personal Psychological | Age, Education, Income Values (LOV) | Product Involvement |
| 9. | Cohen | | | Psychological | Right-Left Symbolism | Responses to Advertising (Interpretive Approach) |
| 10. | Piron & Young | Empirical | USA: Full page ads in *Vogue* & *Mademoiselle* Germany: Full page ads in *Vogue* & *Patra* | Psychological | Frequency & Nature of Visual Sexual Stimuli in Print Magazines (86,89,92) | |

trivialization of consumer life and the hyperreality that is likely to stifle consumer cultures. Belk concludes by suggesting some possible consumer actions to prevent this from happening.

The third paper in this special volume by Wierenga, Pruyn and Waarts discusses the issue of globalization from a marketing strategy perspective. The basic issue that this paper focuses on is that of successful Euromarketing strategies in terms of standardization versus customization of marketing variables. The paper compares EC countries in terms of similarities and differences in the consumers as exhibited in their expenditure and consumption patterns, household appliance ownership, lifestyle, etc. This paper also discusses similarities and differences in the marketing infrastructure, how Europe 92 is likely to shape the marketing infrastructure in future, identifies drives and hurdles in Euromarketing and sets up a research agenda for Euromarketing.

The next paper entitled "Collectivism, Individualism and In-Group Membership: Implications for Consumer Complaining Behaviors in Multicultural Contexts" is authored by Watkins and Liu. This is a conceptual paper which addresses the issue of how culture influences consumer complaining behavior. The authors contrast the individualistic and collectivistic cultural patterns and offer several propositions dealing with the effect of degree of cultural collectivism on three types of consumer complaining behaviors, i.e., exit, negative word-of-mouth and voice. In regards to the conceptual model given in Figure 1, this paper covers the social aspects of the cultural influence and provides examples from multiple cultures.

Abe, Bagozzi and Sadarangani are the authors of the next paper entitled "An Investigation of Construct Validity and Generalizability of the Self-Concept: Self-Consciousness in Japan and the United States." This is an empirical/methodological study in which the authors test for the applicability of a three-dimensional self-consciousness scale by comparing consumers in an interdependent culture, i.e., Japan, with consumers in an independent culture, i.e., U.S. The authors outline a theory of self-concept as it relates to self-conscious for these two types of cultures and test several hypotheses dealing with the relationships among the three dimensions of self-consciousness, i.e., private self-consciousness, public self-consciousness and social anxiety as well as the relationship between these three dimensions and two other scales, ATSCI (Attention to Social Comparison Information) and AC (Action Control). Confirmatory factor analysis models are applied via LISREL for data analysis. This paper covers the social as well as personal aspects of the cultural influence outlined in Figure 1.

The next paper in this special collection entitled "German and American Consumer Orientations to Information Technologies: Implications for Marketing and Public Policy" by Mundorf, Dholakia, Dholakia and Westin is an empirical study that compares German and American consumers in terms of their familiarity with and use of information technology and skepticism of the role of technology in society. The authors draw upon sociopolitical factors in Germany, such as party philosophy/views on dangers of technologies, to predict differences in the responses to information technology between German and American consumers. For each of the two countries, data comprised of a young student sample and a different-aged nonstudent sample. The authors also propose and test hypotheses dealing with the effects of demographics like age and gender on the technology orientation of the consumers in Germany and USA.

The seventh paper in this volume by Lascu, Manrai and Manrai is entitled "Value Differences Between Polish and Romanian Consumers: A Caution Against Using a Regiocentric Marketing Orientation in Eastern Europe." This is an empirical study of instrumental and terminal values (Rokeach 1973) held by different demographic segments in two East European countries, Poland and Romania. The findings indicate that demographics such as age, education and income are useful for value segmentation in Poland but not in Romania. This is attributed to the collectivistic nature of Romanian culture in comparison to which Polish culture is considered to be more individualistic. This paper thus covers the relationship between personal factors (age, education, income) and psychological (values) aspects of the cultural influence drawing upon social (individualism-collectivism) aspects of the two cultures. In conclusion, a caution against regiocentric marketing orientation is offered with several managerial implications.

The next paper entitled "Measuring Values in International Settings: Are Respondents Thinking 'Real' Life or 'Ideal' Life?" by Grunert and Muller also addresses the topic of values but from a methodological point of view. Two alternative approaches to measuring values were tested in an empirical study done in Denmark and Canada. These two alternative approaches consisted of asking the respondents to think of their "real" or day to day values and their "ideal" values using items drawn from LOV (List of Values Scale, Kahle 1983). This study also tested the predictive power of both these types of value measures as these related to the concept of product involvement. The findings indicate that for Denmark, all ideal life values were rated higher than real life values whereas for Canada, this relationship was mixed with some ideal life values rating higher than real life values and vice versa. Both types of value measures were related to product involvement.

The next paper included in this volume, by Cohen, is entitled "The Search for Universal Symbols: The Case of Right and Left." This is a conceptual piece that addresses the topic of right-left symbolism covered under the psychological aspects of cultural influence (Figure 1). The paper takes an interdisciplinary approach to the study of right-left symbolism and provides several examples drawn from a multitude of cultures to demonstrate the universality of preference for right over left. Possible reasons for this universality are discussed and several propositions are offered dealing with marketing implications in the areas of advertising design.

Paper number ten of this special collection is entitled "Consumer Advertising in Germany and the United States: A Study of Sexual Explicitness and Cross-Gender Contact" and is authored by Piron and Young. These authors compared the pervasiveness of seven sexual advertising stimuli in the U.S. and Germany by carrying out a Content Analysis of the full page print ads appearing in selected magazines, i.e., *Vogue* and *Mademoiselle* for the U.S. and *Vogue* and *Patra* for Germany. This analysis covered the years 1986, 1989 and 1992. The seven sexual advertising stimuli were comprised of four variables dealing with dress/undress and three variables dealing with physical contact. The authors report the findings that compare the differences between four magazines (two for each of the two countries) for the three selected years on usage of the seven sexual advertising stimuli separately and also for the composite indexes generated by combing the four types of dress/undress variables and three types of physical contact variables. This research employs an interpretive approach (content analysis) in comparison to other empirical studies included in this special collection which employed a predictive approach. The authors conclude that there is a "softening up" in the use of visual sexual stimuli over the period of study (1986-1992).

## *CONCLUSION*

The research papers included in this special volume *Global Perspectives in Cross-Cultural and Cross-National Consumer Research* cover a variety of important conceptual, methodological and empirical issues related to cross-cultural and cross-national consumer research. In order for development of theories of cross-cultural consumer behavior, effort needs to be undertaken in the following three directions:

1. Development of new theories of consumer behavior which take cultural factors more explicitly into account starting with the conceptual level and subsequent empirical testing.
2. Empirical validation of existing theories of consumer behavior developed mostly in western countries by replicating the studies in

other countries and accounting for the differences in results in terms of cultural factors.
3. Methodological issues in the cross-cultural consumer research such as validation of the scales, personality inventories, etc., across cultures, measurement techniques that are appropriate considering cultural differences, etc.

An overall conceptual level issue that cross-cultural marketers need to address is globalization of marketing strategies. There is a need to examine the impact of such strategies on overall consumer life rather than merely viewing globalization as a strategic concern. The Belk paper contributes to this important understanding. Further, as a strategic concern, the issue of globalization versus adaptation is assuming an ever increasing importance as the world is undergoing rapid and dramatic changes. Events and forces such as the fall of Communism in the Central and European countries, formation of Europe 92, opening up of economies in the Far East, etc., are on one hand opening up huge opportunities for the international marketers and on the other, making competition a global reality. One of these issues, i.e., globalization/standardization versus adaptation/customization for successful Euromarketing, is addressed by the Wierenga, Pruyn and Waarts paper.

While the above two papers address the broader, overall concern with globalization versus adaptation, the rest of the papers deal with more specifically defined conceptual, empirical and methodological issues. In the beginning of this paper, a brief review of the current issues pertinent to cross-cultural consumer research was done identifying the confound that exists between the components of culture and its consequences. Such a confound makes it difficult to understand the contributions made by cross-cultural research studies on account of two reasons: (1) the domain of consumer behavior constructs influenced by culture needs to be clearly identified distinguishing them from the factors influenced by culture such as social, personal and psychological factors, and (2) the nature of this influence needs to be understood in terms of whether it is an intermediary variable or a process. Towards this end, a conceptual model was developed in this paper (Figure 1) and the seven papers summarized using the framework suggested by Figure 1. The seven papers are comprised of two conceptual papers and five empirical/methodological papers. Four of these papers deal with social factors, three deal with personal factors and four deal with psychological factors (these add up to more than seven because some papers cover more than one type of cultural influence as summarized in Table 1). A variety of intermediary variables and processes were covered to develop the rationale for predicted effects. These include constructs such as individualism-collectivism, self-concept, values, symbolism, etc. The consumer behavior domains studied by these papers include consumer complaining behavior, responses to adverting, responses to technology and product involvement.

There is a need for continued emphasis on cross-cultural and cross-national consumer research. Particularly studies that provide a more complete coverage of the model presented in Figure 1, and identify the type of cultural influence, i.e., social, personal, psychological, its nature, i.e., intermediary, process or other as well as the ultimate consumer behavior domain will be particularly useful. Some of these factors may have interactive effect. Also some types of cultural influences could be classified into more than one category, i.e., individualism-collectivism could deal with psychological as well as social aspects of cultural influence thereby suggesting an interactive influence of these two factors. Thus the model developed in Figure 1 needs to be further extended accounting for such interactive effects as well as diverse findings based on an exhaustive coverage of cross-cultural research. However, it provides a useful framework that may be the genesis for the development of a cross-cultural theory of consumer behavior.

## REFERENCES

Assael, H. (1992). *Consumer Behavior and Marketing Action.* Fourth edition, DWS-Kent Publishing Company, Boston, MA: p. 377.

Belk, R. W. (1985). Materialism: Trait Aspects of Living in the Material World. *Journal of Consumer Research,* 14, 26-42.

Belk, R. W. (1990). Materialism and the Modern U.S. Christmas. In Hirschman E. C. (ed.), *Interpretive Consumer Research.* Association for Consumer Research, Provo, UT.

Cateora, P. R. (1993). *International Marketing.* Eighth edition, Irwin, Boston, MA: p. 139.

Czinkota, M. R. and Ronkainen, I. A. (1990). *International Marketing.* Second Edition, Dryden, Hinsdale, IL: p. 134.

Domzal, T. and Unger, L. (1987). Emerging Positioning Strategies in Global Markets. *Journal of Consumer Marketing,* 4 (Fall), 23-40.

Dunn, S. W. (1976). Effect of National Identity on Multinational Promotional Strategy in Europe. *Journal of Marketing,* 40 (October), 50-57.

Engel, J. F., Blackwell, R. D. and Miniard, P. W. (1993). *Consumer Behavior.* Seventh edition, The Dryden Press, New York, NY: p. 61.

Ferraro, G. P. (1990). *The Culture Dimension of International Business.* Prentice Hall, Englewood Cliffs, NJ: p. 18.

Hampton, G. M. and Van Gent, A. P. (1984). International Marketing: 50 Suggested Research Projects for the 1980s. *European Research,* 12 (July), 134-142.

Harris, P. R. and Moran, R. T. (1987). *Managing Cultural Differences.* Gulf Publishing Company, Houston, TX: 190-195.

Herskovitz, M. (1948). *Man and His Works.* New York, NY: p. 634.

Holbrook, M. B. (1989). Seven Routes to Facilitating the Semiological Interpretation of Consumption Symbolism and Marketing Imagery in Works of Art: Some Tips for Wildcats. *Advances in Consumer Research,* 16, 420-425.

Jeannet, J. and Hennessey, H. D. (1988). *International Marketing Management.* Houghton Mifflin, Boston, MA: p. 67.

Kahle, L. (1983). *Social Values and Social Change: Adaptation to Life in America.* Praeger, New York, NY.

Kluckhorn, C. (1951). The Study of Culture. In D. Lewer and H. D. Lasswell (eds.), *The Policy Sciences.* Stanford University Press, Stanford, CA: p. 86.

Kotler, P. (1994). *Marketing Management: Analysis, Planning, Implementation and Control.* Prentice Hall, Englewood Cliffs, NJ: p. 174.

Kroeber, A. and Kluckhorn, C. (1985). *Culture: A Critical Review of Concepts and Definitions.* Random House, New York, NY: p. 11.

McCarty, J. A. (1989). Current Theory and Research on Cross-Cultural Factors in Consumer Behavior. *Advances in Consumer Research,* 16, 127-129.

McCort, D. J. and Malhotra, N. K. (1993). Culture and Consumer Behavior: Toward an Understanding of Cross-Cultural Consumer Behavior in International Marketing. *Journal of International Consumer Marketing,* 6 (2), 91-127.

Murdock, G. P. (1945). The Common Denominator of Culture. In R. Linton (ed.), *Science of Man in the World Crisis.* Columbia University Press, New York, NY: 123-142.

Plummer, J. T. (1977). Consumer Focus in Cross-National Research. *Journal of Advertising,* 6 (Spring), 5-15.

Rokeach, M. (1973). *The Nature of Human Values.* Free Press, New York, NY.

Solomon, M. R. (1992). *Consumer Behavior.* Allyn and Bacon, Boston, MA: p. 478.

Terpstra, V. and Sarathy, R. (1991). *International Marketing.* Dryden, Hinsdale, IL: p. 97.

Triandis, H. C. (1972). *The Analysis of Subjective Culture.* Wiley, New York, NY: pp. 4-10.

Triandis, H. C. (1984). A Theoretical Framework for the More Efficient Construction of Culture Assimilators. *International Journal of Intercultural Relations,* 8, 3, 301-330.

Williams, R. (1977). *Marxism and Literature.* Oxford University Press, Oxford: pp. 79-80.

Winick, C. (1961). Anthropology's Contribution to Marketing. *Journal of Marketing,* 25 (July), 53-60.

Winston, S. (1933). *Culture and Human Behavior.* The Ronald Press Company, New York, NY: pp. 25-26.

Wuthrow, R. (1992). Infrastructure and Superstructure. In Münch, R. and Smelser, N. J. (eds.), *Theory of Culture,* University of California Press, Los Angeles, CA: 145-170.

# Hyperreality and Globalization: Culture in the Age of Ronald McDonald

Russell W. Belk

**SUMMARY.** As the globe shrinks due to multinationalization, world tourism, world sports, and increasingly instantaneous world communication and transportation, there is a threat that cultures will be absorbed into a global commercial culture. This analysis argues that the result is not so much a homogenization and obliteration of cultures marching under the banner of multinational brands, as it is the creation of a sterilized, sanitized, and trivialized version of consumer life as spectacle. This article concludes by noting some possibilities for resisting these trends. *[Article copies available from The Haworth Document Delivery Service: 1-800-342-9678.]*

## A TALE OF ARCHAEOLOGY IN THE YEAR 2995

Archaeologist Gucci Toyota Rolex, a recent graduate of Ralph Lauren University (once Karl Marx University) in Budapest, sits in his IBM sensatorium seeking clues that will help him understand the obscure origins of the major World holidays. He believes that some of these holidays, including Coke Day, Elvis Day, Saint Johnny Walker Day, the Day of the Levi's, Sony Feel-Man Day, and the Feast of the Seven-Eleven, may have originated almost a millennium ago in the 20th or 21st century. But the evi-

---

Russell W. Belk is affiliated with the David Eccles School of Business, University of Utah, Salt Lake City, UT 84112. E-mail MKTRWB@Bus.Buc.Utah.Edu.

[Haworth co-indexing entry note]: "Hyperreality and Globalization: Culture in the Age of Ronald McDonald." Belk, Russell W. Co-published simultaneously in *Journal of International Consumer Marketing* (International Business Press, an imprint of The Haworth Press, Inc.) Vol. 8, No. 3/4, 1996, pp. 23-37; and: *Global Perspectives in Cross-Cultural and Cross-National Consumer Research* (ed: Lalita A. Manrai, and Ajay K. Manrai) International Business Press, an imprint of The Haworth Press, Inc., 1996, pp. 23-37. Single or multiple copies of this article are available from The Haworth Document Delivery Service [1-800-342-9678, 9:00 a.m - 5:00 p.m (EST)].

© 1996 by The Haworth Press, Inc. All rights reserved.

dence is far from clear. No major catastrophe or war has obliterated the relevant data. In fact, the period since the likely origin of these holidays is now known as the Pax McDonald's, due to the extended period of World peace that was ushered in after McDonald's first entered what were then known as China, the Soviet Union, and Eastern Europe. This signalled the peaceful global conquest by Saint Ronald McDonald, at a time when McDonald's sold only food products and the people of the World spoke a variety of languages. No, the lack of data is instead because at some point after the development of United World Government and Entertainment Incorporated, history simply lacked any tension to make it interesting. There was also convincing evidence that history was a source of discontent and neuroses. So when people learned to stop recording the trivia of daily and yearly events, history stopped as well.

As a result, even the details of Saint Ronald's birth and life are lost in the mists of antiquity, along with the biographies of lesser deities such as Colonel Sanders, the Michelin Man, and Mickey Mouse. Although he accepts the catechism that history is bunk, Gucci hopes that if the roots of current celebrations and their patron saints can be pieced together, this proof of divine inspiration will help stop a strange sociopathology spreading among a growing number of the people of the earth: heretic asceticism! Not only does this barbaric and nihilistic cult refuse to worship Saint Ronald, they reject all of our major holidays and refuse to consume the associated products and services to which they are constitutionally entitled. Recently they have also begun to boycott such sacred sites as Marlboro Country, Ford Country, Sesame Street, Disney Universe, and even McDonaldland. What is worse, they fail to show any enthusiasm for the games, even when such arch rivals as Nissan and the Toyota contest. Obviously, such hereticism is dangerous and threatens not only the economy but our essential values. Gucci has no desire to kindle nostalgia for a long dead past, but by returning to the origins of World holidays, perhaps the nonbelievers can be made to accept the legends celebrated by these holidays and their sacrilegious apathetic behavior can be stopped before it spreads farther.

## *GLOBALIZATION THROUGH COMMERCE*

The one-world commercial future envisioned in the preceding story is both less fanciful and less innocent than it may first appear. Sklair (1993) notes that in 1990, 60 countries (excluding Eastern Europe and countries with fewer than one million people) had GNPs of less than ten billion U.S. dollars, while 135 transnational corporations had revenues in excess of this amount. With Ronald McDonald leading the way, multinational consumer goods corporations are now breaking down international barriers that have withstood armies, missionaries, crusaders, and politicians of the past. Historically, soldiers, missionaries, immigrants, and merchant traders have all been influential in diffusing elements of their own cultures to other parts of the world, albeit slowly and gradually. Marshall McLuhan recognized that with innovations in transportation and mass media, tourists, publishers, and broadcasters join this list of change agents and help make the world a global village (McLuhan and Powers 1983). But there is now a new member in this cast who is perhaps the most important cultural ambassador of all: the multinational consumer goods and services corporation and its minion–Ronald McDonald, Mickey Mouse, Colonel Sanders, Big Bird, the Michelin Man, and a host of others. A related type of multinational change agent is the entertainment personality, including the singers, movie and television stars, and sports heroes who increasingly command worldwide followings. Like Ronald and Mickey, Madonna and Péle, command far greater attention and devotion than any of the world's political leaders. In 1986, a survey showed that 96 percent of American school children recognized Ronald McDonald, making him second only to Santa Claus in name recognition (Ritzer 1993). Bibendum, the Michelin Man, is not far behind (Varnedde and Gopnik 1990).

It does not exaggerate to credit such ambassadors for world commercial culture with playing an important role in ending the cold war between the U.S. and the former Soviet Union, reunifying Eastern and Western Europe, stimulating political reform in China, and creating a shifting set of consumer goods that are uniformly desired throughout the world (Kohák 1992, Kozminski 1992, Ostaszewski 1992). With television and the walking billboard of the tourist, the latest desiderata of people in the world's most affluent nations quickly become the desiderata of people in the world's poorest nations (Belk 1988). When McDonald's new Moscow outlet immediately began to outdraw Lenin's tomb and became the chain's largest and busiest outlet, the intensity of world desire for capitalist commercial brands was dramatically demonstrated (Huey 1990, Schudson 1991). Such apparent desire for Western goods is not necessarily benign or innocuous. For instance in Romania it is increasingly common for smokers to opt for American or French cigarettes that are four to five times as expensive as Romanian cigarettes, even though smoking a pack a day of foreign cigarettes demands an entire salary (Ger, Belk, and Lascu 1993). In Bangladesh an adult smoking significantly increases child morbidity and mortality, not due to cigarette smoke, but rather due to the reduction in income to buy food (Belk 1988, Chapman 1986). But in Romania, Bangladesh, and elsewhere, to use the products from the consumer dreamlands of the more developed world is highly alluring. As Wallack and Montgomery (1991, p. 31) observe, "It is highly unlikely that a teenager in a developing country (or anywhere) can easily evaluate the advertising of dangerous products [like cigarettes] promoted with sexy, 'modern' images."

The power of Ronald McDonald has been compared to that of religious leaders, and consumer activities in McDonald's have been seen as sacred rituals (Fishwick 1978, 1983b, Kottak 1981). Similar analyses have been offered of the imaginary characters of the Disney Corporation (e.g., Fjellman 1992, Gould 1979, Mollenhoff 1939), and some have detected a sinister scheme to install worldwide capitalism through Mickey Mouse, Uncle Scrooge, and Donald Duck (Dorfman 1983, Dorfman and Mattelart 1971/1975). With the avidly sought Japanese Disneyland near Tokyo and EuroDisneyland outside of Paris, as well as Disney's media ventures, the scope of Disney consumerism has spread beyond comic book and souvenir sales to worldwide entertainment services as well. Media figures also play an important part in the multinationalization of consumer desires. The worldwide popularity of such television series as "Dallas" and "Dynasty" in the 1980s and early 1990s is a case in point (e.g., Ang 1985, Liebes and Katz 1990, Silj 1988, Thomsen 1989), but other television series and motion pictures echo these influences. In Trinidad, Miller (1990) reports that the U.S. television series "The Young and the Restless" is so popular that in many places work effectively stops when it is aired, and it inspired two calypsos of the same name in 1988. Not the least of its influences, Miller finds, is in stimulating desire for clothing seen on the characters of the series.

Caughey (1984) offers an insightful analysis of how characters seen on television (e.g., series stars, cartoon characters, political figures, musicians, and sports heroes and heroines) can powerfully influence the lives of viewers. Through intense and frequent media exposure to these stars, many viewers feel that they have come to know them. Furthermore, the relationship is often believed to be two-sided. For many, these stars are seen to be talking, singing, or playing just to them. They are believed to somehow know the viewer, and that is presumably why they can speak so clearly and directly to him or her. The media figure enters the viewer's life as a well-known "real" person with whom the viewer interacts in fantasy, including dreams and daydreams. Although this is often a conscious and willing suspension of disbelief, it can also operate outside of consciousness. A number of studies have found evidence of the distorting influence of media viewership on our social construction of reality (e.g., Fox and Phillber 1978, Lee 1989, Mattelart 1989/1991, O'Guinn, Lee, and Faber

1986, Vilanilam 1989), or perhaps more accurately, on our "social construction of unreality" (Duncan 1978).

As a result of such influences, aided by the globalization occurring in mass media, advertising, distribution, tourism, sports, and transportation, cultural and subcultural uniqueness seems to be slowly but inexorably decreasing, or in some cases becoming stylized in ways that bear little resemblance to traditional cultural patterns. Music is increasingly becoming world music. Food is increasingly succumbing to an international cuisine. Clothing styles are becoming a pastiche of worldwide influences. Our heroes are decreasingly likely to be local and increasingly likely to be selected from around the globe. Our shopping malls, franchise outlets, hotels, airports, banks, and gambling casinos are quickly becoming indistinguishable, whether they are in Australia, Europe, Asia, or the Americas (Horne 1992). This in fact is the explicit agenda of Elkin's (1976) Ben Flesh who believes the beauty of the franchises he owns is to homogenize an otherwise ideosyncratic world. If our religions, languages, and currencies continue to act as major points of difference, it may be that it is simply too early in the process of globalization for these differences to have disappeared. Changes planned by the European Economic Community point the way toward eventual global convergence in these areas as well. But globalization through world commerce is only part of the story. To more fully evaluate the changes taking place as we become global citizens, it is necessary to also consider local resistance to globalism and the trend toward hyperreality that seems intimately connected to globalization.

## *LOCAL RESISTANCE TO GLOBALIZATION*

As if in illustration of the Newtonian principle that for every action there is an equal but opposite reaction, the increasingly evident globalism pervading the world has spawned debate as well as various forms of hypothesized resistance including localism, ethnogenesis, and neo-nationalism. While the social and political science debates sparked by globalism offer no consensus on alternatives futures, they cast considerable doubt on the thoroughly global future envisioned in the opening tale (e.g., Featherstone 1990; Sklair 1991). As Thomas (1991, p. 185) concludes,

> ... imperialism is considered one of the most important causes of the "globalization" of culture, a topic that has received increased academic attention. Perhaps in popular perceptions more than scholarly discourse there is a certain crude modernism and Eurocentrism in some views of this process which take it for granted that internationalization entails homogenization, specifically, the assimilation of

other cultures to Euro-American models. It is assumed that the popularity of manufactured consumer items in Asia attests to the immense appeal of Euro-American values and goods, even though East Asian production and technical innovation have eclipsed Europe and the United States as far as many consumer items are concerned. Such notions, like the idea that Eastern Europe has finally been won over to what was all along a better form of sociality and economy, perpetuate the same kind of misreading of others' perceptions and intentions that characterized colonial views. . . .

A part of the argument against inevitable global homogenization is that the presence of foreign brands, theme parks, films, and television programs should not be taken to imply that these things mean the same thing in Bucharest, Kathmandu, or Port Moresby as they mean in Washington, D.C., Paris, or London. Thus, Brannen (1992a, 1992b) shows that the Japanese use the intentionally American facade of Tokyo Disneyland to articulate a particularly Japanese self-concept by using this facade as a caricatured "other." By insisting on an exact copy of the Anaheim Disneyland, the Japanese were able to keep the park exotic and thereby distance themselves from this Americanism in order to maintain the *uchi-soto* (inside-outside) dichotomy (Brannen 1992a; see also Van Maanen 1992). Liebes and Katz (1990) found that the American television drama "Dallas" was interpreted very differently among Japanese, Israelis, Algerians, and Americans. Miller (1990) argues that American soap operas have created a dialogue that has strengthened rather than weakened unique national identity in Trinidad, while Wilk (1993) has made a similar argument concerning the effects of American television programs in Belize.

In addition to the argument that cultures transform and appropriate the global into a unique system of local cultural meaning, another hypothesized type of resistance is seen in the ethnogenesis that has blossomed with the demise of communism in Eastern Europe and the former Soviet Union (Smith 1991). As the breakup of the Soviet Union, Czechoslovakia, and Yugoslavia as well as ethnic disputes elsewhere in Eastern Europe suggest, rather than marching toward a unified world order, ethnic identity has been revivified by the political changes occurring since the 1989 political and economic revolutions. As Belk and Paun (forthcoming) show for Romania, even though there has been an influx of Western soft drinks, liquors, cigarettes, films, television programs, clothing, candies, music, and other consumer goods, significant differences in foods, clothing, religion, vehicles, and celebrations act as ethnic markers that are used by the Romanian majority and the Hungarian and Gypsy minorities to proclaim their ethnic identities and thereby resist assimilation to each other, much less to global culture.

Just as ethnic groups have grown increasingly stronger in the face of global consumer culture, there has also been a rise in nationalism which constitutes a third form of resistance to globalization. While Boorstin (1968) saw Americans being united in "consumption communities" through their shared reverence for national brands, such feelings of kinship exist only superficially, if at all, with global brands that cross national boundaries (see Friedman, Vanden Abeele, and DeVoss 1992, 1993). The one world scenario envisioned in the opening story is not achieved as simply as buying the world a Coke. And the forecasts that the European community would dissolve national boundaries, currencies, and languages, appears premature at best. National tensions may have been sublimated into the Olympics and other international sporting events, but they have hardly disappeared. Thus, as with localism and ethnogenesis, neonationalism offers further evidence of resistance to global consumer culture.

## *HYPERREALITY IN GLOBALIZATION*

If globalism is being resisted to the extent that it clearly does not portend a nationless one world future, what then are the implications of Coca-Cola, Disney, Marlboro, and McDonald's global proliferation? It might seem as we slip into fantasy relationships with media personalities and pay homage, through our spending, to Ronald McDonald, the Marlboro man, and Mickey Mouse, that we are losing touch with reality. However, as Baudrillard (1988) argues, this is not the case. Instead we learn to prefer a certain stylized reality–a hyperreality. Baudrillard cites Disneyland as a quintessential example of hyperreality. In Disneyland's Main Street U.S.A. we find an idealized and romanticized version of small town America at the turn of the last century (Francaviglia 1981, Wallace 1989). This is accomplished through 5/8 to 7/8 scale architecture, exceptionally clean grounds, horse-drawn carriages, and college student employees carefully selected and supervised to be the ideal clean-cut middleclass middle American boy or girl next door (Belk 1991, Van Maanen and Kunda 1989). The fantasy characters who parade through Disneyland must be frequently relieved because people sometimes treat them with the same slapstick violence that these characters meet with in cartoons. Generally, however, people can distinguish the real from the hyperreal, while nevertheless displaying a preference for the idealized version of the latter.

Hyperreality is a sanitized version of reality, cleansed of strife, world problems, dirt, prejudice, exploitation, or other problems of everyday life. It is not restricted to Disneyland and Disney World. Hyperreality is also found in other theme parks and shopping malls, for instance (Belk and Bryce 1993, O'Guinn and Belk 1989). As Bauman (1990, p. 148) sees it,

The most recent invention of 'thematic' shopping malls, with Caribbean villages, Indian reserves and Polynesian shrines closely packed together under one roof, has brought the old technique of institutional separation to the level of perfection reached in the past only by the zoo.

At McDonald's, male employees must keep their hair short and wear well-shined black shoes, while females must wear dark low shoes, hair nets, and only light makeup (Fishwick, 1983a, p. 7). Van Maanen and Kunda (1989) explain the insistence on even stricter employee appearance rules at Disneyland:

> Disneyland management has no desire to staff its attractions with transient roustabouts who, in the eyes of management, might threaten the show by reminding paying guests of sleazy carnival attendants with tattoos of MOTHER on their arms. (p. 86)

Even visitors who are unsuitably punk or countercultural in appearance are turned away from Disney's gates (Van Maanen and Kunda 1989). Disney ventures, in other words, succeed because they are perceived as safe, clean, and innocuous (Zukin 1990). Similarly, Coca-Cola and McDonald's succeed because ". . . there is too little malice and too much ignorance to offend–which is the way many of us feel about Ronald peddling his burgers to the cavernous stomachs of the world" (Fishwick, 1984a, p. 12). Likewise, Honda overcame the image of motorcycle rider as Hell's Angel by substituting a sanitized image of the person next door, in order to sell their motorcycles to a mass market ("You Meet the Nicest People on a Honda"). McDonald's, Disney, and an increasing number of other mass merchandisers are presenting an idealized hyperreal image as they sell their products and services (e.g., Eco 1983). Museum directors worry about the "Disneyfication" of their presentations and becoming more entertaining than enlightening or inspiring (Belk 1991), while officials at historic sites worry about the stylized "touristification" of their facilities (Lanfant 1989, Belk and Costa 1991). In such cases, the interest in presenting history, art, or culture is replaced by an emphasis on fantasy and spectacle (Debord 1970). For instance, it is no longer necessary for tourists to make their way up the Nile river to see the wonders of ancient Egyptian architecture, because they can visit the Pharonic Village theme park on the outskirts of Cairo and witness the gods and crafts of the ancient Egyptian dynasties on a barge in "the Canal of Mythology" (Slyomovics 1989). The Polynesian Cultural Center on Oahu, recreating a village composed of a number of Polynesian cultures is another example (Brameld and Matsuyama 1977; Stanton 1989), among many (see MacCannell 1989).

Hyperreality is not an entirely new phenomenon. In Henry James (1893) story, "The Real Thing," the narrator despairs of trying to successfully illustrate a book about a lady and gentleman by using aristocrats as models and substitutes commoner models who present a more attractive image. Similarly, the delicate foliage in Gainsborough's portraits is reported to have been painted from carefully arranged broccoli on a table (Masuzawa 1989). In Brian Moore's (1976) novel, *The Great Victorian Collection,* the jaded public stops visiting an authentic collection of Victorian artifacts when a stylized pseudo-Victorian shopping village opens nearby. And, arguably, advertising is inherently a hyperreal medium. Still, the presence of hyperrality seems much more pronounced and pervasive in globalized commercial ventures. It is not just that the world is getting smaller; with the aid of global consumer marketers it is becoming more sanitized, stylized, and fantasy-dominated. What remains to be discussed is how this trend toward hyperreality affects culture and whether there are countertrends that may oppose the spread of globalized hyperreality.

## THE COURSE AND EFFECTS OF GLOBALIZED HYPERREALITY

Boorstin (1964) was among the first to detect a movement away from folk culture to a guided pseudo-culture that has been created and packaged by corporate interests, although his analysis was restricted to the United States. Debord (1970) suggests that the illusions created by commercial interests have a religious character and promote a "fallacious paradise." The consumer of things becomes a consumer of illusions. In this sense, hyperreal consumer culture is a religion that is increasingly converting the world to a singular image of paradise as a standard package of branded consumer goods and services. The items in this package are promoted by media images such as Ronald McDonald and his brethren and can be seen on global television programs, movies, sports stars, and tourists.

Three detrimental effects may be charged to result from such developments. One is the banalization of life seen by Debord (1970, p. 55):

> The movement of *banalization,* under the shimmering diversions of the spectacle, dominates modern society the world over and at every point where the developed consumption of commodities has multiplied the roles and the objects to choose from in appearance.

While it seems clear that a world consuming the same Big Macs and Coca-Colas, watching the same television series, listening to the same music, driving the same cars, visiting the same hotels, and wearing interchangeable clothing has lost vitality and originality, we must be careful not to be too nostalgic in our image of the past. And if such nostalgia becomes too tempting, it too is likely to be catered to with a stylized and commercialized version of the past such as that of Disney's Main Street, U.S.A., various shopping malls, and numerous nostalgic motion pictures. Nevertheless, the charge that material life is becoming increasingly uniform and banal is kept in perspective by realizing that it is not a new criticism (e.g., Rilke 1939) and that the nostalgically imagined past always forms a safe refuge for our hopes and ideals (McCracken 1988).

The second major potential detriment that might be extrapolated from the tendency toward globalized commercial hyperreality is the obliteration of cultural differences. Leaving aside the resistance to cultural hegemony discussed in the last section, while the charge of disappearing cultural differences appears to be valid in some respects (e.g., hamburgers, tacos, and pizza are increasingly available throughout the world), it is false in others. The existence of international mixed cuisine depends not on an obliteration of cultural differences but on their highlighting, if often in a stylized hyperreal manner. Thus the taco's popularity depends on its continued association with Mexico and things (stereotypically) Mexican. Similarly, there is little to draw the European tourist to South America if the sights and services there are totally indistinguishable from those at home. Rather, the culture that represents Brazil or Peru in the European's mind is likely to be stylized, exaggerated, and subtly Europeanized. Brazil thus becomes year-round Carnival and samba, while Peru becomes Inca-land and the Andes. In one analysis the new tourist towns of Mexico have been termed "Gringolandia" and regarded as little more than theme parks for Anglo amigos (Shacochis 1989). In these transformations there is indeed a destruction of the former cultures of Central and South America, but not by making them indistinguishable from European cultures. Likewise, international rivalries do not disappear in an age of détente; they are merely stylized and sublimated in sports, entertainment, and other commercial rather than political arenas. Culture is redesigned, packaged, sanitized, and trivialized in the process, but it is not totally homogenized.

And a third concern from the trend toward globalized hyperreality is the commodified rationalization of life. As Ames (1992) warns:

> Quantity, popularity, mass-appeal, customer satisfaction, and majority opinion become the criteria for determining success and goodness, fact and value, art and craft. Thus we see how the ideology of competitive individualism and commodity consumption batter down the marketplace walls to march triumphantly through the streets of everyday life. Ronald McDonald and his hamburgers are but the vanguards of this commodification of everyone. (p. 138)

Ritzer (1993) identifies the elements of formal rationality of this sort as efficiency, predictability, quantification, and control. Van Maanen and Kunda (1989) and Hochschild (1983) suggest that one of the things we give up to achieve this rationality is control of our own emotions in the workplace. And Halton (1992) worries that the cost of this rationality is no less than our humanity. Similar concerns were raised by the rise of Taylorism and Fordism in the workplace earlier in this century. The difference may be that globalized hyperreality in the various forms of Coca-Cola, McDonald's, and Disney, has a much more appealing face and seems far more innocuous than the drab efficiency of the Metropolis assembly line. Rather than our being coerced into compliance, it is more like a seduction.

But one further trend offers a ray of hope in the age of Ronald McDonald. There is a sense in which the same globalized consumer culture that seems to be sweeping the world also offers the opportunity to resist banalization, rationalization, and cultural obliteration. It is seen in microcosm in residents' expensive redecoration of their rented kitchens in the London council housing estate investigated by Miller (1988), even though the original kitchens must be restored before leaving. It is seen in the consumer-empowering sale of goods in the garage sales studied by Soiffer and Herrmann (1987). And it is seen in the regendering of motorscooters by certain British youth chronicled by Hebdige (1988). Although these scooters were originally targeted to women, the Mods in Britain made them a trendy male vehicle. In each case, consumers have used standardized objects of the marketplace in a way that asserts identity, reclaims control, and successfully counters the trends toward globalism, hyperreality, and multinationalization. Such resistance and quiet rebellion, though slight and scattered, offer some small hope that the seemingly inexorable progress toward the age of Ronald McDonald will not go unopposed.

## REFERENCES

Ames, Michael M. (1992), *Canibal Tours and Glass Boxes: The Anthropology of Museums*, Vancouver: UBC Press.

Ang, Ian (1985), *Watching Dallas*, London: Methuen.

Baudrillard, Jean (1988), *Jean Baudrillard: Selected Writings*, Mark Poster, ed., Stanford, CA: Stanford University Press, 119-148, 166-184.

Bauman, Zygmunt (1990), "Modernity and Ambivalence," *Global Culture: Nationalism, Globalism and Modernity*, Mike Featherstone, ed., London: Sage, 143-169.

Belk, Russell W. (1988), "Third World Consumer Culture," *Marketing and Development: Toward Broader Dimensions*, Erdogan Kumcu and A. Fuat Firat, eds., Greenwich, CT: JAI Press, 103-127.

Belk, Russell W. (1991), "Possessions and the Sense of Past," *Highways and*

*Buyways: Naturalistic Research From the Consumer Behavior Odyssey*, Provo, UT: Association for Consumer Research, 114-130.

Belk, Russell W. and Wendy J. Bryce (1993), "Christmas Shopping Scenes: From Modern Miracle to Postmodern Mall," *International Journal of Research in Marketing*, 277-296.

Belk, Russell W. and Janeen A. Costa (1991), "A Critical Assessment of International Tourism," *Proceedings of the Third International Conference on Marketing and Development*, Kiran Bothra and Ruby Roy Dholakia, eds., New Delhi, 371-382.

Belk, Russell W. and Magda Paun (forthcoming), "Ethnicity and Consumption in Romania," in *Consumption and Ethnicity*, Janeen Costa and Gary Bamossy, eds., Newbury Park, CA: Sage.

Boorstin, Daniel J. (1964), *The Image: A Guide to Pseudo-Events in America*, New York: Harper.

Boorstin, Daniel J. (1968), "The Consumption Community," *The Consuming Public*, G. McClellan, ed., New York: H. W. Wilson.

Brameld, Theodore and Midori Matsuyama (1977), *Tourism as Cultural Learning: Two Controversial Case Studies in Educational Anthropology*, Lanham, MD: University Press of America.

Brannen, Mary Yoko (1992a), "'Bwana Mickey': Constructing Cultural Consumption at Tokyo Disneyland," in *Remade in Japan*, Joseph J. Tobin, ed., New Haven, CT: Yale University Press, 216-234.

Brannen, Mary Yoko (1992b), "Cross-Cultural Materialism: Commodifying Culture in Japan," *Meaning, Measure and Morality of Materialism*, Floyd Rudmin and Marsha Richins, eds., Provo, UT: Association for Consumer Research, 167-180.

Chapman, Simon (1986), "The World Tobacco Industry," *Consumer Transnational Corporations and Development*, Ted Wheelwright, ed., Sydney: University of Sydney Press, 191-219.

Debord, Guy (1970), *Society of the Spectacle*, Detroit, MI: Black and Red.

Dorfman, Ariel (1983), *The Empire's Old Clothes: What the Lone Ranger, Babar, and Other Innocent Heroes Do to Our Minds*, New York: Pantheon.

Dorfman, Ariel and Armand Mattelart (1971/1975), *How to Read Donald Duck: Imperialist Ideology in the Disney Comic*, David Kunzle, ed., NY: International General.

Duncan, James S. (1978), "The Social Construction of Unreality," *Humanistic Geography: Prospects and Problems*, David Ley and Marwyn S. Samuels, eds., Maaroufa Press, 269-282.

Eco, Umberto (1983), *Travels in Hyperreality: Essays*, William Weaver, ed., San Diego, CA: Harcourt Brace Jovanovich.

Elkin, Stanley (1976), *The Franchiser*, New York: Farrar, Straus, Giroux.

Featherstone, Mike, ed., (1990), *Global Culture: Nationalism, Globalization and Modernity*, London: Sage.

Fishwick, Marshall, ed., (1978), *The World of Ronald McDonald*, Bowling Green, OH: Bowling Green University Popular Press.

Fishwick, Marshall (1983a), "Introduction," *Ronald Revisited: The World of*

*Ronald McDonald,* Marshall Fishwick, ed., Bowling Green, OH: Bowling Green University Popular Press, 1-13.
Fishwick, Marshall, ed., (1983b), *Ronald Revisited: The World of Ronald McDonald,* Bowling Green, OH: Bowling Green University Popular Press.
Fjellman, Stephen M. (1992), *Vinyl Leaves: Walt Disney World and America,* Boulder, CO: Westview Press.
Fox, William S. and Pilliber, William W. (1978), "Television Viewing and the Perception of Affluence," *Sociological Quarterly,* 19, 103-112.
Francaviglia, Richard V. (1981), " 'Main Street, U.S.A.': A Comparison/Contrast of Streetscapes in Disneyland and Walt Disney World," *Journal of Popular Culture,* 15 (Summer), 141-156.
Friedman, Monroe, Piet Vanden Abeele, and Koen De Vos (1992), "Look at the Consumption Community Concept Through a Psychological Lens," in *Meaning, Measure, and Morality of Materialism,* Floyd Rudmin and Marsha Richins, Eds., Provo, UT: Association for Consumer Research, 126-127.
Friedman, Monroe, Piet Vanden Abeele, and Koen De Vos (1993), "Boorstin's Consumption Community Concept: A Tale of Two Countries," *Journal of Consumer Policy,* 16 (1), 35-60.
Ger, Güliz, Russell W. Belk, and Dana-Nicoleta Lascu (1993), "The Development of Consumer Desire in Marketizing and Developing Economies: The Cases of Romania and Turkey," *Advances in Consumer Research,* Vol. 20, Leigh McAllister and Chris Allen, eds., Provo, UT: Association for Consumer Research, 102-107.
Gould, Stephen J. (1979), "Mickey Mouse Meets Konrad Lorenz," *Natural History,* 88 (May), 20-24.
Halton, Eugene (1992), "A Long Way from Home: Automatic Culture in Domestic and Civic Life," in *Meaning, Measure, and Morality of Materialism,* Floyd Rudmin and Marsha Richins, eds., Provo, UT: Association for Consumer Research, 1-9.
Hebdige, Dick (1988), *Hiding in the Light,* London: Routledge.
Hochschild, Arlie R. (1983), *The Managed Heart: Commercialization of Human Feeling,* Berkeley, CA: University of California Press.
Horne, Donald (1992), *The Intelligent Tourist,* McMahons Point, New South Wales: Margaret Gee.
Huey, John (1990), "America's Hottest Export: Pop Culture," *Fortune,* 122 (December 31), 50-60.
James, Henry (1893), *The Real Thing and Other Tales,* New York: Macmillan.
Kohák, Erazin (1992), "Ashes, Ashes . . . Central Europe After Forty Years," *Daedalus,* 121 (Spring), 197-215.
Kozminski, Andrzej K. (1992), "Consumers in Transition From the Centrally Planned Economy to the Market Economy," *Journal of Consumer Policy,* 14 (4), 351-369.
Kottak, Conrad P. (1981), "Rituals at McDonald's," in *The American Dimension: Cultural Myths and Social Realities,* W. Arens and Susan P. Montagne, eds., Sherman Oaks, CA: Alfred Publishing, 124-136.
Lanfant, Marie-Françoise (1989), "International Tourism Resists the Crisis,"

Anna Olszewska and K. Roberts, eds., *Leisure and Life-Style: A Comparative Analysis of Free Time*, Newbury Park, CA: Sage, 178-193.

Lee, Wei-Na (1989), "The Mass-Mediated Consumption Realities of Three Cultural Groups," *Advances in Consumer Research*, Vol. 16, Thomas Srull, ed., Provo, UT: Association for Consumer Research, 771-778.

Liebes, Tamar and Elihu Katz (1990), *The Export of Meaning: Cross-Cultural Readings of Dallas*, New York: Oxford University Press.

MacCannell, Dean (1989), *The Tourist: A New Theory of the Leisure Class*, 2nd ed., London: Macmillan.

Masuzawa, Tomoko (1989), "Original Lost: An Image of Myth and Ritual in the Age of Mechanical Reproduction," *Journal of Religion*, 69 (July), 307-325.

Mattelart, Armand (1989/1991), *Advertising International: The Privatization of Public Space*, Michael Chanan, trans., London: Routledge.

McCracken, Grant (1988), *Culture and Consumption: New Approaches to the Symbolic Character of Consumer Goods and Activities*, Bloomington, IN: Indiana University Press.

McLuhan, Marshall and Bruce R. Powers (1989), *The Global Village: Transformations in World Life and Media in the 21st Century*, New York: Oxford University Press.

Miller, Daniel (1988), "Appropriating the State on the Council Estate," *Man*, 23, 353- 372.

Miller, Daniel (1990), " 'The Young and the Restless' in Trinidad: A Case of the Local and the Global in Mass Consumption," working paper, Department of Anthropology, University College, London.

Mollenhoff, Fritz (1939), "Remarks on the Popularity of Mickey Mouse," *American Imago*, 1 (3), 19-32.

Moore, Brian (1976), *The Great Victorian Collection*, New York: Farrar, Straus, Giroux.

O'Guinn, Thomas and Russell W. Belk (1989), "Heaven on Earth: Consumption at Heritage Village, U.S.A.," *Journal of Consumer Research*, 16 (September), 227-238.

O'Guinn, Thomas, Wei-Na Lee, and Ronald J. Faber (1986), "Acculturation: The Impact of Divergent Paths on Buyer Behavior," *Advances in Consumer Research*, Vol. 13, Richard J. Lutz, ed., Provo, UT: Association for Consumer Research, 579-583.

Ostaszewski, Krzysztof (1992), "The Boldest Social Experiment of the Twentieth Century," *The Market Solution to Economic Development in Eastern Europe*, Robert W. McGee, ed., Lewiston, Wales, UK: Lamperter, 223-243.

Rilke, Ranier M. (1939), *Duino Elegies*, J. Leishman and S. Spender, translators, New York: W. W. Norton.

Ritzer, George (1993), *The McDonaldization of Society*, Thousand Oaks, CA: Pine Forge Press.

Schudson, Michael (1991), "Delectable Materialism: Were the Critics of Consumer Culture Wrong All Along?" *The American Prospect*, Spring), 26-35.

Shacochis, Bob (1989), "In Deepest Gringolandia; Mexico: The Third World as Tourist Theme Park," *Harper's*, (July), 42-50.

Silj, Alessandro (1988), *East of Dallas: The European Challenge to American Television*, London: British Film Institute.

Sklair, Leslie (1991), *Sociology of the Global System: Social Change in Global Perspective*, Baltimore: Johns Hopkins University Press.

Sklair, Leslie (1993), "Competing Models of Globalization: Theoretical Frameworks and Research Agendas," working paper, London School of Economics and Political Science, University of London, Houghton Street, London 2C2A 2AE.

Slyomovics, Susan (1989), "Cross-Cultural Dress and Tourist Performance in Egypt," *Performing Arts Journal*, 11 (3) and 12 (1), 139-148.

Smith, Anthony D. (1991), *National Identity*, Reno, NV: University of Nevada Press.

Soiffer, Stephen S. and Gretchen M. Herrmann (1987), "Visions of Power: Ideology and Practice in the American Garage Sale," *Sociological Review*, 35 (February), 48-83.

Stanton, Max E. (1989), "The Polynesian Cultural Center: A Multi-Ethnic Model of Seven Pacific Cultures," in *Hosts and Guests: The Anthropology of Tourism*, 2nd ed., Valene L. Smith, ed., Philadelphia, PA: University of Pennsylvania Press, 247-262.

Thomas, Nicholas (1991), *Entangled Objects: Exchange, Material Culture, and Colonialism in the Pacific*, Cambridge, MA: Harvard University Press.

Thomsen, Christian W., ed. (1989), *Cultural Transfer or Electronic Imperialism? The Impact of American Television Programs on European Television*, Heidelberg: Carl Winter Universitätsverlag.

Van Maanen, John (1992), "Displacing Disney: Some Notes on the Flow of Culture," *Qualitative Sociology*, 15 (Spring), 5-35.

Van Maanen, John and Gideon Kunda (1989), " 'Real Feelings': Emotional Expression and Organizational Culture," *Research in Organizational Behavior*, Vol. 11, Greenwich, CT: JAI Press, 43-103.

Varnedde, Kirk and Adam Gopnik (1990), *High & Low: Popular Culture, Modern Art*, New York: Museum of Modern Art.

Vilanilam, John (1989), "Television Advertising and the Indian Poor," *Media, Culture and Society*, 11 (October), 485-497.

Wallace, Michael (1989), "Mickey Mouse History: Portraying the Past in Disney World," *History Museums in the United States: A Critical Assessment*, Warren Leon and Roy Rosenzweig, eds., Urbana, IL: University of Illinois Press, 158-180.

Wallack, Lawrence and Kathryn Montgomery (1991), "Advertising for All by the Year 2000: Public Health Implications for the Third World," working paper, The Marin Institute, 24 Belvedere Street, San Rafael, CA 94901.

Wilk, Richard R. (1993), " 'It's Destroying a Whole Generation': Television and Moral Discourse in Belize," *Visual Anthropology*, 5, 229-244.

Zukin, Sharon (1990), "Socio-Spatial Prototypes of a New Organization of Consumption: The Role of Real Cultural Capital," *Sociology*, 24 (February), 37-56.

# The Key to Successful Euromarketing: Standardization or Customization?

Berend Wierenga
Ad Pruyn
Eric Waarts

**SUMMARY.** Using a framework that incorporates notions from economics and consumer behavior, this paper examines the similarities and differences with respect to consumers and marketing infrastructure in the countries of the European Union. The conclusion is that there are tremendous differences in income levels and income spending patterns among the countries of the European Union and also major differences with respect to consumer values and lifestyles. Furthermore, the distribution and retailing environments as well as the media, differ considerably from one country to the other.

The perspective of completely standardized marketing strategies for the whole European Union is still far removed. If a consumer homogenization process is taking place at all, such a process is likely to be slow. Suppliers (i.e., manufacturers and retailers) adopting Euro-oriented marketing strategies will contribute more to the emergence of the 'European Consumer' than the autonomous cultural homogenization process. *[Article copies available from The Haworth Document Delivery Service: 1-800-342-9678.]*

---

Berend Wierenga is Professor of Marketing, Ad Pruyn is Associate Professor of Marketing, and Eric Waarts is Assistant Professor of Marketing at Erasmus University Rotterdam, Rotterdam School of Marketing, P.O. Box 1738, 3000 DR Rotterdam, The Netherlands.

[Haworth co-indexing entry note]: "The Key to Successful Euromarketing: Standardization or Customization?" Wierenga, Berend, Ad Pruyn, and Eric Waarts. Co-published simultaneously in *Journal of International Consumer Marketing* (International Business Press, an imprint of The Haworth Press, Inc.) Vol. 8, No. 3/4, 1996, pp. 39-67; and: *Global Perspectives in Cross-Cultural and Cross-National Consumer Research* (ed: Lalita A. Manrai, and Ajay K. Manrai) International Business Press, an imprint of The Haworth Press, Inc., 1996, pp. 39-67. Single or multiple copies of this article are available from The Haworth Document Delivery Service [1-800-342-9678, 9:00 a.m - 5:00 p.m. (EST)].

© 1996 by The Haworth Press, Inc. All rights reserved.

## INTRODUCTION

The European Union (EU) of twelve countries constitutes a market of about 325 million consumers. The famous 1985 'White Paper' of Lord Cockfield was aimed at the realization of 300 measures that will bring about a truly European market. Much of this has been realized now. With the disappearance of the legal, fiscal, administrative and institutional thresholds between the national markets it can be expected that an increasing number of companies, many of them operating nationally up to now, will invade new territories and try to market their products and services to customers in other EU-countries.

A fundamental question then is: how should these companies, when directing themselves to buyers in different European countries, design their marketing programs? Should they follow a standardized policy, i.e., apply the same marketing program to the different consumer groups in the different EU-countries, or should they customize their marketing programs and adapt them to the specific needs and wants in the specific countries? With 'marketing program' we mean the complete marketing mix: product design, product positioning, brand name, packaging, retail price, basic advertising message, creative expression, sales promotion, media allocation, salesforce, type of retail outlets and customer service (Jain, 1989).

Within marketing the issue of standardization versus customization has been heavily debated, although not so much in the context of the emerging European market, but more often in the context of American companies going international.

Levitt (1983) has coined the term: 'globalization of markets.' His thesis is that new technological facilities (especially in communication) drive consumers wants and wishes into global commonality. "The world preference structure gets pressed into homogenized commonality." Gone or going rapidly are the accustomed differences in national and regional preferences regarding product or service features. Levitt's message is: perform global marketing, that is: standardization of a firm's marketing programs in different countries.

In Levitt's terminology, the opposite of global marketing is multinational marketing. The multinational corporation operates in a number of countries where in each situation it adjusts to the presumptive special conditions of the particular country: "The multinational corporation's accommodation mode to visible national differences is medieval and so are its offerings and its prices."

A quite opposite view is given by Kotler in his article: 'Global Standardization . . . Courting Danger' (1986). His assertion is that many international product failures have been caused by a lack of product adaptation. His adagium is: international customization, because customer demand in different nations for specific product features is different, consumers differ in resources and behavior and the environmental factors are different. Wind (1986) states that there is no strong empirical evidence that the world is becoming homogeneous.

Sheth (1986) emphasizes the difference between global competition and global marketing. Through worldwide mergers and acquisitions many firms compete globally, but using a customized marketing strategy (i.e., marketing programs adapted to local conditions).

Of course there is no unequivocal answer to the question in the title of this paper. The best that can be said with respect to the choice between standardization and customization is: it will depend. In this contribution an endeavor will be made to take stock of and discuss the factors that should be taken into account when making this choice.

We will ask the question of standardization versus customization in the context of marketing towards the twelve different national consumer populations that constitute the European Union.

The question of global or multinational marketing in Europe has not often been dealt with in the international scientific marketing literature, with some exceptions, e.g., Wills (1991), Guido (1991) and Brown and Burt (1992). Some papers can be found in the literature within individual EU countries, e.g., in Holland: Steenkamp (1992), and Steenkamp et al. (1993). This lack of a substantial literature is surprising since the different EU-countries with their broad variety of ethical, cultural and historical differences offer an ideal opportunity to study the feasibility of standardized marketing programs.

In this paper we deal with the topic of Euromarketing at three levels: European consumers, European marketing infrastructure and European companies.

After developing a conceptual framework based on the (economic) notion of the income allocation process over expenditure categories and the (behavioral) notion of consumer decision processes within product classes, we look at the similarities between European consumers with respect to income level, and expenditure patterns on one hand and factors that influence consumer decision processes (family, values, lifestyle, etc.) on the other hand.

With respect to marketing infrastructure we look at similarities and differences with respect to factors such as retailing structure, media, advertising, distribution networks and their evolution in a European Union context.

As regards the European companies we discuss the major drives and hurdles in going European.

The paper ends with a few summarizing conclusions and the presentation of items for a research agenda on Euromarketing.

## SIMILARITY OF THE EU-MARKETS

For the analysis of the similarity of Euroconsumers we use two frameworks, one economic and one behavioral.

From a marketing point of view important questions are: how much can consumers spend, how do they allocate their expenditures over major consumption categories and within each category over generic product classes; and finally, how do they make their choices within a product class?

Figure 1 is a schematic representation of these different levels in the consumer income allocation process.

Since we would have obtained a huge scheme otherwise, in this figure at level 3 only two items: food and beverages and at level 4 only one: beer have been worked out as examples.

All other things being equal, the more equal the income levels and the more similar the allocation patterns over the several spending categories in the different markets, the better are the perspectives for a standardized marketing approach.

For a marketer the more generic allocation mechanism represented by the levels 2 to 4 of Figure 1 is important because it determines, at least in the short run, the potential of a market. The major interest of a particular brand manufacturer, however, is level 5: the choice by a consumer of a specific brand in a product class. Level 5 refers to the consumer decision process, also called the consumer problem solving process, which has received much attention in the behavioral marketing literature over the last three decades.

To evaluate the effects of specific (country) factors on the consumer decision processes and its outcome, we need a theory or (at least) a model of the way a consumer makes his choice from the alternatives in a product class. For this purpose we developed the schematic representation of Figure 2, which has been adapted from Engel, Blackwell and Miniard (1993).

The 'Engel and Blackwell model' as it is known in the literature, has been around for over twenty-five years and has been applied (with variations) in a huge number of different product classes and countries all over the world. The idea in using it here is that the structure of the model describing the consumer decision process is *universal,* but that the content

FIGURE 1. Different Levels of the Consumer Income Allocation Process

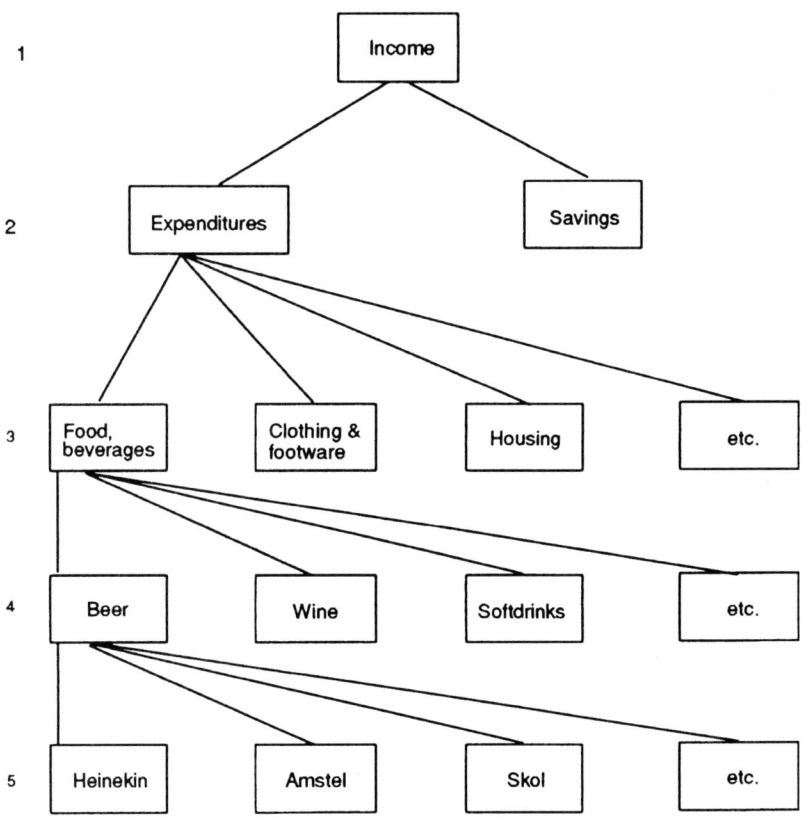

Levels

1 = income
2 = allocation over spending and saving
3 = allocation of expenditures over major consumption categories
4 = generic product class choice
5 = brand choice with product class

FIGURE 2. Abbreviated and Adapted Version of a Universal Consumer Decision Model (After: Engel, Blackwell & Miniard, 1993)

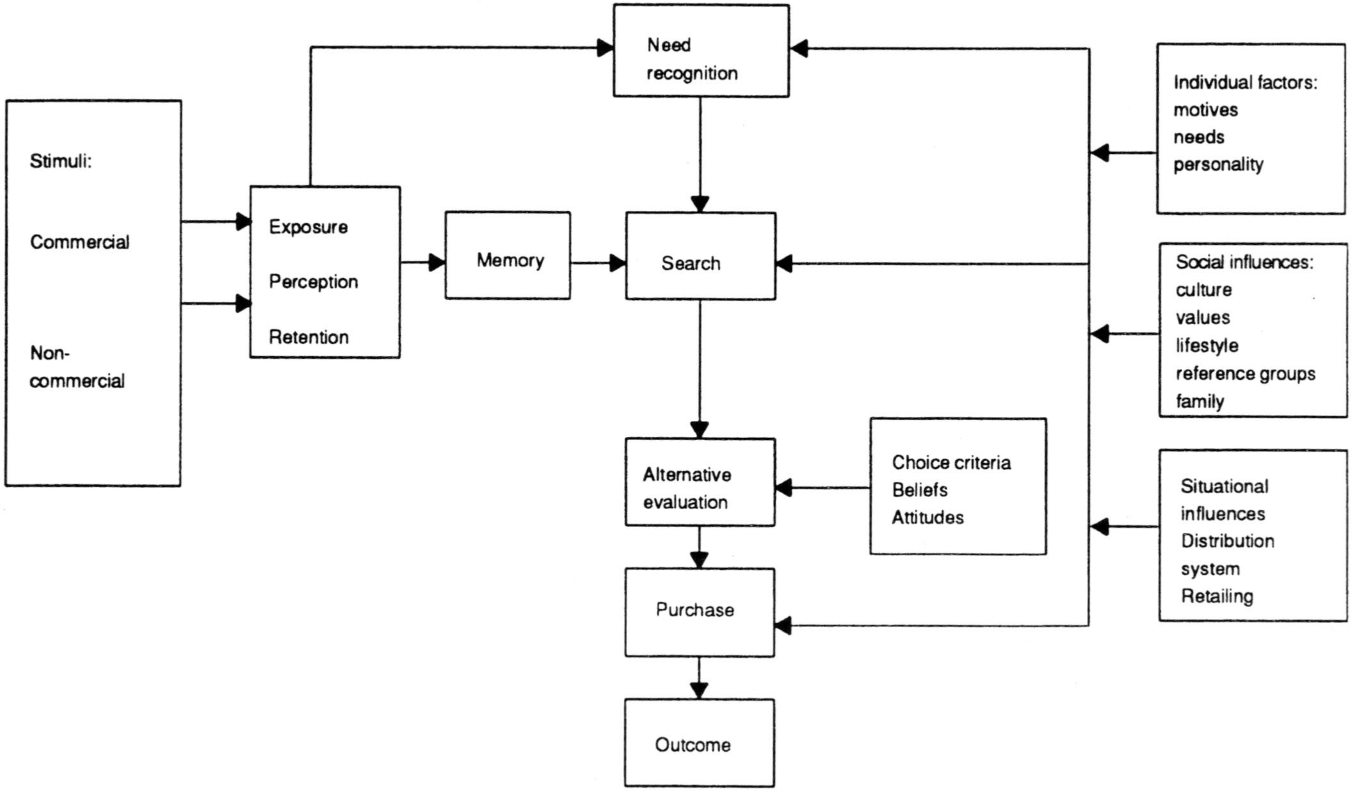

of the several *components* may vary from country to country, depending on the environment of the consumer.

Basically, the model of Figure 2 represents the consumer decision process as a process of problem solving which develops in five steps: need recognition, search, alternative evaluation, choice and outcome. For need recognition the (individual) motives are important. Motives are enduring predispositions that direct behavior toward certain goals (Engel et al., 1993, p. 35). Motives are activated by (i) drive arousal (e.g., hunger, thirst), (ii) 'autistic thinking' or (iii) environmental stimulation. It is clear that the first two are predominantly individual and universal, whereas environmental stimulation has everything to do with the type of society a consumer is in.

For the search-stage the consumer *information* environment is important. The consumer continuously receives stimuli from commercial and non-commercial sources that inform him/her about product, brands, and their attributes. Depending on exposure and attention factors a subset of all these stimuli will ultimately be stored in the consumer memory and constitutes information for his/her choices. Of course, there is also a direct effect of outside stimuli on problem recognition: seeing advertisements may directly trigger the purchase of an item in a product class. So it is clear that the consumer information environment in a country, media (newspapers, magazines, radio, TV) and advertising patterns, have a major impact on the outcome of consumer decision processes.

As Figure 2 indicates, there is a considerable influence of social factors on the consumer decision process: culture, values, lifestyle, reference groups, family, etc. Culture is a fundamental issue, it refers to the complex of values, ideas, artifacts and other meaningful symbols that serve humans to communicate, interpret and evaluate as members of society (Engel et al., 1993, p. 34). They are transmitted from one generation to the next and therefore deeply rooted in a society. Values are shared beliefs or group norms that have been internalized by individuals. For example, as some of the core values of the American society have been mentioned: achievement and success, activity, efficiency and practicality, progress, material comfort and freedom (Schiffman and Kanuk, 1978). As Figure 2 indicates, consumer values affect beliefs and attitudes with respect to products and brands and these are very important for the choices a consumer makes.

Since values are so important for the way consumers make their decisions, differences in consumer values between countries are of utmost relevance for the way the consumer should be approached by the marketer. The same holds for the concept of lifestyle: the patterns in which people live and spend time and money (Engel et al., 1993, p. 369). Lifestyle is a summary construct, reflecting consumer values. Value and lifestyle research (psychographics) may thus serve to analyze differences between countries. In the next paragraph we will give some comparative results from this type of research for different European countries.

Also relevant in the context of social influences on behavior is the concept of 'reference groups': those groups which have the ability to modify or reinforce individual's attitudes. (Robertson et al., 1984, p. 424). One of the major reference groups is the family. Thus differences in family structure between countries can be expected to lead to differences in consumer behavior.

Most European countries represent societies that have evolved in a process of development over many centuries. This causes many differences in cultures, values and lifestyles.

In addition to individual factors, social influences and influences from the information environment, there are other environmental factors that affect consumer behavior. A very important one is the retailing environment in which a customer makes his purchases. It makes quite a difference if he/she buys in a ultra-modern super- or hypermarket or in a traditional small grocery shop.

After having introduced these concepts which offer an analytical framework for studying the differences between European consumers, we will now look at some factual data pertaining to these concepts.

## *Expenditures and Income Allocation Patterns*

Table 1 provides information on an important part of the consumer income allocation process (level 3), as depicted in Figure 1.

The first striking element of Table 1 is the large differences in consumer expenditures between the 12 countries. Total expenditure levels (not included in this table) range from 1654 ecu's per capita in Portugal to 8336 ecu's per capita in Western Germany, which is a ratio of 1 to 5. In studying the figures of Table 1 one should realize that they do not tell the complete story, factors like fax regimes for example may also affect purchasing power of individual consumers.

Differences in purchasing power are of direct interest to the marketer, but in an indirect way, different income levels generally also represent different education levels and different habits with respect to magazine reading and TV-watching which is important for marketing communication.

The second conclusion to be drawn from Table 1 is that there are considerable differences in the allocation patterns over consumption categories. For example, food and beverages as percentage of total expenditures

TABLE 1. Allocation of Expenditures over Major Consumption Categories in the 12 EG-Countries (Ecu's per capita)*

| Spending categories<br>Country: | Food, beverages and tobacco | Clothes and footwear | Gross rent, fuel and power | Furniture, furnishings, households equipment | Medical care and health expenses | Transport and communication | Recreation, entertainment education and cultural services |
|---|---|---|---|---|---|---|---|
| 1 Belgium | 1490 (22) | 514 (7) | 1350 (20) | 696 (10) | 730 (11) | 878 (13) | 419 (6) |
| 2 Denmark | 1961 (24) | 488 (6) | 2049 (25) | 574 (7) | 153 (2) | 1401 (17) | 786 (10) |
| 3 W-Germany | 1443 (17) | 663 (8) | 1650 (20) | 695 (8) | 1176 (14) | 1180 (14) | 731 (9) |
| 4 Greece | 1198 (40) | 254 (9) | 348 (12) | 230 (8) | 90 (3) | 444 (15) | 131 (4) |
| 5 Spain | 1060 (28) | 276 (7) | 604 (16) | 266 (7) | 142 (4) | 525 (14) | 259 (7) |
| 6 France | 1650 (21) | 498 (6) | 1451 (18) | 660 (8) | 1109 (14) | 1101 (14) | 505 (6) |
| 7 Ireland | 1623 (45) | 224 (6) | 474 (13) | 217 (6) | 62 (2) | 475 (13) | 332 (9) |
| 8 Italy | 1504 (29) | 432 (8) | 793 (15) | 338 (6) | 262 (5) | 712 (14) | 402 (8) |
| 9 Luxembourg | 1782 (23) | 503 (7) | 1606 (21) | 704 (9) | 510 (7) | 1295 (17) | 264 (3) |
| 10 Netherlands | 1284 (19) | 450 (7) | 1314 (20) | 485 (7) | 836 (13) | 717 (11) | 620 (9) |
| 11 Portugal | 627 (19) | 152 (9) | 87 (5) | 148 (8) | 73 (4) | 257 (15) | 93 (6) |
| 12 United Kingdom | 1200 (19) | 447 (7) | 1271 (20) | 422 (6) | 86 (1) | 1028 (16) | 588 (9) |

* Source: Eurostat 1989
( ) = percentage of total expenditures

ranges from 17% in West-Germany to 45% in Ireland. Of course this percentage is related to income (Engel's law).

Table 2 gives information about consumption one level deeper: consumption of specific product categories within the category foods and beverages (level 4 of Figure 1). Here again we see tremendous differences, also between countries with similar income levels. For example, consumption of dairy products per head varies from 81 kilogrammes in Italy to 159 in Denmark and 199 in Ireland. Consumption of coffee in the Netherlands is about twice the level in Italy and France. Consumption of wine varies from 8 litres per head in the U.K. to 92 litres per head in France.

Such differences indeed point to fundamental differences in the patterns of consumption in the different EU-countries.

## Factors in the Consumer Decision Process

A marketer is not only interested in consumption levels of product classes as such, but also in the consumer decision processes that ultimately lead to the purchases of specific products and brands. We have information on a number of factors appearing in the consumer decision model of Figure 2.

### Families and Households

One of the basic elements that influences consumer buyer decisions is family structure. Table 3 provides information about numbers of families and average family sizes in the EU-countries.

In consumer research there is a tradition of studying the role of different persons in the household in the decision making process with respect to the purchase of goods and services. It is likely that there are differences with respect to family structures and decision processes among the European countries. There has been some cross-cultural research on this topic (see Robertson et al., 1984, p. 468-471), but to our knowledge no comprehensive comparative studies with respect to the EU-countries. This would constitute a very interesting area of research though.

The numbers in Table 3 on the possession of specific household appliances, give some information about the way the household activities are carried out. Here we see considerable differences between the different countries.

### Consumer Values and Lifestyles

As Figure 2 indicates, consumer values are important since they guide attitude formation and ultimately consumer choice behavior. We have some comparative statistics for European countries here.

TABLE 2. Consumption Per Capita (kg) of Selected Commodities (product classes) in EG-Countries*

| | beef & veal | pork | sheep | poultry | eggs | fresh dairy products | butter | cheese | cereals | potatoes | sugar | vege-tables | fresh fruit | citrus | coffee** | wine** |
|---|---|---|---|---|---|---|---|---|---|---|---|---|---|---|---|---|
| 1 Belgium | 25 | 45 | 2 | 15 | 14 | 86 | 9 | 11 | 72 | 103 | 35 | 86 | 49 | 17 | -- | -- |
| 2 Denmark | 13 | 53 | 1 | 10 | 15 | 159 | 8 | 12 | 72 | 65 | 43 | 60 | 381 | 10 | -- | -- |
| 3 W-Germany | 23 | 59 | 1 | 10 | 17 | 87 | 7 | 14 | 73 | 73 | 36 | 73 | 85 | 26 | 74 | 21 |
| 4 Greece | 22 | 20 | 14 | 16 | 12 | 67 | 1 | 21 | 110 | 83 | 26 | 197 | 75 | 89 | -- | -- |
| 5 Spain | -- | -- | -- | -- | -- | -- | -- | -- | 75 | 97 | 28 | 162 | 67 | 16 | 34 | 61 |
| 6 France | 32 | 38 | 4 | 17 | 15 | 98 | 10 | 20 | 81 | 74 | 36 | 113 | 60 | 18 | 51 | 92 |
| 7 Ireland | 24 | 34 | 6 | 16 | 13 | 199 | 12 | 4 | 90 | 127 | 44 | 85 | 30 | 15 | -- | -- |
| 8 Italy | 26 | 27 | 2 | 18 | 12 | 81 | 2 | 14 | 118 | 38 | 29 | 127 | 68 | 34 | 44 | 90 |
| 9 Luxembourg | -- | -- | -- | -- | -- | -- | -- | -- | -- | -- | -- | -- | -- | -- | -- | -- |
| 10 Netherlands | 19 | 41 | 0 | 13 | 12 | 133 | 4 | 13 | 60 | 87 | 38 | 94 | 64 | 82 | 97 | -- |
| 11 Portugal | -- | -- | -- | -- | -- | -- | -- | -- | 103 | 84 | 28 | 114 | 35 | 13 | -- | 76 |
| 12 United Kingdom | 21 | 24 | 7 | 16 | 13 | 130 | 5 | 6 | 77 | 106 | 36 | 80 | 46 | 13 | 24 | 8 |

\* Source: Landbouwcijfers LEI (Agricultural Economics Research Institute), The Hague, 1987
\*\*Source: Jeannet & Hennesey (1988, Chapter 6)

TABLE 3. Selected Statistics on Households, Ownership of Household Appliances and Abilities to Speak Different Languages in the EG-Countries

| | Number of households (millions) | No. of persons per household | % of household possessing | | | | % of adults who speak | | | | | |
|---|---|---|---|---|---|---|---|---|---|---|---|---|
| | | | Fridge | Freezer | Dish-washer | Microwave oven | English | French | German | Italian | Spanish | Dutch/Flemish |
| Belgium | 3.6 | 2.9 | 97 | 57 | 20 | 7 | 26 | 71 | 22 | 4 | 3 | 68 |
| Denmark | 2.1 | 2.3 | - | - | - | - | 51 | 5 | 48 | 1 | 1 | 1 |
| W-Germany | 25.3 | 2.43 | 95 | 59 | 31 | 7 | 30 | 12 | 100 | 2 | 2 | 3 |
| Greece | - | 3.19 | - | - | - | - | - | - | - | - | - | - |
| Spain | - | 2.70 | 98 | 5 | 9 | 1 | - | - | - | - | - | - |
| France | 20.3 | 2.70 | 97 | 42 | 29 | 6 | 26 | 100 | 11 | 8 | 13 | 1 |
| Ireland | 0.85 | 4.05 | - | - | - | - | 99 | 12 | 2 | 1 | 1 | 0 |
| Italy | 18.5 | 2.98 | 99 | 22 | 21 | 2 | 13 | 27 | 6 | 100 | 5 | 0 |
| Luxembourg | - | 2.81 | - | - | - | - | - | - | - | - | - | - |
| Netherlands | 5.3 | 2.59 | 99 | 43 | - | 2 | 50 | 16 | 61 | 2 | 2 | 100 |
| Portugal | - | 3.24 | - | - | - | - | - | - | - | - | - | - |
| U.K. | 21.0 | 2.67 | 97 | 45 | 4 | 29 | 100 | 16 | 9 | 2 | 3 | 1 |
| Year statistics refer to | 1986 | 1985 | 1986 | 1986 | 1986 | 1986 | 1985 | 1985 | 1985 | 1985 | 1985 | 1985 |
| Source | a | b | c | c | c | c | a | a | a | a | a | a |

Sources:  a. Gallup survey, adapted from Jeannet & Hennesey, 1988, p. 436
 b. Dawson & Burt (1988), The evolution of European retailing, Univ. of Stirling, p. 46 (original source: Euromonitor/Eurostat)
 c. Dawson & Burt (1988), The evolution of European retailing, Univ. of Stirling, p. 46 (original source: AGB/Europanel)

First we give results from a cross-cultural study, organized by the European Value Systems Group, who interviewed 12,000 respondents in 10 European countries (Harding & Phillips, 1986). Table 4 gives their results with respect to personal values, obtained by asking the respondents which qualities should be encouraged in the education of children.

It is clear that there are considerable differences in educational values among the different countries. In the table the countries with the most ○ and/or ☐ scores are the most 'extreme.' In the Netherlands people seem to be the most middle-of-the-road. Denmark has many 'extreme' scores: low for self-control, obedience, hard work, determination and patience but high on responsibility. The U.K. has the largest number of high scores: tolerance, good manners, obedience, unselfishness and patience. In the former West-Germany, leadership capabilities are rather important.

Specific European consumer value studies for marketing purposes have been scarce, with some notable exceptions, for example Boote (1982).

Internationally operating advertising agencies and market research companies are recently developing lifestyle classifications which can be applied to consumers in different countries. One of the purposes of such a classification system is to find similar groups of customers in different countries. Such an analysis could be the starting point for TransEuropean market segmentation. Although such Europewide lifestyle classification instruments are only recently being developed, we can give summary results of an example such as endeavor.

This is the so-called Four-C classification system ('Cross Cultural Consumer Characteristics') developed by the European branch of Young & Rubican.

The Four-C method has seven categories of consumers (see Table 5). The theoretical basis of this classification system is found in the well-known schemes of Riesman and Maslow. Also elements of VALS can be traced.

In fact the seven groups are a more detailed partition of three broader groups. The numbers (1) and (2) of Table 5 are more or less comparable to Riesman's 'tradition directed' and the VALS category: 'need driven.' Number (3) to (5) are comparable to Riesman's 'other-directed' and VALS: 'outer-directed'; (6) and (7) are the 'inner-directed.' From the adjectives given in Table 5, the reader will get some intuitive idea about the characteristics of the seven groups.

Table 5 shows considerable differences among the seven EU-countries. For example the former West-Germany is relative high on mainstreamers and low on reformers, whereas Denmark is low on 'need driven' ( (1) and (2) ) and high on 'inner-directed' ( (6) and (7) ) consumers.

TABLE 4. Qualities Esteemed to Be Important in the Education of Children in Different EC-Countries*

|  | Country | | | | | | | | |
| --- | --- | --- | --- | --- | --- | --- | --- | --- | --- |
|  | EU | FR | UK | WG | IT | NL | DK | BE | SP | IR |
| honesty | 73* | 76 | (79) | 74 | 77 | [79] | 76 | 70 | (47) | 73 |
| tolerance | 51 | 59 | [62] | (42) | 43 | 57 | 58 | 45 | 44 | 56 |
| good manners | 49 | (21) | [68] | 42 | 55 | 59 | 49 | 47 | 54 | 65 |
| responsibility | 46 | 39 | 24 | [63] | 46 | 55 | [63] | 37 | [63] | (22) |
| politeness | 35 | [51] | 27 | 29 | 37 | 42 | 51 | 48 | (20) | 23 |
| loyalty | 32 | 36 | 36 | 22 | [43] | 24 | 24 | 23 | 29 | (19) |
| self-control | 29 | 30 | 33 | 30 | 20 | 34 | (12) | 30 | [37] | 31 |
| independence | 27 | (16) | 23 | [47] | 23 | 27 | 55 | 20 | 24 | 30 |
| obedience | 25 | 18 | [37] | 16 | 27 | 23 | (14) | 28 | 30 | 34 |
| hard work | 23 | 36 | 16 | 22 | 13 | 14 | (2) | 33 | [42] | 24 |
| thrift | 21 | 32 | (9) | 31 | 19 | 17 | 15 | [36] | 11 | 15 |
| determination | 19 | 18 | 17 | [27] | 17 | 16 | (11) | 21 | 13 | 10 |
| religious faith | 17 | 11 | 14 | 17 | 22 | 14 | (8) | 17 | 22 | [41] |
| unselfishness | 15 | 23 | [40] | 4 | (2) | 9 | 23 | 14 | 4 | 22 |
| patience | 14 | 10 | [16] | 14 | [16] | 15 | (9) | 13 | 15 | 12 |
| imagination | 13 | 12 | 11 | 14 | (8) | 11 | 11 | (8) | [24] | (8) |
| leadership | 10 | (2) | 4 | [32] | 3 | 4 | (2) | 6 | 8 | 7 |

\* Source: Halman et al.: Traditie, secularisatie en individualisering, Tilburg University Press 1987, p. 342, see also: Harding & Phillips (1986), p. 20, 21.
In the table: % of respondents that find the specific quality important.

○ = lowest score for the quality
☐ = highest score for the quality

TABLE 5. Distribution of Consumers over 7 Lifestyle Categories of the Four-C-Classification in Seven EC-Countries (percentages)

| | (1) Resigned poor (survival) | (2) Struggling poor (escape) | (3) Main-stream (security) | (4) Aspirers (status) | (5) Succeeders (control) | (6) Transitionals (individuality) | (7) Reformers (self-fulfillment) |
|---|---|---|---|---|---|---|---|
| W. Germany | 11 | 5 | [46] | 11 | 16 | 10 | (2) |
| Italy | 8 | (3) | [40] | 18 | 12 | 13 | 6 |
| Spain | 8 | 7 | (30) | 13 | [17] | 12 | 13 |
| France | [14] | 9 | 33 | 18 | (7) | 10 | 10 |
| Denmark | (4) | 4 | 32 | 11 | (6) | [15] | [28] |
| The Netherlands | 7 | 11 | [44] | [19] | (6) | (4) | 9 |
| United Kingdom | 11 | [13] | 40 | (9) | 12 | 7 | 8 |
| Average 7 countries | 9 | 7 | 38 | 14 | 11 | 10 | 11 |

Source: PMSvW, Y&R Amsterdam
○ = lowest percentage in the group
□ = highest percentage in the group

Of course, such classification systems need further development and validation. It is important that these efforts are being made. For market segmentation across national borders these types of instruments are indispensable.

Finally, a word about language. Language is a very important element of culture. We use language to express our thoughts and beliefs. It is even hypothesized that an individual's perceptions, understanding and relationships are determined by the structure of language (Robertson et al., p. 569). Language differences are very large within Europe. With a few exceptions each country has its own mother's tongue. The right half of Table 3 gives some information about the language speaking abilities in Europe. It is clear from this table that we are far from a situation with a common 'langua franca' spoken by the majority of the people in all EU-countries. This language factor is a tremendous barrier to standardized marketing communication program in the various EU-countries.

## *Fundamental Differences?*

The preceding data about consumer values and lifestyles show clear differences between the EU-countries. However, do these differences point to a fundamental disparity in value systems and lifestyles in the several European countries? No final answers can be given. Some authors (i.e., Harding and Phillips, 1986, p. 213) conclude that the "underlying structure of values is remarkably unified, demonstrating at a number of points an internal logic which clearly transcends national and linguistic boundaries." One of the main findings that led these authors to this conclusion is the fact that the factor analyses of responses revealed consistent and interpretable interrelated patterns of factor structures, even when the analyses were conducted for each country separately.

The resulting factor structures were very similar over countries. Obviously, the structure of values is the same, but the scores on the individual items differ from country to country. According to Harding and Phillips "such homogeneity at the structural level seems likely to reflect a shared cultural inheritance.... 'European civilization' or 'European culture.'" In this view the differences between different European countries should not be over-accentuated.

## *A Homogenization Process?*

Beside the level of homogeneity/heterogeneity at this moment, an interesting question is whether or not a homogenization of cultural values, consumers wants and preferences take place. A possibility to throw light on this issue would be to study tables such as Tables 4 and 5 for different points in time. Unfortunately we are not in the happy position of having such time series data on European values and lifestyles. It is doubtful whether such data exist at all. So we have to turn to other sources.

Maybe we can learn something from unification processes that have taken place in specific countries earlier in history. As our first 'case' we take the authors' own country: the Netherlands. Although many outsiders would suspect that this small country has always been a tightly-knit unified state, the opposite is true. Before 1800 what is now one country was a federation of 'Seven United Netherlands.' At that time there were large differences in language, culture, education, occupation and religion among the different states. Later these states received the much less autonomous status of province.

Knippenberg and de Pater (1988) describe the development from the federation of rather diverse 'Netherlands' into the present unified country. They conclude that on one hand a process of homogenization has occurred, where elements of regional culture gave way to a national culture, dominated by the culture from the former state of Holland, the Western part of the Country. The Holland (Dutch) language also became the official standard all over the country. On the other hand there has been a counter-movement; in a kind of dialectic processes, the nationalization tendency has caused regionalization, for example, in broadcasting: a tendency into the direction of many different regional and local stations is observable.

Knippenberg and de Pater show that infrastructural and economic integration went at a higher speed than cultural and mental integration. Also, people still tend to stay where they are born and the majority of the daily newspapers in the Netherlands is still regional. Outside the Randstad (the former state of Holland), only 20% of the households reads a national newspaper.

Another interesting notion from Knippenberg and de Pater is that only a subgroup of the population takes part in the modernization process of integration and enlargement of scale. This subgroup is called the 'socially mobilized population.' Indicators for belonging to this group are: urbanization, literacy, newspaper reading, listening to the radio, going to the cinema, etc. In analogy, there will probably be only a limited number of 'Europe-mobilized people' in the different EU-countries.

Of course the unification process of the Netherlands can not directly be transmitted to the unification of Europe. Nevertheless, it is striking that cultural integration has taken so long and is still incomplete. This is even more surprising since in the Netherlands the adoption of a common language took place very early in the process.

Our second 'case' is North America, especially the United States of America. To many this country, famous for its 'melting pot' philosophy, is the ultimate example of a homogeneous country. One finds the same types of hotels, shops, fast food restaurants, etc., all over the U.S. The country does not have cultural differences shaped by many centuries of isolated development that inhibited communication and exchange between different regions.

However, there are indications that the differences between regions are increasing instead of diminishing. In a provoking book Garreau (1981) developed his thesis of 'The Nine Nations of North America.' According to this view, North America is not a continent with three nations (i.e., Canada, U.S.A. and Mexico) but consists of 9 different cultural entities of which the boundaries are often quite different from the official national and state boundaries. Garreau comes up with appealing names for his 'nations,' e.g., Foundry, Dixie, Ecotopia, etc.

Another indication for cultural differences within the U.S.A. is the study by Kahle (1986), who found significant differences in values between different regions of the U.S.A. according to the Bureau of Census partition.

From these cases one can learn that there is not a universal one-direction movement towards increasing consumer homogeneity, but that there is a kind of dialectic process. As a reaction to the decreasing emphasis on national differences in Europe, regional differences probably become more important. Perhaps the cities and their surroundings which were so important in Europe in the Middle Ages will see a come-back, now under the more modern term of conurbations.

## SIMILARITY OF MARKETING INFRASTRUCTURE

### *Retailing*

As indicated in Figure 2, one of the most important situational factors that influence consumer behavior is the distribution environment, more specifically the shops where consumers make their purchases, i.e., the retail environment. Some information about grocery shops in the EU-countries is presented in Table 6.

It shows that there are huge differences in retail density: the number of points of sale per 1000 inhabitants ranges from 0.75 in the Netherlands to 4.01 in Portugal. Furthermore, it is shown that the shoptypes are quite

TABLE 6. Information About Grocery Shops in the EC-Countries*

|  | Total number of shops | Hyper-markets | Super-markets | Self-service shops | Traditional shops | Points of sale per 1000 inhabitants |
|---|---|---|---|---|---|---|
| Belgium | 15418 | 81 (1)a (17)b | 1483 (10) (60) | 2930 (19)(12) | 10924 (71) (11) | 1.56 |
| Denmark | 6000 | – | 1100 (18) | 4900 (82) |  | 1.18 |
| W-Germany | 80000 | 383 (0) (12) | 42857 (54) (48) | 14450 (18) (22) | 21270 (27) (18) | 1.31 |
| Greece | 27696 | – | 1273 (5) (56) | 2412 (9) (11) | 24011 (87) (33) | 2.80 |
| Spain | 113636 | 66 (0) (16) | 1485 (1) (19) | 16983 (15) (5) | 95102 (84) (60) | 2.96 |
| France | 76050 | 589 (1) (39) | 5826 (8) (45) | 6653 (9) (7) | 62403 (82) (9) | 1.39 |
| Ireland | 8611 |  |  |  |  | 2.53 |
| Italy | 161954 | – | 2059 (1) (30) | 13943 (9) (17) | 145952 (90) (53) | 2.84 |
| Netherlands | 10740 | 40 (0) | 9200 (86) |  | 1500 (14) | 0.75 |
| Portugal | 40457 | – | 2025 (5) | (34) | 38472 (95) (66) | 4.01 |
| United Kingdom | 50500 | 396 (1) (23) |  |  |  | 0.90 |

Figures in brackets are shares of the shop type to which it refers.
(a) The figure to the left is the share in the total number of shops.
(b) The figure to the right is the share in the total turnover of all grocery shops.
* Source: Saatchi & Saatchi: Compton (1986).
Figures refer to one of the years 1984 to 1986.

different in the different countries: in Greece, Spain, France, Italy and Portugal the traditional shops constitute over 80% of all shops, in West-Germany and the Netherlands their share is under 30%. Perhaps more significant are the shares of the different shoptypes in volume (turnover). For example in Belgium hypermarkets and supermarkets together represent 11% of all shops, nevertheless they represent 77% of total retail volume. For France these figures are still more extreme: 9% of all shops (hypermarkets and supermarkets) account for 89% of retail volume.

These big differences in shopping environment have a major impact on consumer behavior. In a traditional shop for example there is much less confrontation of the consumer with the products and henceforth with alternatives for his planned choice (impulse buying). Also in a traditional shop there are few possibilities for point-of-sale material, displays, product demonstrations, etc. This limits the instruments the marketer has for influencing consumer choice.

Behind a scattered pattern of retailing points usually lies a more scattered pattern of parties a manufacturer has to deal with in getting his products on the retail shelf (wholesalers, head offices of chains, etc.). This has consequences for the way the marketing and sales organisation should be set up. For instance in the Netherlands, an example of a highly concentrated retailing system, the four biggest chains together represent about 50% of all grocery turnover. So a relatively small number of 'account-executives' are responsible for the bulk of the sales volume. In a country with a very dispersed retail pattern this is quite different.

*Media and Advertising Environment*

Figure 2 shows that consumer decision making is heavily influenced by stimuli from the outside world: commercial and noncommercial stimuli. Important carriers of these stimuli are the media: print media, radio and TV to mention the most important ones. Newspapers are present all over the world and the penetration of radio and TV also is practically complete in the sense that almost 100% of all households have radio and TV (Douglas & Craig, 1983, p. 10). With respect to the intensity with which these media are used for advertising Table 7 gives information.

We see that not only the absolute levels of advertising spending vary heavily from country to country, but that advertising intensity per capita also differs a great deal. Based on advertising/capita it can be concluded that consumers in Denmark, West-Germany, the Netherlands and U.K. are much more heavily exposed to advertising than consumers in Portugal, Greece, Italy and Ireland. Further we see considerable differences in allocation spending over media.

For an explanation, legal and institutional factors have to be taken into account. For example, the low figures for TV advertising in Denmark, Belgium and the Netherlands, have to do with the nonexistence of TV or radio advertising in Denmark and in Belgium, (until January 1, 1989; the Belgians made use of the commercial station Luxemburg though) and the limited amount of TV-advertising capacity in the Netherlands (the latter limit has been lifted substantially now). Some countries such as Greece, Ireland and Portugal, with low absolute levels of advertising have a surprisingly large share of TV-advertising.

TABLE 7. Advertising Expenditures and Allocation over Media in the EC-Countries*

|  | Total advertising expenditure (million Ecu's) | Advertising expenditure per capita (Ecu's) | printed media (%) | TV (%) | Radio (%) | Cinema billboards, etc. (%) |
|---|---|---|---|---|---|---|
| Belgium/Luxembourg | 633 | 62 | 68 | 13 | 1 | 17 |
| Denmark | 664 | 130 | 96 | 0 | 0 | 4 |
| W-Germany | 6825 | 112 | 81 | 10 | 4 | 5 |
| Greece | 159 | 16 | 40 | 53 | 7 | 0 |
| Spain | 2306 | 60 | 50 | 32 | 13 | 5 |
| France | 4508 | 82 | 59 | 19 | 8 | 14 |
| Ireland | 159 | 44 | 43 | 36 | 11 | 9 |
| Italy | 3089 | 54 | 42 | 49 | 4 | 5 |
| Netherlands | 1749 | 121 | 83 | 10 | 2 | 4 |
| Portugal | 99 | 8 | 27 | 54 | 13 | 6 |
| United Kingdom | 7620 | 135 | 61 | 33 | 2 | 4 |

* Source: The Advertising Association London 1987, taken here from Adformatie Bureau Bijlage 1989.
The data refer to 1986.

## *The Impact of European Union on the Marketing Infrastructure*

The effects of removing the barriers between the EU-countries are most relevant for the market infrastructure factors. We discuss them following the elements of the marketing mix.

### *Product*

In terms of marketing, the 'product' is more than just the physical good: it also implies packaging, servicing, branding, delivery and installation. Beside regulations on package-information, the European Commission's proposals predominantly focus on just the physical aspect. The two most important regulation areas with direct consequences for a firm's physical products are: technical harmonization and the regulation of competition. The first deals with the current differences between the Member States with respect to product standards, health, safety and environmental standards. Famous in this respect was the German 'purity' law prohibiting the sale of beer brewed in other countries than Germany. The number of these so-called 'non-tariff barriers' is very high: over 200 according to the Cecchini report and it has increased since 1970. Proposals of the Commission were and are aimed on reducing the unnecessary national protections.

The national legislations are relatively detailed for health-sensitive products such as food and pharmaceuticals. Here the rules under which a product is allowed to the market can vary a great deal. For pharmaceuticals the national regimes differ completely from one country to the other. (For the latter category, see De Wolf (1988).)

For product policy also the protection of products and brands under the still national patents laws deserves attention. For example to register a brand a registration is needed for each EU-country separately. Belgium, the Netherlands and Luxemburg have a common Benelux regime since 1971. The help of specialized trademark agencies is indispensable here (Markgraaf 1988).

*Price*

Important for a marketer's pricing decisions is the removal of fiscal barriers, like VAT and duties, from across the Member States. Frontier controls enabled the direction of VAT payments and incomes to the consuming country. Since January 1, 1993 most of these frontier controls have been removed. Europe has harmonized the taxation-systems among the countries. The aim is not to reach one uniform system of taxes and duties. With respect to the VAT, the Member States will be free to fix their own VAT-rate within a band of 14-20% for the standard rate and 4-9% for the reduced rate.

*Distribution*

Distribution of goods and services through Europe will be dramatically affected by the removal of administrative barriers. The welter of papers and checks processed at country frontiers used to be a nightmare for exporters and transporters. Starting in 1988 the majority of the separate forms have been replaced by the 'Single Administrative Document,' which regulates transport much more efficiently. Also intra-community transport regulations will be changed. A 'common transport policy' is aimed at avoiding local quotas and allowing hauliers to operate in freedom throughout the common market. Last but not least, the intention is to deregulate all modes of transport. For instance, air travelling within Europe is priced too high as compared to flights with a destination outside Europe. This is caused by mutual agreements between the Member States. For all modes of transport the level of competition is likely to increase, resulting in cheaper distribution of goods and services.

It should be noted that it will take time to reach the full advantage of distribution in a large EU. Distribution networks often have been established over a long period of time and are much dependent on long-standing personal relationships between members in the various channels. Dealing in international networks will take time to develop. Moreover the infrastructure of railways, roads and waterways has been shaped by the national needs: a region use to be connected with the major centers in the own country. To take advantage in a physical distribution sense from the greater Europe, new developments, such as the Channel Tunnel and the Trans-Europe TGV, are very important.

*Promotion and Advertising*

Marketers can make use of a variety of promotion tools, such as advertising, sales promotion, publicity and personal selling. With respect to personal selling, door-to-door selling has been regulated already. Other regulations predominantly concern the advertising aspect, where pan-European broadcasting is one of the most frequently discussed topics. Motive for the emphasis on broadcasting (only a minor percentage of the total expenditure of firms on promotion instruments) is the appearance of direct television satellites. This new technology seems to enhance the Commission's goal of stimulating free circulation of programmes throughout the Community and coordinating national laws on advertising, sponsorship and the protection of young people. There is not much agreement among experts whether or not Satellite television will be a success in the near future: the current penetration of cabling in Europe is limited; the quality of programmes is perceived to be low and cultural and language barriers block the reach of the medium. Therefore, the incentive for a advertiser to go on satellite is still minor. Nevertheless, the discussion on this topic has speeded up the pace of regulating broadcasting. For instance, the minutage of advertising on television has been agreed to be 15% at the maximum. The regulation of tariffs will probably disappear, as will be the case with the Sunday-ban and the introduction of natural breaks is likely. This implies changes for advertising firms as well as advertising agencies.

From this discussion of the different marketing mix instruments, it is clear that the European Union will significantly increase the possibilities for more standardized marketing programs. However, it will also be clear that many of the changes will have its impact only gradually over time.

## *DRIVES AND HURDLES FOR COMPANIES GOING INTERNATIONAL*

Many companies in European countries have been operating national up to now. What will make them go European?

Firms are not internationalizing just because of the fun of it. There are some driving forces contributing to the growth of a business, but there also are restraining factors, 'hurdles' for going abroad. The balance of 'drives' and 'hurdles' is continually shifting. Generally 'Europe' will cause the balance to shift in favour of internationalization. This does not mean, however, that for each individual firm the drives are strong enough to leap over the hurdles. In Figure 3 an overview is presented of the main driving and restraining factors influencing the process of Europeanization of individual firms. Drives as well as hurdles can be divided into two categories: Drives and hurdles from within the company ('internal'), inherent in the firm but to a certain extent controllable, and from outside the company ('external') which are only slightly or not controllable for the firm.

Some of those drives and hurdles are influenced by the coming changes in the EU. This leads to a change in the internationalization potential (balance of drives and hurdles) of an particular enterprise, but all depends on the company and the specific business it is operating in. Therefore, here we only briefly discuss the effects of 'Europe' on the driving and restraining factors in general.

When looking at the drives, one can expect that a more international oriented competitive environment will lead to at least a thorough discussion within companies with respect to their strategies regarding internationalization. Internal drives towards internationalization may be more prevalent when managements' prestige is at stake, non-local competing products are entering the market or when the stock of products becomes large enough to drive the firm to operating abroad. Naturally, also external drives are changing: There is no boundary on the dispersion of technology, there will be more opportunities to advertise internationally and probably more foreign trade intermediairies become interested in trading products all over the EU, as such an opportunity to internationalise.

As regards the hurdles, often the internal ones are the most difficult to overcome: limited management skills, difficulty in getting foreign ventures financed, lacking production capacity or, more importantly, lacking production flexibility. It seems that those internal hurdles will not spontaneously be changed to the good of such companies, but constitute more crucial weaknesses as foreign competition draws near. Regarding the external hurdles, without doubt some of those will diminish as the unification process goes ahead: Troubles with taxations and transportation will no longer be too worrying and foreign product specifications will be less hindering for adapting local products to the various markets in the Community. At the other hand some substantial external hurdles will remain or may even increase. Very often it is extremely difficult for a company to market its products to foreign countries because of history and habits. This does no only refer to differences in consumer buying behavior, brand

## FIGURE 3. Drives and Hurdles for Going European

|  | Drives | Hurdles |
|---|---|---|
| Internal | * ambition<br>* obsolescence<br>* economies of scale<br>* risk dispersion | * org. capacities<br>* political dependence<br>* product modifications<br>* financing and risks |
| External | * escaping local competition<br>* subsidies<br>* invading foreign competition<br>* market pull<br>* global technology<br>* demand for quality<br>* international communication<br>* leverage | * national regulations<br>* transport barriers<br>* market history<br>* local competition<br>* cultural differences |

loyalty and shop loyalty. Foreign trade history is also a problem: One has to adapt to foreign trade cultures and to try to penetrate into foreign distribution channels (wholesaling and retailing). Moreover, as international competition will become more fierce, those hurdles will not diminish and will certainly not disappear.

Each individual company will have to draw up the balance of its internal and external drives and hurdles for internationalisation. Much is dependent on the type of product a company offers. For example industrial products are easier marketed at an international scale than fast moving consumer goods. And within the latter group non foods (e.g., detergents) because of their lower cultural content are more suitable for a Euromarketing strategy than foods (e.g., packaged meat). The outcome of the considerations will either push the company abroad or force the company to focus on local markets.

## CONCLUSIONS AND RESEARCH AGENDA

Using a framework that incorporates notions from economics and consumer behavior, we examined the similarity of consumers in the different countries of the European Union. There are tremendous differences in income levels, expenditure patterns and consumption levels of individual products among the EU-countries. Furthermore there are major differences in consumer values and lifestyles. However experts on cultural values think that at the basis there is something like a 'European culture.'

If a homogenization process among the countries in the European Union is taking place at all, from drawing historical parallels it becomes clear that this process is likely to be very slow and dialectic in nature.

With respect to marketing infrastructure there exist huge differences in distribution systems, especially at the retailing level. Also large differences exist in the advertising and media environment.

To refer back to the title of this paper, these findings imply that one standardized marketing approach for the whole EU is still a far away perspective for most manufacturers.

Also we found that there are several other hurdles (apart from heterogeneity in customers) for companies that want to go European.

Nevertheless it might well be that it is more the supply side (i.e., manufacturers, retailers) than the demand side (autonomous cultural homogenization) that will ultimately produce the 'European Consumer.' Infrastructural and economic integration usually occur at a higher speed than the cultural and mental integration of consumers. Signs that companies increasingly take a Euro-wide approach (without necessarily adopting one standard marketing policy) are visible all over Europe.

From this paper it is clear that the state of knowledge, in terms of conceptual/theoretical frameworks as well as in terms of facts and data on European marketing, is rather low. In the following we mention three research areas which are interesting and have an urgent need for attention.

First there is the topic of *cross-cultural analysis of European consumers in the various EU-countries*. As we have seen in this paper there are only a few studies at this moment that make an effort to compare consumer values and lifestyles in different EU-countries. Much more attention is needed for the theoretical basis of this type of analysis and a lot of work has to be done in the area of validation of lifestyle groupings, standardization (in content) of questionnaires, etc. Also the question whether or not a homogenization process among the consumers in the different EU-countries takes place should get proper attention. For that purpose comparative lifestyle and value studies at regular times intervals are needed. Furthermore reliable instruments for carrying out trans-European market segmentation have to be developed.

Other topics in consumer behavior have received some, but only scarce attention. Cross-European studies of family structure and its impact on household decision making, patterns of brand loyalty and its causes, reference groups and their impact on the consumption decisions of the individual, and the relative importance of various information sources for the consumer, to mention just a few. It is necessary that after the business companies also the academics take the European perspective needed to deal with the issues just mentioned.

A second area is *European brand strategies*. There is a normative and a positive approach here. With respect to the first, an interesting question is under which conditions it is recommendable to adopt Euro-branding instead of maintaining national brands?

A positive approach would deal with the observation, analysis and explanation of brand strategies actually followed by suppliers in the various Euro-countries. Starting from a framework as given in this paper, a theoretical model could be developed with the purpose to explain and predict Euromarketing strategies actually followed by companies, dependent on the industry, the size, the country and other characteristics of the firm. This will enrich our insights in the actual determinants of strategies and in the critical factors for success in the European arena. Also the concept of brand equity (i.e., the value of a brand to a company) gets a special dimension in the Euromarket context. What is the value of a 'Eurobrand,' compared to a set of different national brands?

Thirdly, the European marketing scene is an ideal source for *theory formation and testing for international marketing*. In this stage of development the field of international marketing predominantly has a prescriptive orientation: what to do, how to act, and which aspects to pay attention to when a company is entering other markets than its home market. There has not been much development in terms of specific concepts, theories, etc. Europe offers a natural laboratory where comparative analysis can be carried out on a large number of factors. This can contribute significantly to the body-of-knowledge of international marketing. One relevant topic is the relationship between country image and product image. Why is it that German products are perceived as strong in precision and Italian products as strong in design? Will these perceptions change as Europe gains more unity? Europe is an ideal field for such country-of-origin studies.

Of course this list of Euromarketing research topics is by far not exhausting. One other obvious topic is the effect of the extension of the EU with four member states: Norway, Sweden, Finland and Austria.

We hope that this article will trigger interest and lead researchers to European marketing topics. Many 'green pastures' are out there, as well as many fields 'ripe to be reaped.'

## REFERENCES

Boote, A. S. (1982), Psychographic Segmentation in Europe, *Journal of Advertising Research*, 22, No. 6 (Dec/Jan), pp. 19-25.
Brown, S. & S. Burt (1992), Conclusion-Retail Internationalization: Past Imperfect, Future Imparative, *European Journal of Marketing*, Vol. 26, 135. 8, 9, pp. 80-84.
Douglas, S. P. & C. S. Craig (1983), *International Marketing Research*, Prentice Hall, Englewood Cliffs.
Engel, J. F., R. D. Blackwell & P. W. Miniard (1993), *Consumer Behavior*, 7th Ed., The Dryden Press.
Garreau, J. (1981), *The Nine Nations of North America*, New York: Avon.
Guido, G (1991), Implementing a Pan European Marketing Strategy, *Long Range Planning*, Vol. 25, 5, pp. 23-33.
Halman, L., F. Heunks, R. de Moore & H. Zanders, (1987), *Traditie, secularisatie en individualisering*, Tilburg Universiteits Press, Tilburg.
Harding, S. & D. Phillips (1986), *Contrasting Values in Western Europe, Unity, Diversity & Change*, MacMitlan, London.
Jain, S. C. (1989), 'Standardization of International Marketing Strategy: Some Research Hypotheses,' *Journal of Marketing*, 53, No. 1 (January), pp. 70-79.
Jeannet, J. P. and H. D. Hennessey (1988), *International Marketing Management*, Houghton Mifflin, Boston.
Kahle, Lynn R. (1986), The nine nations of North America and the Value Basis of Geographic Segmentation, *Journal of Marketing*, 50, (April), pp. 37-47.
Knippenberg, H. & B. de Pater (1988), *Deeenwording van Nederland*, SUN, Nijmegen.
Kotler, P. (1986), 'Global standardization-courting danger,' *Journal of Consumer Marketing*, 3, No. 2 (Spring), pp. 13-15.
Levitt, T. (1983), *The Marketing Imagination*, The Free Press, New York.
Markgraaf (1988), *Effektieve bescherming van merken en modellen*, (brochure), Amsterdam.
Robertson, T. S., J. Zielinski & S. Ward (1984), *Consumer Behavior*, Scott, Foresman & Company.
Saatchi & Saatchi Compton (1986), *Distributie van Levensmiddelen in Nederland + EG landen 1986*, Amsterdam, pp. 113.
Schiffman, L. G. & L. L. Kanuk (1978), *Consumer Behavior*, Prentice Hall, Englewood Cliffs.
Sheth, J. (1986), 'Global markets or global competition?' *Journal of Consumer Marketing*, 3, No. 2 (Spring), pp. 9-11.
Steenkamp, J. E. B. M. (1992), *De Europese Consument: Feit of Fictie*, (The European consumer: fact or fiction), Wageningen Agricultural University.
Steenkamp, J. E. B. M., Th. M. M. Verhallen, J. H. Gouda, W. A. Kamakura & Th.P. Novak (1993), De zoektocht naar de Europese consument: heilige graal of kansrijke missie? (The search for the European consumer: Holy Grail or promising mission?), *Tijdschrift voor Marketing*, Vol. 27, September, pp. 17-23.

Wills, G. (1991), The Single Market and National Marketing Thinking, *European Journal of Marketing,* Vol. 25, No. 4, pp. 148-156.

Wind, Y. (1986), 'The myth of globalization,' *Journal of Consumer Marketing,* 3, No. 2 (Spring), pp. 23-25.

De Wolf, P. (1988), 'The pharmaceutical industry: structure, intervention and competitive strength,' in H. W. de Jong (ed.) *The Structure of European Industry,* Kluwer Academic Publishers, Dordrecht, pp. 211-244.

# Collectivism, Individualism and In-Group Membership: Implications for Consumer Complaining Behaviors in Multicultural Contexts

Harry S. Watkins
Raymond Liu

**SUMMARY.** Effective implementation of a customer relationship management strategy rests on understanding and managing customer satisfaction/dissatisfaction and complaining behavior processes. However, the extensive consumer complaining behavior (CCB) literature that has emerged since the 1970s has focused almost exclusively on U.S. consumers, and the few CCB studies conducted outside of the United States have suffered from a lack of an integrating theory of how culture influences CCB. This paper builds from the cultural psychology and CCB literatures to contrast individualist and

---

Harry S. Watkins is Associate Professor of Marketing in the Business Administration Department, California State Polytechnic University, San Luis Obispo, CA 93407. Raymond Liu is Assistant Professor of Marketing in the College of Management, University of Massachusetts-Boston, Boston, MA 02125-3393.

Our thanks to Dr. Shinobu Kitayama and two anonymous reviewers for their constructive comments on earlier versions of this paper.

This research was partially supported by research grants from the California State University and the University of Massachusetts at Boston.

[Haworth co-indexing entry note]: "Collectivism, Individualism and In-Group Membership: Implications for Consumer Complaining Behaviors in Multicultural Contexts." Watkins, Harry S., and Raymond Liu. Co-published simultaneously in *Journal of International Consumer Marketing* (International Business Press, an imprint of The Haworth Press, Inc.) Vol. 8, No. 3/4, 1996, pp. 69-96; and: *Global Perspectives in Cross-Cultural and Cross-National Consumer Research* (ed: Lalita A. Manrai and Ajay K. Manrai) International Business Press, an imprint of The Haworth Press, Inc., 1996, pp. 69-96. Single or multiple copies of this article are available form The Haworth Document Delivery Service [1-800-342-9678, 9:00 a.m - 5:00 p.m. (EST)].

© 1996 by The Haworth Press, Inc. All rights reserved.

collectivist cultural patterns and to argue that a consumer's behavioral responses to post-purchase dissatisfaction will be strongly influenced by this aspect of their cultural identity. Working models of voice, exit and negative word-of-mouth complaining behaviors are offered which can test the impacts of this dimension of culture on CCB. A number of propositions are derived from the models, and their implications for management are discussed. *[Article copies available from The Haworth Document Delivery Service: 1-800-342-9678.]*

## INTRODUCTION

Over the last decade, the importance of effective business-customer relationship management has been increasingly recognized by both academia and marketing practitioners. The core argument is that business success in most industries depends on the supplier's ability to successfully develop and maintain long term relationships with customers (Jackson 1985). Support for this thesis has been found in industrial markets (Jackson 1985) and in consumer product and services markets (cf. Crosby, Evans and Cowles 1990, Levitt 1983).

A central aspect of successful relationship management is the effective management of post-purchase satisfaction on the part of the customer. The managerial importance of understanding dissatisfaction and its outcomes goes beyond the truism that satisfied customers are loyal customers. Rather, it lies in the fact that dissatisfied customers represent a key opportunity for cost-effective marketing. More than 15 years ago, Fornell (1976) documented the value of complaints, both as a communication mechanism and as a means of giving the firm an opportunity to turn an unhappy customer into a satisfied, loyal customer. Since then research has shown that customers who complain are *more* brand loyal than customers who do not complain, especially if their complaints are handled effectively (TARP 1985). Fornell and Wernerfelt (1987) use economic theory and formal analysis to demonstrate how complaint management can become a tool of defensive marketing and conclude that, in general, it is cost effective for a firm to spend 200% of the profit margin associated with a sale to turn a dissatisfied customer into a satisfied customer.

Thus, outcomes of customer dissatisfaction, or "consumer complaint behaviors" (CCB) have been of increasing interest to marketing firms and marketing researchers over the last decade (Bearden and Teel 1983; *Business Week* 1984; Day 1984; Resnik and Harmon 1983; Richins 1983, 1987, Singh 1988, 1990a, 1990b, TARP 1979, 1986, Westbrook 1987). Practitioners are focusing on CCB research in their attempts to understand marketplace dissatisfaction and to develop programs to address consumer complaints (Clark and Kaminski 1989; Gilly 1987; Goodwin et al. 1989; Lewis 1982; Ross and Oliver 1984; TARP 1979, 1986). From a theoretical point of view, an understanding of CCB is central to an understanding of brand loyalty and consumer repurchase intentions (cf. Oliver 1980; Richins 1983) and is relevant to macromarketing issues of consumer and social welfare (Andreasen 1985).

The research in CCB grew primarily out of the U.S.-based consumer movement of the 70s, and thus has had a strong U.S. domestic (vs. international) orientation. In recent years, CCB researchers have moved beyond the measurement of rates of voice, word-of-mouth (WOM) and exit behaviors to develop taxonomies and typologies of CCB (cf. Richins 1987, Singh 1988,1989) and to develop and test theories of the antecedents to CCB (cf. Swan and Oliver 1989, Goodwin and Wallace 1989, Singh 1989, Westbrook 1987). However, the North American focus of most of the CCB research to date poses a substantial threat to its validity in an increasingly worldwide economy. Research in cultural psychology has found that individuals' values, concepts of the self, perceptions of others, and patterns of interaction with their environment are profoundly affected by the "cultural meaning systems" (Triandis 1989) in which they operate. Similarly, patterns of response to post-purchase dissatisfaction may be expected to be affected by culture.

International research on CCB has been limited. Studies have investigated consumer dissatisfaction and complaint behaviors in various countries (e.g., Francken 1983, in The Netherlands; Lliker et al. 1969, in Britain; Meffert and Bruhn 1983, in Germany; Ash and Quelch 1980, in Canada, and Bodur et al. 1982 in Turkey and the U.S). A series of studies by the Commission of the European Communities (1976) studied dissatisfaction and complaint behavior across nine countries from the European Common Market. In general, these studies have found that the incidence of dissatisfaction and complaint rates varied widely, but no explanations were offered for this variation.

While negative word-of-mouth hasn't been explicitly studied in cross-cultural sense, a few studies have studied diffusion of innovations in various cultures. For example, Takada and Jain (1991) found higher rates of diffusion of innovations in Japan, Taiwan and Korea than in the United States. This difference was attributed to the stronger societal bonds and associated higher rates of positive word-of-mouth communications in the Asian countries.

A few cross-cultural studies have also examined *attitudes* towards complaining. Thorelli (1983) studied attitudes towards complaining in China and Thailand, while Arndt, Barksdale, and Perreault (1982) compared attitudes in the United States, Norway, and Venezuela. In these studies, positive attitudes towards complaining were found to be positively associated with the level of a country's economic development. More recently, Richins and Verhage (1985) found that U.S. and Dutch consumers hold different attitudes towards complaining. They found that Dutch consumers were more concerned about negative social consequences (being looked down on or suffering embarrassment when complaining) and less motivated by a sense of accomplishment for themselves or for society than were U.S. consumers. They, like earlier researchers, conclude that attitudes towards complaining are likely to vary across cultures. However, they had little to say about *how* culture affects CCB.

All of these studies have suffered from the lack of any integrating theory concerning the impact of culture on CCB. In the absence of such a theory, research on international CCB has been descriptive only and the results of cross-cultural studies have been limited in their generalizability beyond the countries/cultures studied. This paper seeks to begin the process of addressing this problem by exploring the relevance of concepts drawn from cultural psychology to the phenomenon of CCB. In particular, we will explore the potential relationship between the widely studied collectivism/individualism dimension of culture and CCB.

The paper is organized around four sections. First the cultural psychology literature concerning the core concepts of collectivism, individualism, and construals of the self is discussed in some detail. Then the empirical findings of CCB literature is reviewed with an emphasis on identifying those factors that have been found to be significant antecedents of CCB (at least in the United States). Next the potential impact of the collectivism/individualism dimension of culture on CCB and its antecedents is explored and a set of propositions are presented for future research. Finally, the implications for management are briefly discussed.

## *INDIVIDUALISM, COLLECTIVISM AND THE IMPORTANCE OF IN-GROUPS*

In America, "the squeaky wheel gets the grease." In Japan, "the nail that stands out gets pounded down." With these two examples Markus and Kitayama (1990) point out that people in different cultures may hold dramatically divergent views about the self. Nevertheless, they point out that "most of what psychologists currently know about human nature is based on one particular view–the so-called 'Western' view of the individual as an independent, self-contained, autonomous entity who (a) comprises a unique configuration of internal attributes (e.g., traits, abilities, motives, values), and (b) behaves primarily as a consequence of these internal attributes" (Markus and Kitayama 1990, pg. 224). This independent self construal is most commonly found in highly individualistic cultures such as are found in the United States and Canada, Northern Europe, Australia and New Zealand (Hofstede 1980).

Markus and Kitayama draw on a wide range of authors from psychology and anthropology (e.g., Bond 1986, Cousins 1989; Maehr & Nicholls 1980; Stevenson et al. 1986; Triandis 1989; Triandis et al. 1988) to develop and compare with the independent view of the self, another, contrasting view–an *interdependent view*. According to Markus and Kitayama (1990, pg. 224), "experiencing interdependence entails seeing oneself as part of an encompassing social relation and recognizing that one's behavior is determined, contingent on and, to a large extent, organized by what the actor perceives to be the thoughts, feelings, and actions of *others* in the relationship." This interdependent construal of the self is characteristically found in collectivist cultures such as are found in Asia, Africa, Mediterranean Europe, the Middle East, and in Latin America (Hofstede 1980, Markus and Kitayama 1990).

While a detailed characterization of the differences between the cultural patterns of individualism and collectivism is beyond the scope of this paper (see Markus and Kitayama 1990, Triandis 1989 for reviews), a number of salient observations may be made (Table 1). First, it must be noted that the individualism/collectivism construct is useful both for comparing cultures and, for comparing differences among individuals and populations within a particular culture (e.g., Triandis et al. 1988). The United States may be described as having a relatively individualist culture, and Japan as having a collectivist culture; members of each country will tend to exhibit their respective cultural pattern. However, there are also individual differences within cultures. That is, in both collectivist and individualist cultures one can find individuals who are collectivist or individualist in their attitudes and behavior (Triandis et al. 1988, Triandis, Brislin and Hui 1988). This paper is primarily concerned with contrasting the overall cultural patterns of individualism and collectivism, and then examining how these patterns are likely to differentially impact the complaining behaviors of consumers. However, much of the discussion that follows may be equally salient for understanding within-culture differences among individuals based on the individualism/collectivism dimension (see Implications for Management and Conclusion).

A fundamental attribute of collectivist cultures is that individuals are

TABLE 1. Examples and Characteristics of Individualist and Collectivist Cultures

|  | Individualist Cultures | Collectivist Cultures |
|---|---|---|
| **Examples** | U.S.A. and Canada; Northern Europe (e.g., Great Britain, Germany, Scandanavia); Australia, New Zealand | Asia (e.g., Japan, China, Korea, India); Africa; Mediterranean Europe and Middle East (e.g., Turkey, Greece, Portugul, Egypt); Mexico; Central and South America (e.g., Brazil, Chile, Argentina, etc.) |
| **Summary of Differences** | Goals of collectives are subordinated to individual's goals | Goals of individuals are subordinated to collective's goals |
| **Aspects of the Self** | Separate from social context, constant and stable. Internal, private (abilities, thoughts, feelings) | Connected with social context, flexible and variable. External, public (statuses, roles, relations) |
|  | Key tasks: be unique, express self, realize internal attributes, be direct– "say what's on your mind." | Key tasks: belong, fit-in, occupy one's proper place, engage in appropriate action, be indirect–"read other's mind." |
|  | Role of others: self-evaluation | Role of others: self-definition |
|  | Self-esteem depends on ability to express self, to validate internal attributes. Negative emotions should be expressed | Self-esteem depends on ability to adjust, to restrain self, to maintain harmony with social context. Negative emotions should be repressed |
| **Group Membership, Influences & Interactions** | Membership in many "in-groups." Join and leave groups, and make friends easily. Relative preference for short-term, "shallow" relationships. | Membership in few "in-groups." Join and leave groups, and make friends slowly and with difficulty. Relative preference for long-term "deep" relationships. |
|  | In-group norms and expectations have *weak* influence on attitudes and behavior. | In-group norms and expectations have *strong* influence on attitudes and behavior. |
|  | Competition and conflict often occurs among in-group members. Acceptance of in-group power differences | Competition and conflict are rare among in-group members, relatively common without-groups. Acceptance of in-group power differences is high. |

typically induced to subordinate their personal needs to the needs of one or (at most) a few collectives, which are usually stable in-groups (e.g., family, tribe, company, etc.). Self-definition and self-esteem among collectivists depend on succeeding at belonging, fitting-in, engaging in actions that are contextually appropriate, maintaining social harmony, and saving face for self and others. Emotions, particularly negative emotions, tend not to be outwardly expressed, and are often repressed in intimate social contexts. (Markus and Kitayama 1990).

In contrast, individuals raised in individualist cultures tend to subordinate group needs and goals to their own personal goals. An individualist's self-construal is relatively independent of social context and depends instead on success in being unique, in self-expression (including expressing negative emotions), and in validating internal attributes. While for collectivists, others aide in self-definition, for individualists, others are relatively more important for self-evaluation (Markus and Kitayama 1990).

Not surprisingly, these differences have profound impacts on group membership and social interaction. For example, collectivists tend to be concerned about the results of their actions on members of their in-groups, tend to share resources with in-group members, and typically go to great lengths to maintain harmonious relationships with in-group members. In collectivist cultures, the relationship of the individual to the in-group tends to be stable, entry and exit are difficult and rare, acceptance of in-group power differences is high, and even when the in-group makes extensive demands, the individual remains loyal (Triandis 1989). This contrasts with individualist cultures where there are typically many more in-groups, emotional detachment from in-groups is greater, and acceptance of in-group power differences is low. Participation in any particular in-group is more heavily contingent on the continuing ability of that in-group to contribute to the individual's positive social identity without making excessive, broad-based demands. (Triandis et al. 1988).

## Social Interactions Within and Between In-Groups

The quality of social interactions between individuals in a collectivist culture depends heavily on whether or not they belong to the same in-group. Thus, various researchers (Sinha 1982, Triandis, et al. 1988) have reported results suggesting that compared with individualistic cultures, cooperation in collectivist cultures is higher with in-group members, but lower with out-group members. Markus and Kitayama (1990) conclude that "not only the expression but also the experience of . . . anger is effectively averted within an interdependent structure of relationship." In contrast, Matsumoto et al. (1988) noted that Japanese respondents to a study of the eliciting conditions of several emotions, reported feeling anger primarily in the presence of strangers (non-in-group members). Moreover, collectivists are relatively ineffective in meeting strangers (Gabrenya and Barba 1987), avoidance relationships and behaviors are common in collectivist cultures (Triandis 1989), and competition with and manipulation and exploitation of out-groups is more extensive in collectivist cultures than individualistic cultures (Espinoza & Garza 1985).

## Membership in In-Groups

Given that collectivist cultures treat in-group and out-group profoundly differently, *who* is in the in-group(s) is particularly important. In individualistic cultures, people define the in-group (Triandis 1972) as "people who are like me in social class, race, beliefs, attitudes, and values." Most interpersonal behavior occurs within this huge group. In contrast, the in-group in a collectivist culture is more intimately defined as "family and friends and other people concerned with my welfare" (Triandis 1972). This would imply that in some collectivist cultures, where most interactions with businesses (particularly multi-national firms), government representatives, policemen, and so on are outgroup interactions, the amount of inter-group conflict and distrust is necessarily high. This conclusion has some empirical support. For example, in a relatively old cross-national survey Almond and Verba (1963) found the Italians as providing a picture "of relatively unrelieved political alienation and of social isolation and distrust."

The traditional collectivist response to this distrust of strangers and out-group members is to restrict social and economic exchanges to in-group (family, tribe, etc.) members wherever possible (Triandis 1989). However, as the socio-economic structures of many collectivist cultures have become more complex and broad-based (e.g., in Japan, China, Korea, India, etc.), their members have increasingly pursued a strategy of broadening the membership and types of in-groups that they define as relevant while maintaining their characteristic loyalty to those groups (Triandis 1989). Thus, in these countries, conflict and friction are avoided because social and economic exchanges are still occurring primarily between members of (more broadly defined) in-groups.

The most thoroughly investigated example of this collectivist cultural strategy comes from Japan. The Japanese define a broad range of persons with whom they interact as "in-group." For example, in a comparative study of the U.S., and Japan, Gudykunst and Nishida (1986) found that the Japanese seem to develop relatively more intimacy (measured as ratings of the "intimacy" of relationships on a 9-point scale) with acquaintances, co-workers, colleagues, best friends, and close friends. Similarly, the Japanese desire to form trusting (amae) in-group relationships with their customers and suppliers. Picken (1987) cites a Japanese proverb that shows that Japanese firms regard their customers as high status members of their in-group that goes "The customer is to be revered as a divine being" *(kami)* which differs significantly from "the customer is always right." Pickens (1987) points out that:

> The Western version is a rule of prudence for abrasive sales clerks to be reminded of from time to time. The Japanese one implies that the company that treats its customers with the degree of respect they would give to a *kami* will in turn receive protection. The complete mutuality of the relation is stressed.

The widely publicized focus of Japanese firms on building close customer and supplier relationships and on delivering superior product quality and service, is at least partially an outgrowth of perceiving their exchange partners as being part of the firm's in-group (cf. Campbell 1985, Darling & Arnold 1988). Similarly, the desire of Japanese consumers to establish trusting (*amae,* in-group-like) relationships with suppliers and their products is reflected in the tendency of Japanese advertising to focus on inducing positive feelings rather than to provide information. Many other collectivist cultures appear to exhibit analogous propensities for exchange partners to develop similar, trusting, in-group-like relationships (cf. Triandis, Lisansky and Betancourt 1984).

In summary, the collectivist or interdependent self view is widespread among the nations. It drives many dimensions of human experience in these cultures including perceptions of the self, and patterns of social interaction and exchange, along paths that are notably distinct from the more individualist cultures (e.g., the United States) where most marketing theory development and empirical research have been conducted. In particular, the individualist/collectivist dimension of culture can be expected to have far reaching implications for the management of customer relationships and of consumer complaining behavior. We turn now to a brief review of the CCB literature.

## COMPLAINING BEHAVIOR RESEARCH

### Conceptual and Taxonomical Issues

Singh (1988) has pointed out that there is substantial agreement in conceptualizing the CCB phenomenon "as a set of multiple (behavioral and non-behavioral) responses, some or all of which are triggered by perceived dissatisfaction with a purchase episode." These responses may be behavioral, involving any and all actions intended as an "expression of dissatisfaction" (Landon 1980) or nonbehavioral, such as when the problem is forgotten and no action is taken. CCB behaviors have been generally viewed as falling into one of three categories: "exit" or the failure to rebuy the offending product, "voice" or complaining behavior addressed to the manufacturer or retail outlet, or "negative word-of-mouth" to friends and associates (Richins 1983, 1986; Singh 1990a). Importantly, these are largely independent behaviors; a consumer may complain to a retailer, or tell friends about the problem, or switch products, or do any combination of the three, in response to a single dissatisfying consumption incident (cf. Richins 1986).[1]

Most CCB research has concerned itself with one or more of these outcomes and their antecedents without exploring the taxonomy of the CCB construct itself. Several authors have pointed to the importance of properly defining and conceptualizing CCB (Bearden and Teel 1983, Landon 1980, Singh 1988) and various formal classification approaches or taxonomies of CCB behaviors have been suggested. Using cluster analytic techniques and a U.S. sample, Singh (1988) found empirical support for a three dimensional taxonomy involving "voice responses" (e.g., seek redress from seller, no-action), "private responses" (e.g., word-of-mouth communication), and "third party responses" (e.g., take legal action). Significantly, however, Singh's results may have limited applicability outside the United States where less well developed consumer advocacy infrastructures exist. Moreover, what concepts like voice or exit mean in terms of behavior in other national/cultural contexts may be different from in the United States. For example, in the United States, exit usually implies switching to another supplier of the product category, whereas, in countries where fewer alternatives exist, exit may involve boycotting the product category entirely. Finally, it is possible that other culturally-driven complaint options are possible. However, for the purposes of this paper, the traditional voice, negative word-of-mouth, exit taxonomy remains a useful starting point for examining the impact of culture on complaining behaviors.

## *CCB Incidence Rates and Antecedents*

Much of the early CCB research was concerned with measuring the rates of incidence of exit, voice and word-of-mouth behaviors for various categories of goods and services. In general, they found that customers dissatisfied with durables will typically exhibit higher levels of voice and lower levels of exit than customers experiencing problems with non-durables (e.g., Ash and Quelch 1980; Day & Bodur 1977; TARP 1979, 1986).

These results have been explained in terms of the relative investment the customer has in the product or service and, thus, the perceived value of redress (cf. Singh 1990a). Of key importance from a managerial viewpoint, these studies found in general that dissatisfied consumers are unlikely to voice complaints, and very likely to either do nothing or "exit."

More recently, attention has turned to understanding the antecedents of exit, voice, and word-of-mouth behaviors. First of all, the core findings in the literature are that all forms of CCB increase as dissatisfaction (e.g., Bearden and Teel 1983; Singh 1989b; Swan and Oliver 1989) and the perceived importance of the problem (e.g., Folkes et al. 1987; Richins 1983; Singh 1990a) increase. However, a variety of other variables that lead to or moderate CCB have been proposed. These variables can be categorized as involving various attributes (1) of the complaining environment, (2) of the dissatisfaction-causing event or situation, and (3) of the dissatisfied consumer. Table 2 summarizes some of the key findings in the CCB literature.

The next section discusses these findings in the light of the individualism/collectivism literature (Table 3), and develops propositions concerning the impacts of this dimension of culture on CCB. These propositions are organized into models of exit, negative word-of-mouth and voice in Figure 1.

## IMPLICATIONS OF INDIVIDUALISM/COLLECTIVISM FOR CCB

### Collectivism, Economic Development and CCB

Table 2 shows that various attributes of the complaining environment have been found to impact CCB. In particular, the likelihoods of voice and negative word-of-mouth (exit) vary directly (inversely) with the degree of industry concentration (which influences the availability of alternatives to the dissatisfying product) (Fornell and Didow 1980, Singh 1990a). Similarly, as the perceived difficulty or costs of complaining increases, the probability of voice decreases and the probability of exit increases (Richins 1983, 1987). However, both industry concentration and the availability of voice mechanisms (e.g., 1-800 numbers, consumer affairs organizations, etc.) are likely to be a function of the complexity and state of development of a nation's economic infrastructure (Table 3). Similarly, individualism has been shown to be strongly correlated to measures of national economic development such as GNP per capita (e.g., $r = .82$–Hofstede 1980). Moreover, even within broadly collectivist cultures, individuals living in cities tend to be more individualist than their more rural peers (Triandis et al. 1988). Triandis and his colleagues (1988) argue that

TABLE 2. Summary of Selected Research Results Concerning Antecedents of Voice, Negative Word-of-Mouth, and Exit Behaviors in Response to Consumer Dissatisfaction

| CCB Antecedents | Authors | Voice | Neg. W-O-M | Exit |
|---|---|---|---|---|
| **Attributes of Complaining Environment** | | | | |
| Industry Concentration (Alternatives) | Singh 1990a<br>Fornell & Didow 1980 | + | + | – |
| Perceived Difficulty/Costs of Complaining | Richins 1983, 1987<br>Bearden 1983 | – | NS | + |
| Perceived Responsiveness of Supplier | Singh 1990a<br>Richins 1983, 1987 | + | – | – |
| **Situational Attributes** | | | | |
| External Blame Attributions | Folkes et al. 1987<br>Richins 1987, 1983 | + | + | + |
| Negative Affect re: Supplier | Westbrook 1987<br>Singh 1989b<br>Folkes et al. 1987 | + | + | + |
| **Personal and Social Attributes** | | | | |
| Strength of Social Ties | Richins 1985, 1987 | NS | + | NS |
| Social Class | Bearden & Oliver 1985<br>Warland et al. 1975 | + | NS | NS |
| Personal Approval of Voice Behavior | Day 1984, Richins 1982<br>Singh 1989a | + | NS | NS |

Note: Entries indicate where significant relationships between each antecedent and the outcome have been found: "+" = positive relationship; "–" = negative relationship; "NS" = not significant.

economic development is an antecedent of individualism in that increased personal affluence and societal resources lead to greater personal independence from in-groups (and gradually, towards more individualist behavior patterns). Nevertheless, cultures change slowly (e.g., Japan). Thus, studies of the impacts of the individualist/collectivist dimension of culture on CCB need to control for the independent effects of economic development on CCB by way of industry concentration (availability of alternatives) and perceived difficulty of voicing complaints.

## Collectivism and In-Group Perceptions of Supplier

Other aspects of the complaint environment and problem situation that have been found by CCB researchers to impact complaining behaviors deal directly with the consumer's perceptions of and attitudes towards the supplier (see Table 2). For example, the likelihood of voice (negative word-of-mouth and exit) has been found to vary directly (inversely) with consumer perceptions of supplier responsiveness to complaints (Richins 1983, 1987, Singh 1990a). Moreover, voice, negative word-of-mouth, and exit behaviors are all more likely when the blame for the problem is attributed to the supplier (Folkes et al. 1987, Richins 1983, 1987), and when negative affect towards the supplier is high (Folkes et al. 1987, Singh 1989, Westbrook 1987).

However, a consumer's perceptions of suppliers with whom they do business is likely to be influenced by their cultural pattern and the degree to which their self-construals are independent or interdependent (Table 3). The concept of products as part of the "extended self" which has been discussed with respect to (predominantly individualist) U.S. consumers (Belk 1988; McCracken 1990) may be even more relevant for collectivist consumers. As was discussed earlier, collectivists assign strong emotional meanings to the products they buy, and place particular importance on developing close, trusting relationships with their exchange partners. Accordingly, they prefer to do business with existing in-group members, and failing that, they seek to bring exchange partners into an in-group-like (e.g., "amae" in Japan) relationship. In contrast, in individualist cultures like the U.S., consumers are more likely to assume that their relationship with a company from whom they purchase a product or service will be "exchange-based," that is, relatively distant. The following proposition is suggested (see Figure 1):

P1: Consumers in collectivist cultures will have stronger in-group perceptions of the suppliers from which they buy goods and services than will consumers in individualist cultures.

In general, if a consumer perceives a company as in-group and that company's products as part of the consumer's extended self (Belk 1988), then that company will be expected to have the consumer's best interests at heart, and the relationship between the consumer and that company is liable to take on a relatively communal, uncritical nature. In particular, consumer perceptions of supplier responsiveness to complaints might be expected to be higher when the supplier is perceived as in-group (which from P1 is more likely among collectivists) than when the supplier is perceived as outgroup (which will be more likely among individualists).

P2a: The more consumers perceive a firm to be in-group, the more they will perceive the firm to be responsive to complaints.

P2b: Voice (exit and negative word-of-mouth) will vary directly (inversely) with the perceived responsiveness of a supplier to complaints.

TABLE 3. Implications of Cross-Cultural Literature on Collectivism for CCB and Its Antecedents

| CCB Antecedents | Relevant Findings from Individualism/Collectivism Cross-Cultural Literature | Hypothesized Effects of the Degree of Cultural Collectivism on CCB and CCB Antecedents |
|---|---|---|
| **Attributes of Complaining Environment** | | |
| Industry Concentration (Alternatives) | Collectivist cultural patterns are negatively correlated with economic complexity. | None predicted. However, this is an important co-variate. |
| Perceived Difficulty & Costs of Complaining | Less developed economic systems may have fewer channels for voicing complaints. | None predicted. However, this may be an important co-variate. |
| Perceived Supplier Responsiveness | Collectivists are more likely than Individualists to define social and economic exchange partners as in-group. In-group members are assumed to be concerned with each other's well-being. | Perceived Supplier Responsiveness will vary directly with Perceptions of Supplier as In-group, which will vary directly with Degree of Collectivism. Via these mediating variables, Collectivism reduces the likelihood of Exit and Neg. WOM, but *increases* the likelihood of voice behavior. |
| **Situational Attributes** | | |
| External Blame Attributions | Collectivists are more likely than Individualists to accept personal responsibility for failures, particularly when in-group members are involved. | External Blame Attributions will vary inversely with Degree of Collectivism and with Perceptions of Supplier as In-group. Thus, via these mediating variables, Collectivism reduces the likelihood of all CCB. |

| | | |
|---|---|---|
| Negative Affect re: Supplier | Collectivists avoid expressing (or even feeling) negative emotions towards in-group members. | Negative Affect will vary inversely with Perceptions of Supplier as In-group. Via these mediating variables, Collectivism reduces the likelihood of all CCB. |
| **Personal & Social Attributes** | | |
| Strength of Social Ties | Social ties are relatively strong, involving, and central to personal functioning in Collectivist cultures. Innovations diffuse relatively rapidly in collectivist cultures. | The likelihood and extent of Negative WOM will vary directly with Strength of Social Ties, which will vary directly with Degree of Cultural Collectivism. |
| Social Class | The degree and acceptance of power differences in Collectivist cultures is relatively high. | The Social Class/Voice relationship will be stronger in Collectivist cultures than in Individualist Cultures |
| Personal Approval of Voice Behavior | Personal attitudes are affected by perceptions social norms in all cultures. Collectivists place relatively high value on avoiding conflict and on maintaining harmony. Relative to Individualists, Collectivists' behavior is more influenced by group norms and less influenced by personal attitudes. | Personal Approval of Voice will vary directly with Perceived Social Approval of Voice, which will vary inversely with Degree of Cultural Collectivism. The likelihood of Voice behavior will vary positively with both Personal Approval of Voice and Perceived Social Approval of Voice. However, Personal Approval will have less impact and Social Approval more impact on Voice in Collectivist cultures than in Individualist cultures. |

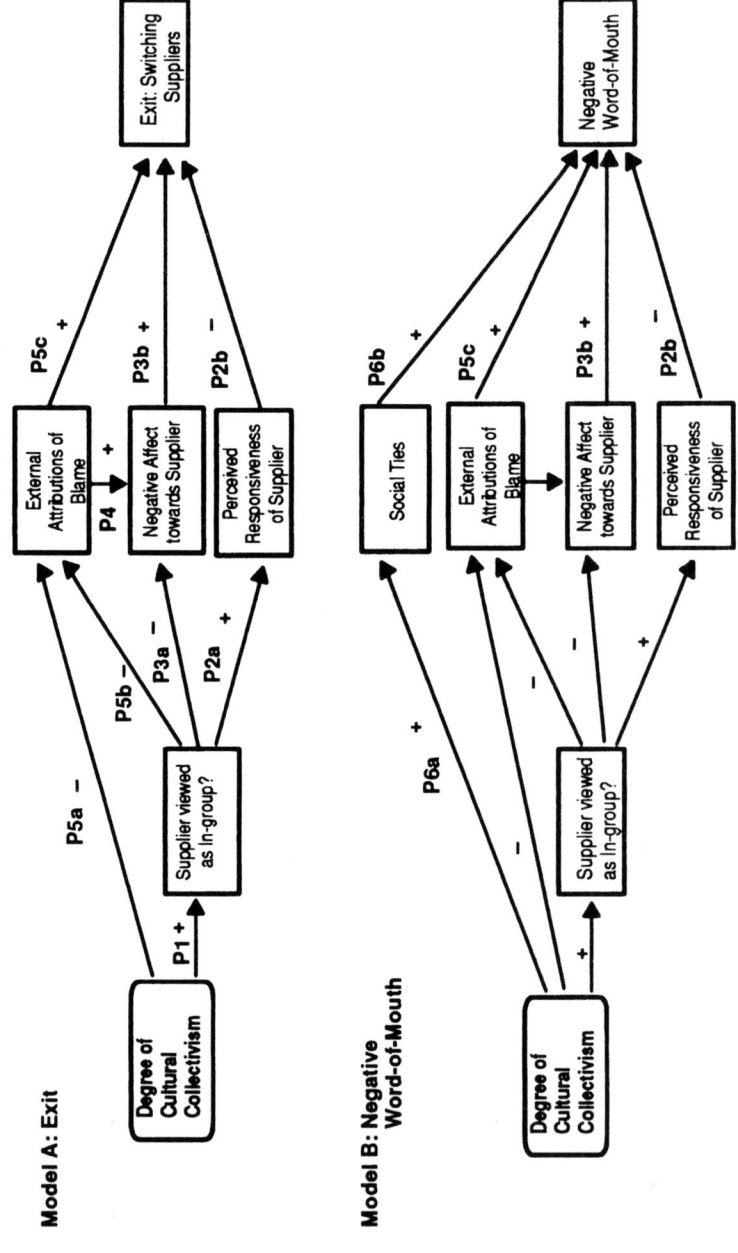

FIGURE 1. Preliminary Models of the Impacts of Collectivism on Exit, Negative Word-of-Mouth, and Voice

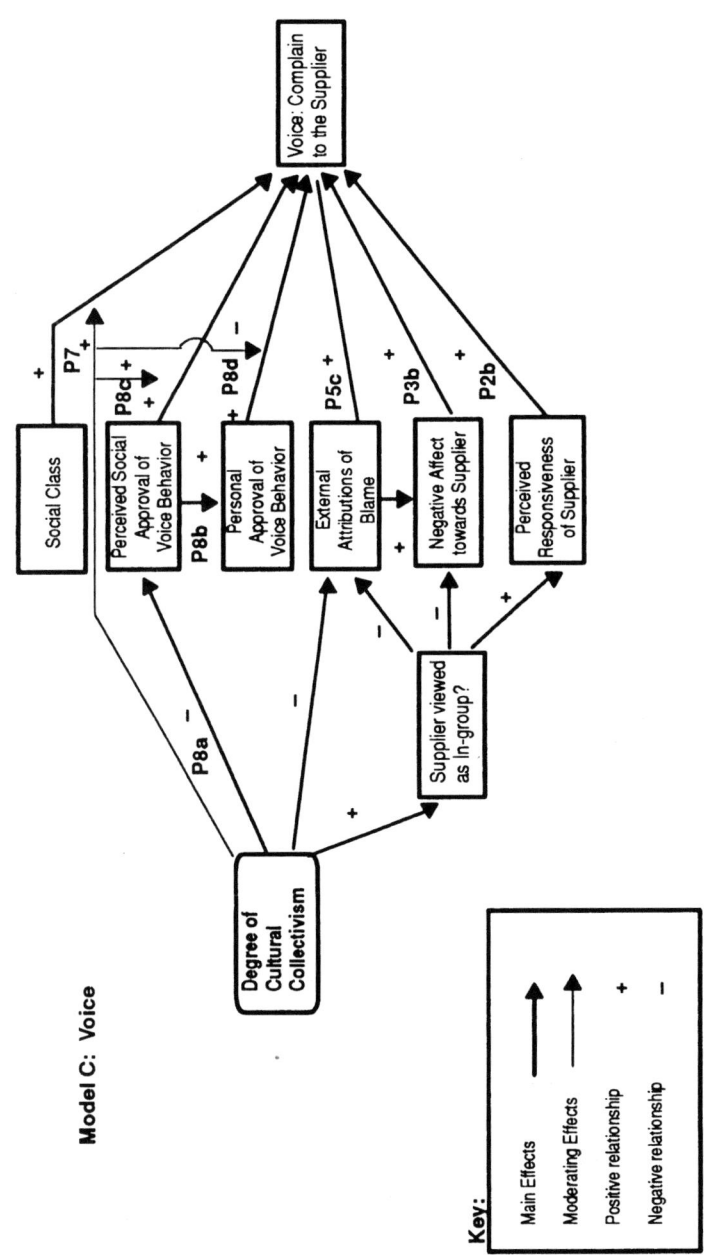

Similarly, while "negative affect" (e.g., anger) towards the supplier has been found to lead to CCB (Table 2), one would expect less critical evaluations of the supplier, and less anger in response to problems with a "in-group" product or service (Table 3 and Figure 1). This would be especially true among collectivists for whom the maintenance of harmonious in-group relationships is particularly important. Thus:

P3a: The more consumers perceive a firm to be in-group, the less anger they will direct at the firm when post-purchase problems occur.

P3b: Negative word-of-mouth, voice and exit will all vary directly with anger (negative affect) towards the firm.

Negative affect towards the firm has also been shown by many CCB researchers (e.g., Curren and Folkes 1987; Westbrook 1987) to vary directly with the degree to which consumers make external attributions concerning the causes of their post-purchase dissatisfaction (Figure 1):

P4: The more consumers blame the problem on the firm (i.e., make external attributions of blame), the greater the anger they will direct at the firm.

## Self- or Other-Serving Bias, Attributions of Blame and CCB

In addition to having an indirect effect on CCB via negative affect towards the firm, external attributions of blame for problems have also been shown to lead directly to greater amounts of voice, negative WOM, and exit behaviors (Table 2). While a consumer's blame attributions concerning a particular problem will be driven largely by the facts surrounding the situation, they may also be affected by a consumer's attributional style which in turn may be influenced by enduring cultural norms (Table 3). In this regard, another important difference between independent and interdependent cultures is the presence or absence of self-enhancing biases. Markus and Kitiyama (1990) note that "Studies with American (individualistic) subjects demonstrate that they take credit for their successes, explain away their failures, and in various ways try to aggrandize themselves." In contrast, they suggest, in collectivistic/interdependent cultures self-enhancement is strongly discouraged and "instead, positive feelings about the self . . . derive from fulfilling the tasks associated with being interdependent with relevant others–belonging, fitting-in, occupying one's proper place, engaging in appropriate action, promoting others' goals, and maintaining harmony." They cite a series of studies (Markus 1990; Takata 1987; Goethals 1989; Wylie 1979; Shikani 1978 and others) that show that individualists tend to attribute their successes to their own internal attributes, while blaming their failures on external causes, while interdependent collectivists tend to be more self-effacing. For example in a study by Shikanai (1978) examining the causal attribution for one's own success or failure in an ability task, Japanese students were variously led to believe that they had "succeeded" or "failed" at an anagram task. Failure was attributed mainly to the lack of effort, success was attributed primarily to the ease of the task. Ability was largely discounted as an explanation for success.

This self-effacing tendency among collectivists may reasonably be expected to extend to the choice of whom to blame for product or service problems. When an individualist experiences a product/service problem that has an unclear cause (e.g., difficulty assembling a children's toy) s/he is likely to seek an external explanation, i.e., to blame the problem on the manufacturer. However, (1) because collectivists have no culturally induced tendency to deflect blame away from themselves and (2) because the problems they experience with products are relatively likely to occur in the context of an in-group exchange relationship, they are more likely to assume personal responsibility for the problem. The above discussion suggests that the individualism/collectivism dimension of culture may effect attributions of blame both directly, and indirectly by way of perceptions of the supplier as ingroup (Figure 1):

P5a: The greater the degree of collectivism in a culture, the less likely are that culture's consumers to make external attributions of blame (i.e., they are more likely to assume personal responsibility) when they experience product problems.

P5b: The more consumers perceive a firm to be in-group, the less likely they are to make external attributions of blame when they experience a problem with a product.

P5c: Voice, negative word-of-mouth, and exit will all vary directly with the degree to which consumers make external attributions (i.e., blame the firm) for their product-related problem.

## *Collectivism, Social Ties and Negative Word-of-Mouth*

CCB researchers have found that certain aspects of consumers' social position, social connections and attitudes towards complaining affect how they respond to post-purchase dissatisfaction. For example, Richins (1985, 1987) found that strong social ties increase the likelihood of negative word-of-mouth, but had no impact on voice or exit (Table 2).

Even within individualist cultures (i.e., the U.S.), the related concepts of tie strength (i.e., the force of the bond between two people–Granovetter 1973) and homophily (i.e., source/receiver similarity on attributes such as beliefs, education and status–Engel, Blackwell and Miniard 1986) have been used to predict the amount and impact of WOM behaviors (Bristor 1989). Information exchanges, including negative communications about products, have been shown to occur more readily among groups of homophilous (similar) people sharing strong ties. In collectivist cultures, relationships within in-groups are obviously strongly homophilous with relatively strong ties and good communications (Table 3), while individual/out-group relationships are profoundly heterophilous. These observations account for recent empirical findings that innovations diffuse relatively rapidly in collectivist countries such as Japan, Taiwan and Korea (Liu and Kahle 1989, Takada and Jain 1991). Further, they suggest that negative word-of-mouth communications, at least with in-group members, are more likely as an outcome of post purchase dissatisfaction in collectivist cultures than in individualistic cultures. This discussion and the CCB literature suggest the following propositions (Figure 1, Model B):

P6a: The greater the degree of collectivism in a culture, the stronger will be the social ties among consumers in that culture.

P6b: The stronger a consumer's social ties, the more likely the consumer is to engage in negative word-of-mouth in response to post-purchase dissatisfaction.

## Collectivism, Social Class and Voice Behavior

A consumer's social class has been shown to be moderately related to the likelihood of voice behavior; as education and income levels increase, voice becomes more likely (e.g., Bearden and Oliver 1985; Warland et al. 1975–see Table 2). This relationship was found to be relatively weak in U.S. samples. However, in collectivist cultures both the degree and the acceptance of power differences within in-groups tend to be relatively high. Low status individuals are expected to be especially deferential in their interactions with higher status individuals, and high status collectivists feel particularly empowered to act (although they are still concerned with maintaining in-group harmony). This suggests that the degree of collectivism in a culture may serve to moderate the strength of the social class/voice relationship; one would expect to find a stronger relationship between social class and the likelihood of voice among collectivists than among individualists (Figure 1, Model C).

P7: The likelihood of voice behavior will vary directly with the social class of the individual consumer. This relationship will be stronger in collectivist cultures than in individualistic cultures.

## *Social Norms, Personal Attitudes About Complaining, and Voice Behavior*

In the U.S., positive personal attitudes towards complaining have been shown to affect voice intentions and behaviors (Day 1984; Richins 1982; Singh 1989a). However, even in the relatively individualistic Netherlands, social norms concerning complaining behavior have been shown to affect personal attitudes (Richins and Verhage 1985). Personal attitudes about complaining are even more likely to conform with social norms about complaining among collectivists than among individualists. Moreover, in a collectivist culture, individuals are less likely to "sample their private self" and more likely to "sample their collective self" i.e., to attend to the attitudes of their in-group(s) for guidance as to whether or not complaining to a supplier or to a third party are appropriate behaviors (Triandis 1989). This is important because collectivist cultures in general tend to value conformity and harmony; complaining behavior in general (as distinguished from consumer voice) is discouraged (Triandis et al. 1988). In summary, among collectivists, there may be little difference between perceived social norms and personal attitudes about complaining, and to the extent that there is a difference, social norms will weigh relatively heavily in effecting (discouraging) their decision to voice complaints to suppliers (Figure 1, Model C). Thus:

P8a: Perceived social approval of voice behavior will be lower in collectivist cultures than in individualist cultures.

P8b: Personal approval of voice behavior will vary directly with perceived social approval of voice behavior.

P8c: The likelihood of voice behavior will vary directly with the degree of perceived social approval of voice behavior. This relationship will be stronger in collectivist cultures than in individualistic cultures.

P8d: The likelihood of voice behavior will vary directly with the degree of personal approval of voice behavior. This relationship will be weaker in collectivist cultures than in individualistic cultures.

## Overall Rates of Voice, Negative Word-of-Mouth and Exit in Collectivist and Individualist Cultures

Finally, we turn to the managerially significant question of how the individualism-collectivism dimension of culture is liable to affect overall rates of voice, negative word-of-mouth. The models presented in Figure 1 are suggestive, but not conclusive.

A review of the causal paths of the Voice model (Figure 1, Model C) suggest that the net impact of cultural collectivism is to make voice a relatively unacceptable response to dissatisfaction. Voice behavior is inherently confrontational. It involves telling a firm's representative that something is wrong with their product or service, and (often) that some action to correct the problem is desired. In general, collectivists will be less likely to engage in voice behavior than individualists because confrontation (voice) is relatively unacceptable, particularly where in-group members are involved.

The negative word-of-mouth model (Figure 1, Model B) suggests that collectivism has mixed impacts on negative word-of-mouth: compared with individualists, collectivists' strong social ties would seem to make negative word-of-mouth more likely, while their propensity to view suppliers as in-group would seem to have the opposite effect. In the final analysis, however, collectivists depend on regular communication with members of their in-groups in order to evaluate their world and to define and manage their self-view. Accordingly, we argue that, overall, collectivists are more likely to engage in negative word-of-mouth behavior, and will engage in more extensive negative word-of-mouth behavior than individualists when problems occur (see Figure 2).[2]

Finally, as was discussed earlier (Table 1), collectivists are relatively slow to enter or exit in-group relationships. From this alone, one would expect that they would be less likely than individualists to engage in exit behavior. Similarly, the model for exit and its antecedents presented above (Figure 1, Model A) suggests that exit is a relatively unlikely response to post-purchase dissatisfaction in collectivist cultures.[3] In summary:

P9a: Voice behavior will be less common in collectivist cultures than in individualist cultures.

P9b: Negative word-of-mouth will be more common and more extensive (i.e., more individuals will be involved) in collectivist cultures than in individualist cultures.

P9c: (Even after controlling for the perceived availability of alternatives), exit behavior will be less common in collectivist cultures than in individualist cultures.

## IMPLICATIONS FOR MANAGEMENT AND CONCLUSION

In recent years, academicians and managers alike have devoted increasing attention to the challenges of managing customer relationships. Central to this effort is developing an understanding of how consumers respond when dissatisfied with a product or service. However, the growing importance of international and multinational trade, and the increasing size and economic significance of subcultures (i.e., Hispanic, Asian, etc.) within the U.S., make it imperative that CCB researchers study the impact of cultural differences on dissatisfaction and CCB. This article has sought to explore some ways in which the individualist/collectivist dimension of culture is useful (1) in explaining the results of much of the limited cross-cultural CCB research that has been conducted to date, and more importantly, (2) in suggesting theory-driven, testable propositions for future research.

FIGURE 2. A Summary Model of the Impacts of Collectivism on Consumer Complaining Behaviors

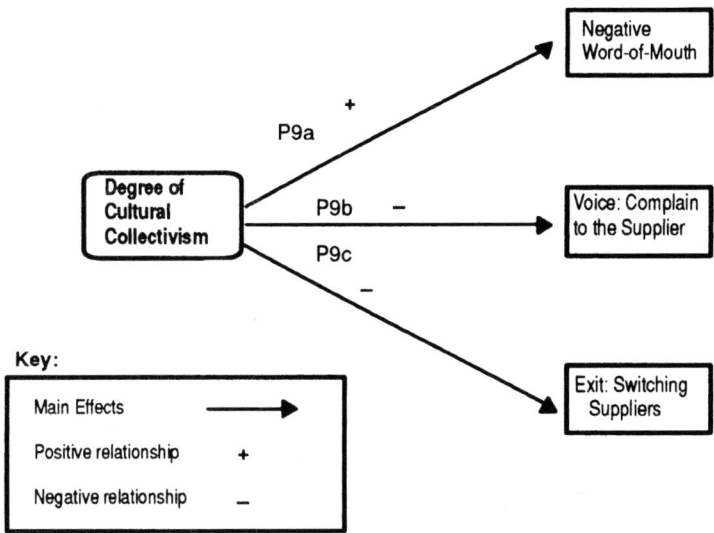

The models proposed in this paper suggest that compared with individualists, collectivist consumers are relatively loyal, and are even less likely to voice complaints when they experience post-purchase problems. In contrast, they are more likely to engage in negative word-of-mouth to in-group members, and these negative communications are more likely to be attended to by other members of their in-group(s). Moreover, when collectivists do exit, it is likely to be particularly difficult for the offending supplier to regain them as customers. Managers are going to have to work especially hard to encourage voice when collectivists experience problems. Attitudes and feelings concerning the supplier and complaining behaviors among collectivists will be strongly affected by whether management can cause the supplier and its products to be identified by consumers as a member of a relevant "in-group," that is, to be perceived as trustworthy, and intimately concerned with the particular consumer's well-being. The implication is that effective relationship management is both especially demanding and particularly critical to long term business success in collectivist cultures.

This paper just begins the process of relating the concepts of cultural psychology to the problem of understanding consumer complaining behaviors. Its focus has been cross-cultural, that is, it has sought to compare and contrast consumer behavior across cultures rather than within them. However, Triandis and his colleagues have demonstrated that substantial variance along the individualist/collectivist dimension exits within cultures (particularly in heterogeneous cultures such as is found in the United States). Many of the propositions in this paper may also hold for CCB differences between collectivists and individualists *within* a given culture. Further, the paper has dealt with only one dimension of culture. For example, several other dimensions of culture have been identified (e.g., power-distance, risk avoidance, and masculinity-femininity–Hofstede 1980) that should be studied for their potential impact on CCB. Nevertheless, the fruitfulness of this brief review of the implications of just one dimension of culture for understanding consumer complaining behavior strongly suggests that such research efforts, directed toward the goal of developing a theory of multicultural consumer complaining behavior, will be well worthwhile.

## NOTES

1. The limited research on consumer satisfaction with suppliers' responses to voice suggests that *successful* voice may lead to less exit behavior. For example, Gilly (1987) demonstrated that positive consumer perceptions of supplier responses to complaints resulted in high satisfaction and increased repurchase intentions and behaviors. This suggests that for some consumers, voice precedes and (depending on supplier response) impacts the probability of exit. This possible

relationship between voice and exit merits further research, but lies beyond the scope of this paper. In the interests of clarity and of facilitating comparisons with the existing CCB literature, we have chosen to focus on the impacts of culture on exit, voice and negative word-of-mouth considered as independent outcomes of dissatisfaction.

2. However, perceptions of the supplier as in-group may have the effect of moderating the purpose and content of the negative word-of-mouth communications, for example, by making them less punitive.

3. A possible alternative view is suggested from the observation in footnote 1 that *successful* voice has been found to reduce the subsequent probability of exit by the voicing consumer (Gilly 1987, TARP 1985). The implication is that collectivists' reluctance to voice complaints (thus eliminating the possibility of an appropriate supplier response) may counterbalance their natural loyalty to their in-group supplier: in severe situations, exit may be perceived as their only acceptable recourse. The net balance between these influences necessarily must be determined empirically.

## REFERENCES

Almond, G. A. and S. Verba (1963). *The Civic Culture*. Princeton, NJ: Princeton University Press.

Andreasen, Alan (1985). "Consumer Responses to Dissatisfaction in Loose Monopolies," *Journal of Consumer Research*, 12 (September), 135-41.

Arndt, Johan, H. C. Barksdale and W. D. Perreault (1982). "Comparative Study of Attitudes Toward Marketing, Consumerism, and Government Regulation." In *New Findings on Consumer Satisfaction and Complaining*, R. L. Day and H. K. Hunt, eds., Bloomington, IN: Indiana University.

Ash, S. B. and J. A. Quelch (1980). "Consumer Satisfaction, Dissatisfaction and Complaining Behavior: A Comprehensive Study of Rentals, Public Transportation and Utilities." In *Refining Concepts and Measures of Consumer Satisfaction and Complaining Behavior*, Bloomington, IN: Indiana University.

Bearden, William O., and Richard L. Oliver (1985). "The Role of Public and Private Complaining in Satisfaction with Problem Resolution." *Journal of Consumer Affairs*. 19 (Winter) 222-240.

_____, and Jesse E. Teel (1983). "Selected Determinants of Consumer Satisfaction and Complaint Reports," *Journal of Marketing Research*. 20 (February), 21-28.

Belk, Russel W. (1988). "Possessions and the Extended Self," *Journal of Consumer Research*, 15 (September) 139-168.

Bodur, M., E. Borak and K. Kurlukus (1983). "A Comparative Study of Satisfaction/Dissatisfaction and Complaining Behavior with Consumer Services." In *New Findings on Consumer Satisfaction and Complaining*, R. L. Day and H. K. Hunt, eds., Bloomington, IN: Indiana University.

Bond, M. H. (1986). *The Psychology of the Chinese People*. New York: Oxford University Press.

Bristor, Julia M. (1989). "Word of Mouth Communications and their Effects in Consumer Networks," American Marketing Association, Winter Educator's Conference.

*Business Week* (1984). "Making Service a Potent Marketing Tool" (June 11), 164-170.

Campbell, N. C. G. (1985). "Buyer/Seller Relationships in Japan and Germany: An Interaction Approach," *European Journal of Marketing*, 19, 3, 56-66.

Clark, Clark L., and Peter F. Kaminski (1989). "Consumer Complaints: Advice on How Companies Should Respond Based on an Empirical Study," American Marketing Association, Summer Educator's Conference Proceedings, 159.

Commission of the European Communities (1976). *European Consumers: Their Interests, Aspirations, and Knowledge on Consumer Affairs*. Brussels.

Cousins, S. (1989). "Personality Research in a Non-Western Culture: The Philippines," *Psychological Bulletin*, 102, 272-292.

Day, Ralph L. (1984). "Modeling Choices Among Alternative Responses to Dissatisfaction." In *Theoretical Developments in Marketing*, Charles Lamb and Patrick Dunne, eds. Chicago: American Marketing Association, 211-215.

_____, and Muzzaffar Bodur (1977). "A Comprehensive Study of Satisfaction with Consumer Services," *Consumer Satisfaction, Dissatisfaction and Complaining Behavior*, Day (ed.): 64-70.

Espinoza, J. A., and R. T. Garza (1985). "Social Group Salience and Inter-ethnic Cooperation," *Journal of Experimental Social Psychology*, 231, 380-392.

Folkes, Valerie, Susan Koletsky and John L. Graham (1987). "A Field Study of Causal Inferences and Consumer Reaction: The View from the Airport," *Journal of Consumer Research*, Vol. 13 (March), 534-539.

Fornell, Claes (1976). *Consumer Input for Marketing Decisions: A Study of Corporate Departments for Consumer Affairs*, New York, Praeger Publishers.

_____, and Nicholas M. Didow (1980). "Economic Constraints on Consumer Complaining Behavior." In *Advances in Consumer Research*, Vol. 7, Jerry C. Olson, ed. Ann Arbor, MI: Association for Consumer Research, 318-23.

_____, and Birger Wernerfelt (1986). "A Model for Customer Complaint Management," working paper, Graduate School of Business Administration, University of Michigan.

Francken, Dick A. (1983). "Postpurchase Consumer Evaluations, Complaint Actions and Repurchase Behavior." *Journal of Economic Psychology*, 4: 273-290.

Gilly, Mary C. (1987). "Postcomplaint Processes: From Organizational Response to Repurchase Behavior," *Journal of Consumer Affairs*, 21 (Winter), 293-311.

Goodwin, Cathy, Kelly L. Smith, and Ivan Ross (1989). "Responses to Consumer Service Complaints: A Procedural Fairness Approach," American Marketing Association Summer Educator's Conference Proceedings. Goodwin and Ross.

Granovetter, Mark S. (1973). "The Strength of Weak Ties," *American Journal of Sociology*, Vol. 78(6), 1361-80.

Gudykunst, W. B., and T. Nishida (1986). "The Influence of Cultural Variability on Perceptions of Communication Behavior Associated with Relationship Terms," *Human Communication Research*, 13, 147-166.

Hofstede, Seert (1980). *Culture's Consequences: International Differences in Work-Related Values*. Beverly Hills, CA: Sage Publications, Inc.

Kaiser, R. G. (1984). *Russia: The People and the Power*, New York: Washington Square Press.

Lewis, Robert C. (1982). "Consumers Complain–What Happens When Business Responds?" In *Consumer Satisfaction/Dissatisfaction and Complaining Behavior Conference Proceedings*, Ralph Day and Keith Hunt, eds. Bloomington: Indiana University, 88-94.

Liu, R. and L. Kahle (1989). "Consumer Social Values in the People's Republic of China," *Proceedings of the American Psychology Association*, Division 23.

Markus, H. and S. Kitayama (1990). "Culture and the Self: Implications for Cognition, Emotion, and Motivation," *Psychological Review*, 98, No. 2, 224-253.

Matsumoto, D., T. Kudoh, K. Scherer, and H. Wallbott (1988). "Antecedents of and Reactions to Emotions in the United States and Japan," *Journal of Cross-Cultural Psychology*, 19, 267-286.

McCracken, Grant (1990). "Culture and Consumer Behavior: an Anthropological Perspective," *Journal of the Market Research Society*, Vol. 32, 1, 3-11.

Meffert, H. and M. Bruhn (1983). "Complaining Behavior and Satisfaction of Consumers." In *International Fare in Consumer Satisfaction and Complaining Behavior*, R. L. Day and H. K. Hunt, eds., Bloomington, IN: Indiana University.

Oliver, Richard L. (1980). "A Cognitive Model of the Antecedents and Consequences of Satisfaction Decisions," *Journal of Marketing Research*, 17 (November), 460-9.

Picken, Stuart D. B. (1987). "Values and Value Related Strategies in Japanese Corporate Culture," *Journal of Business Ethics*, 6, 137-143.

Resnik, Alan J. and Robert R. Harmon, (1983). "Consumer Complaints and Managerial Response: A Holistic Approach," *Journal of Marketing*, 47 (March), 86-97.

Richins, Marsha L. (1982). "An Investigation of Consumers' Attitudes Toward Complaining," In *Advances in Consumer Research*, A. Mitchel, ed., Vol. 9, Ann Arbor, MI: Association for Consumer Research.

_____, (1987). "A Multivariate Analysis of Responses to Dissatisfaction," *Journal of the Academy of Marketing Science*, 15 (Fall), 24-31.

_____, (1983). "Negative Word-of-Mouth by Dissatisfied Consumers: A Pilot Study," *Journal of Marketing*, 47 (Winter), 68-78.

_____, and Bronislaw J. Verhage (1985). "Cross-cultural Differences in Consumer Attitudes and Their Implications for Complaint Management," *International Journal of Research in Marketing*, 2, 197-206.

_____, (1987). "A Multivariate Analysis of Responses to Dissatisfaction," *Journal of the Academy of Marketing Science*, 15 (Fall), 24-31.

Ross, I. and R. L. Oliver (1984). "The Accuracy of Unsolicited Consumer Communications as Indicators of True Consumer Satisfaction/Dissatisfaction. In *Advances in Consumer Research*, T. C. Kinnaer, ed., Vol. 11. Ann Arbor, MI: Association for Consumer Research.

Singh, Jagdip (1988). "Consumer Complaint Intentions and Behavior: Definitional and Taxonomical Issues," *Journal of Marketing*, 52 (January): 93-107.

_____, (1989a). "Determinants of Consumers' Decisions to Seek Third Party Redress: An Empirical Study of Dissatisfied Patients," *Journal of Consumer Affairs*, Vol. 23, 2, 329-363.

_____, (1989b). "The Role of Dissatisfaction in Consumer Complaint Behaviors: An Exploratory Study," In American Marketing Association Summer Educator's Conference Proceedings, pg. 290.

_____, (1990a). "Voice, Exit, and Negative Word-of Mouth Behaviors: An Investigation Across Three Service Categories," *Journal of the Academy of Marketing Science*, 18 (Winter): 1-16.

_____, (1990b). "A Typology of Consumer Dissatisfaction Response Styles," *Journal of Retailing*, 66 (Spring), 57-99.

Sinha, J. B. P. (1982). "The Hindu (Indian) Identity," *Dynamisch Psychiatrie*, 15, 148-160.

Swan, John E. and Richard L. Oliver, (1989). "Postpurchase Communications by Consumers," *Journal of Retailing*, 65 (Winter), 516-533.

Takada, Hirokazu and Dipak Jain, (1991). "Cross-National Analysis of Diffusion of Consumer Durable Goods in Pacific Rim Countries," *Journal of Marketing*, 55 (April), 2, 48-54.

Takata, T. (1987). "Self-Deprecative Tendencies in Self-Evaluation Through Social Comparison," *Japanese Journal of Experimental Social Psychology*, 27, 27-36.

TARP (1979). *Consumer Complaint Handling in America: Summary of Findings and Recommendations*, Washington, DC: US Office of Consumer Affairs.

_____, (1986). *Consumer Complaint Handling in America: An Updated Study*, White House Office of Consumer Affairs, Washington, D.C.

Thorelli, H. B. (1983). "China: Consumer Voice and Exit." In *Consumer Satisfaction/Dissatisfaction and Complaining Behavior*, H. K. Hunt and R. L. Day, eds., Bloomington, IN: Indiana University.

Triandis, H. C. (1967). "Interpersonal Relations in International Organizations," *Journal of Organizational Behavior and Human Performance*, 2, 26-55.

_____, (1989). "The Self and Social Behavior in Differing Cultural Contexts," *Psychological Review*, Vol. 96, 3, 506-520.

_____, (1972). *The Analysis of Subjective Culture*, New York: Wiley.

_____, G. Marin, J. Lisansky, and H. Betancourt (1984). "*Simpatia* as a Cultural Script of Hispanics," *Journal of Personality and Social Psychology*, 47, 1364-1375.

_____, R. Bontempo, M. J. Villareal, M. Asai, and N. Lucca (1988). "Individualism and Collectivism: Cross-Cultural Perspectives on Self-Ingroup Relationships," *Journal of Personality and Social Psychology*, 54, 323-338.

Warland, Rex H., Robert O. Herrmann and Jane Willitts (1975). "Dissatisfied Consumers: Who Gets Upset and Who Takes Action," *Journal of Consumer Affairs*, 9 (Winter), 148-163.

Westbrook, Robert A. (1987). "Product Consumption-based Affective Responses and Post-Purchase Processes," *Journal of Marketing Research*, 24 (August), 258-270.

# An Investigation of Construct Validity and Generalizability of the Self-Concept: Self-Consciousness in Japan and the United States

Shuzo Abe
Richard P. Bagozzi
Pradip Sadarangani

**SUMMARY.** This article presents an investigation of the self-concept in independent and interdependent cultures. Hypotheses are tested based on differences expected between Japanese ($N = 402$) and American ($N = 233$) consumers. Japanese conceptualizations of the self were found to be more integrated and less distinct in the sense that self-images of private and public self-consciousness were more strongly correlated. Japanese also experienced higher levels of social anxiety but lower levels of private self-consciousness than Americans. Attention to social comparison information was positively related to public self-consciousness and social anxiety, but unrelated to private self-consciousness, for both Americans and Japanese. Ac-

---

Shuzo Abe is affiliated with the Faculty of Business Administration, Yokohama National University, Yokohama 240, Japan. Richard P. Bagozzi and Pradip Sadarangani are affiliated with the School of Business Administration, University of Michigan, Ann Arbor, MI 48109-1234.

Appreciation is expressed to Yoshida Hideo Kinen Jigyo-Zaidan for a research grant to Shuzo Abe and to the Center for International Business Education, University of Michigan, for a research grant to Richard Bagozzi.

[Haworth co-indexing entry note]: "An Investigation of Construct Validity and Generalizability of the Self-Concept: Self-Consciousness in Japan and the United States." Abe, Shuzo, Richard P. Bagozzi, and Pradip Sadarangani. Co-published simultaneously in *Journal of International Consumer Marketing* (International Business press, an imprint of The Haworth Press, Inc.) Vol. 8, No. 3/4, 1996, pp. 97-123; and: *Global Perspectives in Cross-Cultural and Cross-National Consumer Research* (ed: Lalita A. Manrai, and Ajay K. Manrai) International Business Press, an imprint of The Haworth Press, Inc., 1996, pp. 97-123. Single or multiple copies of this article are available form The Haworth Document Delivery Service [1-800-342-9678, 9:00 a.m - 5:00 p.m. (EST)].

© 1996 by The Haworth Press, Inc. All rights reserved.

tion control was negatively related to public and private self-consciousness and social anxiety for both Americans and Japanese. The attention to social comparison information was more strongly positively correlated with social anxiety and public self-consciousness for American as opposed to Japanese consumers. Action control was more strongly negatively correlated with social anxiety and public self-consciousness for Japanese as opposed to American consumers. The findings are interpreted from recent theories of interdependent and independent conceptualizations of the self. *[Article copies available from The Haworth Document Delivery Service: 1-800-342-9678.]*

## SELF-CONSCIOUSNESS IN JAPAN AND THE UNITED STATES

### The Self-Concept

William James (1890) was an earlier theorist to define the self as an object of self-perception and self-knowledge (Smith, 1992). For him, the "empirical self or me" was the concept most central to personal experience. James maintained that the empirical self has three main divisions: the material self (i.e., one's body and possessions), the social self (i.e., the impression one conveys to others), and the spiritual self (i.e., one's inner or subjective being). Today the study of the self has a rich tradition in both psychology, where the self-concept is represented by such labels as self-schemas (e.g., Markus, 1977) and self-esteem (e.g., Fleming & Courtney, 1984), and sociology, where the self-concept is investigated as part of social-identity theory (e.g., Stryker, 1987).

We can think of the self-concept as a cognitive appraisal of the attributes about oneself (Hattie, 1992). The self-concept both mediates and regulates behavior: "It interprets and organizes self-relevant actions and experiences; it has motivational consequences, providing the incentives, standards, plans, rules, and scripts for behavior; and it adjusts in response to challenges from the social environment" (Markus & Wurf, 1987, pp. 299-230; see also Markus & Nurius, 1986).

Researchers have found that two construals of the self can be identified in people, depending on the culture within which one has been raised (Markus & Kitayama, 1991; see also Triandis, 1989). The *independent self-concept* is common in many Western cultures and is characterized by an emphasis on personal goals, personal achievement, and appreciation of one's differences from others. People with an independent self-concept tend to be individualistic, egocentric, autonomous, self-reliant, and self-contained. They place considerable importance on asserting the self and are driven by self-serving motives. The individual is the primary unit of consciousness, with the self coterminous with one's own body. Relationships with others frequently serve as standards of self-appraisal, and the independent self takes a strategic posture vis-à-vis others in an effort to express or assert one's internal attributes. One's personal attributes are primary and are seen as relatively stable from context to context. Emphasis is placed on displaying or showing one's attributes (e.g., pride, anger). The normative imperative is to become independent from others and discover one's uniqueness.

The *interdependent self-concept* is common in many non-Western cultures and is characterized by stress on goals of a group to which one belongs, attention to fitting in with others, and appreciation of commonalities with others. People with an interdependent self-concept tend to be obedient, sociocentric, holistic, connected, and relation oriented. They place much importance on social harmony and are driven by other-serving motives. The relationships one has are the primary unit of consciousness, with the self coterminous with either a group or the set of roles one has with individuals across multiple groups. Relationships with others are ends in and of themselves, and the interdependent self takes a stance vis-à-vis others of giving and receiving social support. One's personal attributes are secondary and are allowed to change as needed in response to situational demands. Emphasis is placed on controlling one's attributes (e.g., avoiding the display of anger). The normative imperative is to maintain one's interdependence with others and contribute to the welfare of the group.

The categories of independent and interdependent selves are, of course, ideal types and some variability is to be expected within any particular culture characterized by one or the other. Nevertheless, the distinctions are very real as general tendencies. Triandis (1989) describes how cultures shape either an independent or interdependent self. Markus and Kitayama (1991) argue that independent and interdependent selves have specific consequences for the acquisition and experience of cognition, emotion, and motivation. However, very little cross-cultural research can be found testing the existence of differences in the self-concept and their implications.

## *Self-Consciousness*

We chose the self-consciousness scale as our specific operationalization of the self-concept. The self-consciousness scale is a 23-item inventory designed to measure the tendency or disposition to direct attention inward towards oneself or outward towards others (e.g., Fenigstein, Scheier, & Buss, 1975).

Self-consciousness has three dimensions or components. *Private self-consciousness* refers to attentiveness to covert aspects of the self and is manifest in one's inner thoughts and feelings. *Public self-consciousness* denotes attentiveness to overt aspects of the self reflected in one's expressed behavior, particular that which others can observe. Finally, *social anxiety* is the degree of discomfort one feels in the presence of others.

A considerable body of research has addressed the self-consciousness scale. In addition to the results supporting the three dimensions of self-consciousness reported by Fenigstein et al. (1975), which arose from factor analyses performed on nine different samples, Carver and Glass (1976), Turner, Carver, Scheier, and Ickes (1978), and Carver and Scheier (1978) presented evidence confirming construct validity. More recently, Nasby (1989) found support for convergent, discriminant, and predictive validity of private self-consciousness and public self-consciousness (social anxiety was not examined). Likewise, Abrams (1988) found support for the three-factor self-consciousness representation by use of CFA and discriminant validity of public and private self-consciousness (poor discriminant validity was found for social anxiety). Although debate can be found on conceptual aspects of self-consciousness and the 23-item scale (e.g., Carver & Scheier, 1987; Fenigstein, 1987; Wicklund & Gollwitzer, 1987), the balance of empirical research is supportive and the "scales have become an established part of self-awareness research" in the field of psychology (Abrams, 1988, p. 12).

The self-consciousness scale has not been investigated much in consumer research. Burnkrant and Page (1982) predicted, but failed to find, that "people who are high in public self-consciousness should be more sensitive to the type of impression called for in social situations and more inclined to act in accord with these impressions than people who are low in public self-consciousness" (p. 454). Solomon and Schopler (1982) found that women, but not men, who were higher in public self-consciousness evaluated clothing fashions more favorably. Bearden and Rose (1990) found that public self-consciousness correlated .60 with the attention to social comparison information scale in their Study 1, .40 in their Study 2, and .46 in their Study 3. This was taken as evidence for discriminant validity. Finally, Bagozzi, Baumgartner, and Yi (1992) found that public self-consciousness and action control were correlated −.21, thus showing discriminant validity. With one exception, no studies could be found examining hypotheses with all three dimensions of self-consciousness,[1] and none could be found investigating self-consciousness in cross-cultural consumer contexts. Our hypotheses concerning the self-consciousness scale and its components in a cross-cultural setting are described in the next titled section.

It should be mentioned as well that little cross-cultural research can be found with the self-consciousness scale in the psychology literature. Early research attempted to see if the self-consciousness scale "works" in other cultures. Typically, the studies limited inquiry to a single, non-English speaking culture, which, while addressing the viability of the scale within that culture, leaves cultural differences unexplored (e.g., Heinemann, 1979). More recent research looking at cross-cultural administrations of the self-consciousness scale has not formally examined hypotheses based on cultural differences nor compared psychometric properties (e.g., factor structure, loadings, error variances, correlations across factors) between cultures (e.g., Abrams, 1988; cf., Gudykunst, Yang, & Nashida, 1987). The present study attempts to do these things.

## Hypotheses

The following hypotheses are presented in summary form in the left-hand column of Table 5.

*Self-integration.* We predict that the correlation between public and private self-consciousness will be greater for Japanese than American subjects. The Japanese function in an interdependent culture where self-control of personal attributes (e.g., emotions, vocalizations, and even thoughts) is performed in order to adjust oneself to social exigencies. The Japanese work to maintain a balance between private and public cognitions of self (e.g., Doi, 1986). This tends to bring private and public self-concepts in-line, so to speak. Indeed, the Japanese word for the self, *jibun,* means "one's share of the shared life space" (Hamaguchi, 1985). Personal attributes are not conceived in rigid, unchanging ways, but rather are fluid and situation specific. The need to fit in with others and the importance placed on harmonious relations produce public conformity and avoidance of both idiosyncratic responses and the expression of ego-focused emotions. For example, the Japanese strive to avoid displays of anger or self-pride in close relationships, because they often threaten to disrupt orderliness. When asked to express their "private" thoughts or feelings, Japanese subjects are likely to give the responses they feel are called for by the social situation at hand (i.e., their public self-consciousness). As a consequence, one expects a high correlation between private and public selves for Japanese subjects.

Americans, in contrast, live in a relatively independent culture. They are expected on the one hand to strive for individual goals, uniqueness, independence, and self-actualization. Rather than practicing self-control, per se, Americans are taught to be assertive, speak their own minds, and in general, stand out from the crowd. These characteristics require that more attention be paid to the private self and help to develop a more crystallized and distinctive self-image than Japanese. On the other hand, when Americans do function in social situations, they often create a social persona designed to enhance their self-image and maintain their individuality. Instead of searching for commonalities and assimilating oneself in the social situation, however, Americans strive to use the setting to reaffirm differences. Emphasis is on give and take rather than mutual gain or submission. When asked to express their "private" thoughts or feelings, Americans often give a response sampled from traits, states, or behaviors characteristic of their personal, unique identity and not necessarily as demanded by any particular situation. As a result, one anticipates a relatively low correlation between private and public selves for Americans.

No differences in correlations are expected between Japanese and American subjects for private self-consciousness and social anxiety or for public self-consciousness and social anxiety. We expect small to moderate positive correlations between social anxiety and public and private self-consciousness because greater inward focus should exacerbate worry associated with shyness, embarrassment, and related social fears. But because Americans and Japanese both function in social situations, albeit in different ways, the *association* between anxiety and self-consciousness should not differ between the cultures (see below, however, where differences in the *magnitude* of anxiety are predicted).

*Levels of self-consciousness.* The following predictions are made on differences between the average levels of self-consciousness for Americans and Japanese. Americans are expected to have higher levels of private self-consciousness than Japanese. This is a straightforward prediction based on the greater emphasis placed on discovering and expressing individual attributes by Americans. Americans see themselves as relatively separate from the social context and strive to project their individuality into it. Indeed, Americans sometimes attempt to change or control the outer world (e.g., one's public behaviors or even the social situation) by affirming their inner attributes or even on occasion imposing these on others in a group context (e.g., Weisz, Rothbaum, & Blackburn, 1984). The Japanese, in contrast, place much less emphasis on personal attributes and in addition experience more variability in personal attributes because these are very much situation specific. When personal attributes become salient, more often than not effort is expended to control them so as to blend in with others and not disrupt social harmony. Hence, Americans are expected to reveal higher levels of private self-consciousness than Japanese.

We predict that the mean level of social anxiety experienced by the Japanese will be higher than that experienced by Americans. In an interdependent or collectivistic culture, considerable energy is expended in monitoring the needs and expectations of others and in regulating one's own feelings and behavior so as to fit in. Relationships are of central importance and place much demands and stress on the members of a group. This alone tends to increase social anxiety. At the same time, the possibility of social disapproval or the threat of rejection, even ostracism, makes social anxiety high in an interdependent culture (DeVos, 1985; Lebra, 1976). Japanese children, for example, are taught to fear the pain of loneliness. In contrast, Americans are taught how to be comfortable with being alone, a frequent consequence of struggling for autonomy, individuality, and self-actualization. Moreover, Americans are less dependent on, and integrated with, groups. All of these things make for lower levels of social anxiety for Americans compared to Japanese.

No differences are expected in the level of public self-consciousness between Americans and Japanese. Americans achieve a relatively high level of public self-consciousness because social relations are used in a strategic sense to express or exert personal attributes or to define the self in relation to others as a personal standard. Japanese achieve a relatively high level of public self-consciousness because social relations are ends in and of themselves and are central to the self concept. As a consequence, public self-consciousness is important for both Americans and Japanese, albeit for different reasons. Thus, the mean levels of public self-consciousness are predicted to be the same for Americans and Japanese.

*Self-consciousness and attention to social comparison information.* The attention to social comparison information scale was developed as a measure of long-run predispositions toward conformity (Lennox & Wolfe, 1984). Reflecting the negative motivational character of the scale, Lennox and Wolfe (1984) found that it correlated .64 with the fear of negative evaluation. We therefore expect that the scale will correlate positively with social anxiety. However, we anticipate that the scales will be correlated at a moderate level. Finally, because of greater commitment to and involvement with social relations by Japanese and because of their higher levels of social anxiety, we predict that the attention to social comparison information scale will correlate more highly with social anxiety for Japanese than Americans.

The attention to social comparison information scale is designed to also capture the degree to which people are aware of the reactions of others to one's own behavior. Therefore, it should correlate highly with public self-consciousness. Both scales measure aspects of attentiveness to others. Nevertheless if the constructs are distinct, they should not correlate too highly (and thus show discriminant validity). No differences are expected in correlations between the two constructs for Americans and Japanese.

Finally, the attention to social comparison information scale should be unrelated or related at a low level to private self-consciousness. The constructs represent entirely distinct phenomena.

*Self-consciousness and action control.* Action control refers to self-regulatory mechanisms that mediate (i.e., help overcome the difficulties inherent in) the enactment of action-related mental structures, particularly intentions (e.g., Kuhl, 1985). In Kuhl's (1985) decision-related state-versus action-oriented version of the action control scale, people are scaled by their readiness to make a decision and to implement that decision. People who are low in self-regulatory capacity are called state oriented. State orientation reflects inertia to act and is characterized by excessive deliberation. People who are high in self-regulatory capacity are called action oriented. Action orientation reflects a readiness to act and is characterized by nondeliberative, even automatic responding.

We expect that action control and social anxiety will be negatively related. The greater the social anxiety, the less one will be action oriented. Social anxiety should be associated with a tendency to deliberate and perhaps exhibit a certain degree of indecisiveness. Hence, social anxiety should be associated with state orientation. We predict further that the negative correlation between action control and social anxiety should be greater for Japanese than Americans. Japanese experience greater social anxiety and spend more time and energy interpreting and accommodating to their social relations than Americans. This makes it more likely that they will also be more state oriented. The greater the tendency to act automatically (i.e., to be action as opposed to state oriented), the less the likelihood of being socially anxious for Japanese as opposed to Americans.

Action orientation is also expected to be negatively related to public and private self-consciousness. Self-consciousness implies an inward focus, and the deliberation so manifested should be related to state orientation. Nevertheless, no differences in these relations are expected between Americans and Japanese.

## *Representation of Self-Consciousness*

Based on the large body of research on the self-consciousness scale, a three-factor CFA model will be used to represent the three dimensions. To reduce the number of parameters to be estimated and to capitalize on the increase in reliability resulting when items on sub-scales are summed, each dimension will be measured with two indicators wherein each indicator is itself the sum of multiple items (see Method for specific CFA model and specification of indicators). This approach is a compromise to the often unwieldy and ill-fitting practice based on treating all items in a scale as separate indicators. This "partial disaggregation" approach has been used before by Marsh and Hocevar (1985) and Hull, Lehn, and Tedlie (1991), and its underlying logic, as well as pros and cons, are discussed in Bagozzi and Heatherton (1994).

## METHOD

### Subjects and Procedure

Subjects in Japan were undergraduates from Aoyama-Gakuin University, Senshu University, and Yokohama National University. A total of 419 students responded (88 female). Subjects in the United States were undergraduates from a single university. The sample size was 246 (86 female). After elimination of subjects who did not follow instructions or who failed to answer all items investigated herein, the final sample sizes were 402 and 233 in Japan and the United States, respectively.

Questionnaires were administered during class in Japan and in scheduled group sessions in the United States. Two weeks following administration of the main questionnaire, subjects filled-out a short form soliciting their extent of patronage of fast-food restaurants during the previous 14 days. Only the data gathered at the first wave are relevant to the study at hand. Subjects in the Untied States were paid $7 US for participation.

For preparation of the questionnaires, the back-translation procedure was used, as recommended by Brislin (1986). Questionnaire items were first prepared in English. Next, a bilingual individual translated the items into Japanese. Then another bilingual person blindly translated the Japanese version back into English. Finally, inconsistencies were reconciled by making changes until "decentered" versions in Japanese and English were achieved.

### Questionnaire

*Self-consciousness.* The 23-item self-consciousness scale developed by Fenigstein, Scheier, and Buss (1975) was used. Ten items measure private, 7 measure public, and 6 measure social anxiety aspects of self-consciousness. Subjects were asked to rate the extent to which each item is characteristic of them on 5-point "extremely uncharacteristic" (1) to "extremely characteristic" (5) scales. Sample items include: "I am generally attentive to my inner feelings" (private self-consciousness); "I am concerned about the way I present myself" (public self-consciousness); "It takes me time to overcome my shyness in new situations" (social anxiety).

*Attention to social comparison information (ATSCI).* The 13-item attention to social comparison information scale developed by Lennox and Wolfe (1984) was used. This scale is a revision of Snyder's (1974) self-monitoring scale. Subjects were asked to indicate the extent to which each item applies to them on 6-point "always false" (1) to "always true" (6) scales. An example item is, "If I am the least bit uncertain how to act in a social situation, I look to the behavior of others for cues."

*Action control (AC).* The action control scale developed by Kuhl (1985) was used. This scale consists of 20 forced-choice items, one response alternative in each case reflecting state orientation and the other action orientation. For instance, one item reads: "When I have to do something important that is unpleasant, (a) I would rather do it right away; (b) I avoid doing it until it is absolutely necessary."

## Confirmatory Factor Analysis Models

Figure 1 presents the confirmatory factor analysis model for examining reliability, convergent validity, and uniqueness of components of self-consciousness. In this model, the circles are latent variables and correspond to factors in factor analysis. Each component of self-consciousness is represented as a latent variable and designated as $\xi_i$. The components are each shown connected to two boxes with arrows. The boxes indicate actual observed measurements of the components. Each operationalization (i.e., $pr_i$, $pu_i$, $sa_i$) is a composite drawn from the appropriate items in the scale. For private self-consciousness (i.e., $\xi_1$), $pr_1$ and $pr_2$ are the sums of 5 items each taken at random from the 10 items designed to measure the component. For public self-consciousness (i.e., $\xi_2$), $pu_1$ and $pu_2$ are similarly formed as the sums of 3 and 4 items, respectively, from the total domain of 7 items corresponding to this component. Likewise for social anxiety (i.e., $\xi_3$), $sa_1$ and $sa_2$ are computed as the sum of 3 items each from the total set of 6 measuring this component. As discussed earlier, this represents an intermediary level of analysis between the total scale approach and the total disaggregation of items. This procedure has been advocated by psychometricians and used to investigate similar hypotheses in the personality literature (e.g., Bagozzi & Heatherton, 1994; Hull, Lehn, & Tedlie, 1991; Marsh, 1994; Marsh & Hocevar, 1985). The Greek letters ($\lambda_k$s) adjacent to the arrows connecting latent variables to measurements are factor load-

FIGURE 1. Confirmatory Factor Analysis Model for Examining Reliability, Convergent Validity and Uniqueness of Components of Self-Consciousness (pr = private self-consciousness, pu = public self consciousness, sa = social anxiety; Greek letters are defined in text)

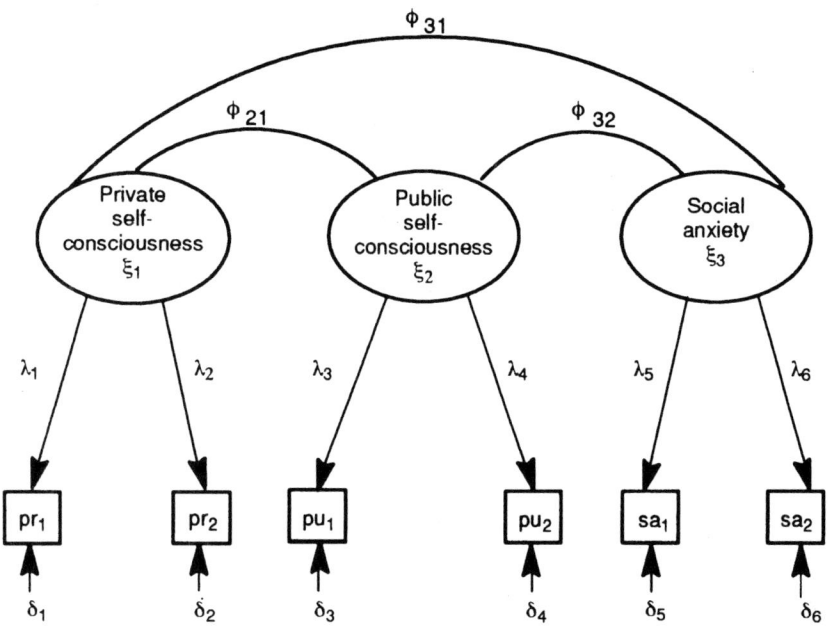

ings. In standardized form, they vary from 0 to 1 inclusive and express the degree of correspondence between latent variables and measurements. The square of the $\lambda_k$s indicate the amount of variance in the measurements as a function of the underlying latent components. They are measures of the reliability of each item. The reliability of the composite of items for each component can be computed as

$$P\xi_i = \frac{(\Sigma\lambda_k)^2 \; \text{var}\,(\xi_i)}{(\Sigma\lambda_k)^2 \; \text{var}(\xi_i) + \Sigma(\theta_{\delta_{kk}})}$$

where $\theta_{\delta kk}$ stands for the error variance of the kth measure. The curved lines in Figure 1 connecting pairs of factors indicate correlations between components. These are designated $\phi_{ij}$. As a consequence of the estimation procedures used to infer values for the $\phi_{ij}$s, the correlations are corrected for attenuation due to the unreliability in the measurements. To the extent that the $\phi_{ij}$s are less than 1.00 by an amount greater than two standard errors, the factors can be considered distinct in a strict statistical sense. The smaller the $\phi_{ij}$s, the greater the achievement of distinctiveness among components. Convergent validity is attained when the model shown in Figure 1 fits the data and the $\lambda_k$s are significant.

To test for (a) discriminant validity between the components of self-consciousness and attention to social comparison information and (b) predictive validity (or criterion related validity) between the components and action control, confirmatory factor analysis was also used. The model is similar to the one shown in Figure 1 but in addition includes separate factors for ATSCI and AC, where two composite measures are used for each. Hence, a five-factor model is investigated where each factor has two indicators.

## Statistical Procedures

*Estimation of models and assessment of fit.* The confirmatory factor analysis models investigated herein were estimated with LISREL (Jöreskog & Sörbom, 1989). One measure of fit that was employed is the likelihood ratio $\chi^2$ statistic which can be used to test the null hypothesis that a specified model reproduces the population covariance matrix of the observed variables. By convention, an acceptable model is one where the $p$-value is greater than or equal to .05. Reliance on the $\chi^2$ test as the sole measure of fit is not recommended because of its dependence on sample size. For example in large samples, even trivial deviations of a hypothesized model from a true model can lead to rejection of the hypothesized model; or for very small samples, large deviations of a hypothesized model from a true model may go undetected. Therefore, it is desirable to examine other measures of fit not as sensitive to sample size (Gerbing & Anderson, 1992). Another drawback with the $\chi^2$ test is that it does not directly provide an indication of the degree of fit such as is available with indices normed from 0 to 1.

Another approach to the assessment of goodness-of-fit is to use an index which is based on the comparison of the fit of a hypothesized model to the fit of a baseline model, such as the null model, where the latter assumes that all variables are uncorrelated (i.e., only error variances are estimated). Such an approach is termed, an incremental fit index, in that a hypothesized model is compared to a more restricted, nested model. The best known index in this regard is the relative noncentrality index (RNI) developed by McDonald and Marsh (1990; see also Bentler, 1990):

$$\text{RNI} = \frac{(\chi_0^2 - df_0 - \chi_f^2 - df_f)}{\chi_0^2 - df_0}$$

where $\chi_0^2$ and $\chi_f^2$ are for the null and focal models, respectively. The RNI is normed in the population and thus has values bounded by 0 and 1. Equally important, the RNI provides an unbiased estimate of its corresponding population value, and therefore it should be independent of sample size. Monte Carlo studies show that the RNI performed well for sample sizes varying from 50 to 1,600, in the sense of producing unbiased estimates and estimates low in variability (e.g., Bentler, 1990).

From an intuitive perspective, the RNI can be thought of as a measure of how much variation in measures is accounted for from a practical standpoint. A rough rule-of-thumb is that the RNI should be greater than or equal to about .90, where values less than .90 suggest that significant amounts of variance remain to be explained and values greater than or equal to .90 imply that further relaxation of parameter constraints are not warranted and might lead to overfitting (Bentler & Bonett, 1980).

Although there are no universal guidelines for evaluating alternative models, we have chosen to use the general approach recently proposed by Marsh (1990, pp. 678-679). Marsh suggested that three steps be employed when evaluating the goodness-of-fit of any model. First, one should ascertain whether the solutions are well-defined. In particular, the iterative procedures in LISREL should converge to a proper solution, parameter estimates should lie within their permissible ranges, and standard errors of parameter estimates should not be too large. Second, parameter estimates should be examined in relation to the substantive, a priori model and common sense. Finally, the $\chi^2$ test and the indices mentioned above should be evaluated and compared to alternative models where appropriate.

*Tests of hypotheses.* Chi-square difference tests are used to test hypotheses concerning the equivalence of models and parameters for Japan and the United States (e.g., Anderson & Gerbing, 1988). A sequence of hypotheses is examined to explore generalizability in this sense. Marsh (1994) notes that "there is no clear consensus in recommendations about the ordering" of hypotheses concerning invariance constraints and the "choice of a particular ordering . . . must be evaluated in relation to the aims of a particular study" (p. 14). There is consensus, however, on the first two steps: one should begin with a test of invariance of variance-covariance matrices and, then, if the matrices are found to differ, tests of invariance of the factor pattern and the factor loadings should be performed. Marsh (1994) points out that "(t)he minimal condition for 'factorial invariance' is the equivalence of all factor loadings in the multiple groups" (p. 11). For the subsequent tests of invariance, we next examine whether error variances are equal across groups, and then we investigate the invariance of factor variances and the hypothesized relations among factors.

More specifically, the following sequence of invariance constraints is examined. First, a test is performed of the equality of variance-covariance matrices across samples. A failure to reject this hypothesis means that the measures are equivalent and relate among each other in identical ways. The data could be pooled, and no further cross-sample analyses are warranted on the differences between psychometric properties of the scales (the means of variables can differ even if the psychometric properties of scales are invariant, however). Rejection of the hypothesis of the equality of variance-covariance matrices sets the stage for investigation of specific differences between the samples. The next hypothesis is to scrutinize whether the same factor structure exists for the samples. This is done by doing a multiple sample analysis on the model shown in Figure 1. A satisfactory fit implies that the identical three factors are reasonable representations of the data in both samples. Given equal factor patterns, we turn to a test of whether the factor loadings are equal across samples. Invariant factor loadings show that the measures indicate the same factors and do so in an equal way. In other words, the evidence supports the conclusion that the hypothesized relationships between measures and constructs generalize across samples. This is tested with a chi-square difference test comparing the chi-squares for the equal factor loadings model to the equal factor pattern model. Given equal factor loadings, it is meaningful to look at the equality of error variances. This is done by comparing the chi-square for the model with both factor loadings and error variances constrained to be equal across samples to the chi-square for the model where only factor loadings are constrained to be equal. A failure to reject the hypothesis of equal error variances, given equal factor loadings, suggests that the measures are equally reliable. Next, a test can be performed on the invariance of factor variances and covariances. This is accomplished by constraining the $\phi_{ii}$s and $\phi_{ij}$s to be equal across samples and comparing the chi-square test so obtained to the chi-square for the model where factor loadings and error variances are not constrained to be equal across samples.

The aforementioned hypotheses examine the generalizability of the psychometric properties of the model in Figure 1. The tests must be performed on the covariance matrices as input (see Cudeck, 1989). To fix the scales of measurement for each factor, one factor loading per factor was constrained to be 1.00. Given the invariance of key structural parameters across samples, it is meaningful to investigate the differences in means of factors. This is done by use of the procedures described in Jöreskog and Sörbom (1989, pp. 245-253).

## RESULTS

### Tests of Basic Models for the Organization of Self-Consciousness

*Japan.* Table 1 presents the findings for the three-factor model in Figure 1 as well as the null and single-factor models. The null model is used in the computation of the RNI, which we will turn to in a moment. The single factor model hypothesizes that all measures of self-consciousness load on one factor. In other words, self-consciousness is considered to be unidimensional. For the factor analyses of the individual samples, correlation matrices were used for ease of interpretation. It can be seen that this model must be rejected ($\chi^2(9) = 295.66$, $p \simeq .00$) and that error variances are generally quite high. The three-factor model (see Figure 1) fits quite well: $\chi^2(6) = 7.13$, $p \simeq .31$, and RMR = .02. This is confirmed by the RNI = 1.00, which indicates that no variance remains to be explained as a practical matter. Factor loadings are high and error variances low to moderate. Private and public self-consciousness correlate moderately high ($\phi_{21} = .55$), while social anxiety correlates relatively low with private ($\phi_{31} = .20$) and moderately with public ($\phi_{32} = .38$) self-consciousness. All correlations are statistically significant. The composite reliabilities for the private, public, and social anxiety components of self-consciousness are $\rho_{pr} = .71$, $\rho_{pu} = .77$, and $\rho_{sa} = .82$, respectively.

*United States.* It can be seen in Table 1 that the single-factor model fits poorly ($\chi^2(9) = 200.54$, $p \simeq .00$) and error variances are quite high. The three-factor model fits quite well indeed: $\chi^2(6) = 2.17$, $p \simeq .90$, and RMR = .02. The RNI = 1.00 and suggests that no variance remains to be explained from a pragmatic standpoint.[2] Factor loadings are quite high and error variances low to moderate. Private and public self-consciousness correlate moderately ($\phi_{21} = .33$), as do public self-consciousness and social anxiety ($\phi_{32} = .30$). Private self-consciousness and social anxiety correlate at a low level ($\phi_{31} = .19$). All correlations are statistically significant. The composite reliabilities for the private, public, and social anxiety components of self-consciousness are $\rho_{pr} = .76$, $\rho_{pu} = .79$, and $\rho_{sa} = .78$, respectively.

### Tests of Generality of the Three-Factor Model Across Samples

Table 2 shows the results for the comparison of the three-factor model of self-consciousness in Japan and the United States. The test of equal variance-covariance matrices shows that $\chi^2(21) = 75.45$, $p \simeq .00$. Therefore, we must reject the hypothesis that the measures of self-consciousness are equivalent for Japanese and Americans. Next we investigate whether any aspects of the measurement properties of the three factor model are equivalent across samples.

TABLE 1. Confirmatory Factor Analysis Findings for Three Factor Model: Individual Samples

| | Goodness-of-Fit | | Factor Loadings | | | | Factor Correlations | | |
|---|---|---|---|---|---|---|---|---|---|
| Model | $x^2$ (df) | RMR[a] | Private self | Public self | Social anxiety | Error variances | Private self | Public self | Social anxiety |
| Japan ($N$ = 402) | | | | | | | | | |
| Null | 709.46 (15) | .30 | | | | | | | |
| Single factor | 295.66 (9) | .14 | .45(.05)[b] .50(.05) | .76(.05) .76(.05) | .42(.05) .34(.06) | .80(.06) .75(.06) .42(.05) .42(.05) .82(.06) .88(.06) | | | |
| Three factor | 7.13 (6) | .02 | .68(.06) .81(.06) .00 .00 .00 .00 | .00 .00 .78(.05) .80(.05) .00 .00 | .00 .00 .00 .00 .94(.08) .71(.07) | .54(.07) .35(.08) .38(.06) .36(.06) .12(.13) .49(.08) | 1.00 .55(.05) .20(.06) | 1.00 .38(.06) | 1.00 |
| United States ($N$ = 233) | | | | | | | | | |
| Null | 381.64 (15) | .27 | | | | | | | |
| Single factor | 200.54 (9) | .16 | .34(.07) .30(.07) | .80(.07) .76(.07) | .34(.07) .29(.07) | .88(.08) .91(.09) .37(.08) .42(.08) .89(.09) .92(.09) | | | |
| Three factor | 2.17 (6) | .02 | .84(.11) .72(.10) .00 .00 .00 .00 | .00 .00 .85(.09) .75(.09) .00 .00 | .00 .00 .00 .00 .87(.12) .73(.11) | .30(.17) .48(.13) .28(.13) .42(.11) .24(.19) .47(.14) | 1.00 .33(.08) .19(.08) | 1.00 .30(.08) | 1.00 |

[a] Root mean square residual; [b] Standard errors in parentheses

TABLE 2. Findings for Multiple Sample Analysis Comparisons Between Japanese and Americans–Three Factor Model

| Model | Goodness-of-fit | Test of hypotheses |
|---|---|---|
| $M_1$: Equal covariance matrices | $\chi^2(21) = 75.45$<br>$p \simeq .00$ | -- |
| $M_2$: Equal factor pattern | $\chi^2(12) = 9.31$<br>$p \simeq .68$ | -- |
| $M_3$: Equal factor loadings | $\chi^2(15) = 16.42$<br>$p \simeq .35$ | $M_3 - M_2$:<br>$\chi_d^2(3) = 7.11$<br>$p > .05$ |
| $M_4$: Equal factor loadings and equal error variances | $\chi^2(21) = 58.48$<br>$p \simeq .00$ | $M_4 - M_3$:<br>$\chi_d^2(6) = 42.06$<br>$p < .001$ |
| $M_5$: Equal factor loadings and equal factor variances and covariances of factors | $\chi^2(21) = 31.40$<br>$p \simeq .07$ | $M_5 - M_3$:<br>$\chi_d^2(6) = 14.98$<br>$p < .02$ |
| $M_6$: Equal factor loadings and equal variances of factors | $\chi^2(18) = 19.72$<br>$p \simeq .35$ | $M_6 - M_3$:<br>$\chi_d^2(3) = 3.30$<br>$p > .30$ |
| $M_7$: Equal factor loadings and equal covariance between public and private self-consciousness | $\chi^2(19) = 30.44$<br>$p \simeq .05$ | $M_7 - M_6$:<br>$\chi_d^2(1) = 10.72$<br>$p < .001$ |
| $M_8$: Equal factor loadings and equal covariance between private self-conscious and social anxiety | $\chi^2(19) = 19.86$<br>$p \simeq .40$ | $M_8 - M_6$:<br>$\chi_d^2(1) = .14$<br>$p > .70$ |
| $M_9$: Equal factor loadings and equal covariance between public self-consciousness and social anxiety | $\chi^2(19) = 20.91$<br>$p \simeq .34$ | $M_9 - M_6$:<br>$\chi_d^2(1) = 1.19$<br>$p > .25$ |

Model $M_2$ hypothesizes that the same factor pattern occurs for Japanese and Americans. The findings reveal that we cannot reject this hypothesis: $\chi^2(12) = 9.31, p \approx .68$. Thus, the same three factors underlie responses in both samples.

The model ($M_3$) that further constrains factor loadings to be equal for Japanese and Americans fits well: $\chi^2(15) = 16.42, p \approx .35$. As this model is nested in $M_2$, a chi-square difference can be computed to formally test the hypothesis of equal factor loadings. The test shows that the hypothesis is supported: $\chi_d^2(3) = 7.11, p > .05$. Hence, we conclude that the same constructs are measured in Japan and the United States. The relationship between measures and factors are equivalent in Japan and the United States.

Given equal factor loadings, we test further whether the error variances are equal across samples ($M_4$). The model making these constraints, in fact, fits poorly ($\chi^2(21) = 58.48, p \approx .00$), and the chi-square difference test demonstrates that error variances are not equal for Japanese and Americans $\chi_d^2(6) = 42.06\ p < .001$.

Likewise, the model ($M_5$) hypothesizing equal variances and covariances across samples indicates that this must be rejected: $\chi_d^2(6) = 14.98, p < .02$. However, we can not reject the hypothesis ($M_6$) of equal variances of factors across samples: $\chi_d^2(3) = 3.30, p > .30$. Next we test whether the covariances among factors are equal in models $M_7$-$M_9$ (see Table 2). Although the covariance between public and private self-consciousness is not equal in Japan and the United States ($\chi_d^2(1) = 10.72, p < .001$), the covariances are equal for private self-consciousness and social anxiety($\chi_d^2(1) = .14, p > .70$) public self-consciousness and social anxiety and for ($\chi_d^2(1) = 1.19, p > .25$). The correlation between public and private self-consciousness is thus higher in a statistical sense for Japanese ($\phi_{21} = .55$) than for Americans ($\phi_{21} = .33$), but the other covariances are invariant.

The findings show that the pattern of factors, factor loadings, and correlations between public self-consciousness and social anxiety and between private self-consciousness and social anxiety are identical for Japan and the United States. In these senses, the three-factor model of self-consciousness can be said to generalize. In addition to tests of structural parameters across groups, it is also interesting to examine differences in factor means. It is not possible to estimate absolute values of factor means for both samples. Rather in confirmatory factor analysis, it is only possible to investigate the increase or decrease in factor means for one sample in comparison to another sample. The results show, as hypothesized, that the mean of private self-consciousness is significantly lower for Japanese than Americans ($\Delta\mu = -.64$, s.e. $= .10$), and the mean of social anxiety is significantly higher for Japanese than Americans ($\Delta\mu = .37$, s.e. $= .09$).

The means of public self-consciousness do not differ significantly between Japan and the United States ($\Delta\mu = .00$, s.e. $= .09$).

## Discriminant and Predictive Validity of the Three-Factor Model

Table 3 summarizes the associations between the components of self-consciousness and attention to social comparison information and action control. We expect that the components of self-consciousness will be distinct from measures of ATSCI. At the same time, we expect private self-consciousness to display the strongest degree of discriminant validity and public self-consciousness to show the weakest, with social anxiety in the middle. Indeed, significant correlations of ATSCI are expected with public self-consciousness and social anxiety, given the common focus on self concepts in relations with others. We expect action control to be negatively related to all components of self-consciousness. This is a consequence of the interference that self-reflection and rumination have on activation of automatic schemata related to the initiation of behavior.

We see in Table 3 that private self-consciousness shows strong discriminant validity from ATSCI in that the association is nonsignificant for Japanese ($\phi_{41} = .08$, s.e. $= .06$) and Americans ($\phi_{41} = .01$, s.e. $= .08$). Public self-consciousness, in contrast, is correlated moderately high with ATSCI in Japan ($\phi_{42} = .62$, s.e. $= .04$) and the United States ($\phi_{42} = .68$, s.e. $= .05$). Finally, social anxiety is correlated at a low level with ATSCI in Japan ($\phi_{43} = .23$, s.e. $= .06$) and at a moderate level with ATSCI in the United States ($\phi_{43} = .45$, s.e. $= .07$). Therefore, while the ATSCI is distinct from public self-consciousness and social anxiety, the significant correlations support a certain degree of criterion related validity for these aspects of self-consciousness.

As hypothesized, action control is negatively related to all facets of self-consciousness. The correlation of AC is low with private self-consciousness in Japan ($\phi_{51} = -.20$, s.e. $= .06$) and the United States ($\phi_{51} = -.16$, s.e. $= .08$). The correlation of AC with public self-consciousness is somewhat higher in Japan ($\phi_{52} = -.35$, s.e. $= .05$) and the United States ($\phi_{52} = -.27$, s.e. $= .05$). Finally, the correlation of AC is stronger yet with social anxiety in Japan ($\phi_{53} = -.62$, s.e. $= .05$) and the United States ($\phi_{53} = -.45$, s.e. $= .06$).

The last set of analyses is an exploration of differences in correlations of self-consciousness with ATSCI and AC between Japan and the United States. Table 4 presents the findings. The baseline model hypothesizing that factor loadings are equal between Japan and the United States reveals that this cannot be rejected. This model is then compared individually with each remaining model listed in Table 4. It can be seen that the correlation between public self-consciousness and ATSCI is greater in the United States ($\phi_{42} = .68$) than Japan ($\phi_{42} = .62$), though the differ-

TABLE 3. Factor Intercorrelations for Tests of Discriminant Validity and Predictive Validity

| | Japan (N = 402) | | |
|---|---|---|---|
| | Private self-consciousness | Public self-consciousness | Social Anxiety |
| Attention to social comparison information | .08 (.06)[a] | .62 (.04) | .23 (.06) |
| Action control | −.20 (.06) | −.35 (.05) | −.62 (.05) |
| | United States (N = 233) | | |
| Attention to social comparison information | .01 (.08) | .68 (.05) | .45 (.07) |
| Action control | −.16 (.08) | −.27 (.06) | −.45 (.06) |

[a] Standard errors in parentheses

ence is small. Likewise, the correlation between social anxiety and ATSCI is greater in the United States ($\phi_{43} = .45$) than in Japan ($\phi_{43} = .23$). Next it can be seen that the correlation between public self-consciousness and action control is greater in Japan ($\phi_{52} = -.35$) than the United States ($\phi_{52} = -.27$). Finally, the correlation between social anxiety and AC is greater in Japan ($\phi_{53} = -.62$) than in the United States ($\phi_{53} = -.45$), and the correlation between private self-consciousness and action control is greater in Japan ($\phi_{51} = -.20$) than in the United States ($\phi_{51} = -.16$), although the latter difference is quite small as a practical matter. The correlations between private self-conscious and ATSCI in Japan ($\phi_{41} = .08$) and the United States ($\phi_{41} = .01$) fail to differ.

## DISCUSSION

The framework used in this article provides a useful approach for examining reliability, validity, and generalizability of personality and related constructs in cross-cultural consumer research. It overcomes drawbacks with past practice which tended to ignore reliability, the dimensionality of concepts and scales, and the relationship between constructs and measurements. The hierarchy of hypotheses used in this article also gives the researcher a way of investigating important measurement properties and their equivalence across cultural groups. Measure equivalence or factorial invariance must be established before substantive hypotheses (e.g., tests of differences in factor means, associations between factors, and causal or functional relations) can be validly examined. In the past, cross-cultural researchers often examined regression and other parameters across cultural groups without demonstrating measure equivalence (e.g., Poortinga, 1975). Without showing measure equivalence, it is impossible to know whether differences found in parameter estimates are a result of valid differences in the substance under investigation or the consequence of measurement differences. The framework introduced in this article provides a means of avoiding this problem.

The application of the multiple group CFA model to the self-consciousness scale revealed interesting differences. Although Japanese and Americans had similar self concepts in the sense that self-consciousness could be represented in a three-dimensional structure and factor loadings relating measures to their respective dimensions were equivalent (as were the variances of factors), the integration, level, and association of the dimensions with other criteria were different in important respects. The Japanese, in comparison to Americans, showed a stronger integration of public and private self-consciousness. They also exhibited lower levels of private self-consciousness and higher levels of social anxiety. In addition, the Japanese revealed stronger associations between action control and public

TABLE 4. Findings for Multiple Sample Analysis Comparisons of Japanese and Americans on Correlations Between Self-Consciousness Components and (a) Attention to Social Comparison Information and (b) Action Control

| Model | Goodness-of-fit | Test of hypotheses |
|---|---|---|
| $M_1$: Equal factor loadings | $\chi^2(55) = 73.22$<br>$p \simeq .05$ | -- |
| $M_2$: $\phi_{PR,ATSCI}$ equal | $\chi^2(56) = 73.31$<br>$p \simeq .06$ | $M_2 - M_1$:<br>$\chi^2_d(1) = .09$<br>$p > .75$ |
| $M_3$: $\phi_{PU,ATSCI}$ equal | $\chi^2(56) = 86.69$<br>$p \simeq .01$ | $M_3 - M_1$:<br>$\chi^2_d(1) = 13.47$<br>$p < .001$ |
| $M_4$: $\phi_{SA,ATSCI}$ equal | $\chi^2(56) = 95.48$<br>$p \simeq .00$ | $M_4 - M_1$:<br>$\chi^2_d(1) = 22.26$<br>$p < .001$ |
| $M_5$: $\phi_{PR,AC}$ equal | $\chi^2(56) = 83.82$<br>$p \simeq .01$ | $M_5 - M_1$:<br>$\chi^2_d(1) = 10.60$<br>$p < .001$ |
| $M_6$: $\phi_{PU,AC}$ equal | $\chi^2(56) = 84.34$<br>$p \simeq .01$ | $M_6 - M_1$:<br>$\chi^2_d(1) = 11.12$<br>$p < .001$ |
| $M_7$: $\phi_{SA,AC}$ equal | $\chi^2(56) = 94.91$<br>$p \simeq .00$ | $M_7 - M_1$:<br>$\chi^2_d(1) = 21.69$<br>$p < .001$ |

Note: PR = private self-consciousness, PU = public self-consciousness, SA = social anxiety, ATSCI = attention of social comparison information, and AC = action control

self-consciousness and between action control and social anxiety than Americans. Finally, the Japanese experienced weaker levels of associations between attention to social comparison information and public self-consciousness and between attention to social comparison information and social anxiety than Americans.

Table 5 summarizes the hypotheses and findings. With respect to the levels of self-consciousness, all hypotheses were confirmed. With regard to the associations among the dimensions of self-consciousness, all hypotheses also were confirmed. With respect to the associations between dimensions of self-consciousness and attention to social comparison information, the hypothesis for private self-consciousness was fully confirmed and the hypotheses for public self-consciousness and social anxiety were partially confirmed. The correlation between social anxiety and

## TABLE 5. Summary of Hypotheses and Results

| Prediction | Result |
|---|---|
| **Levels of Self-Consciousness** | |
| Private self-consciousness greater for Americans than Japanese | Confirmed |
| Social anxiety higher for Japanese than for Americans | Confirmed |
| Public self-consciousness the same for Americans and Japanese | Confirmed |
| **Associations Among Dimensions of Self-Consciousness** | |
| Public and private self-consciousness correlate higher for Japanese than Americans | Confirmed |
| Private self-consciousness and social anxiety correlate same for Japanese and Americans | Confirmed |
| Public self-consciousness and social anxiety correlate same for Japanese and Americans | Confirmed |
| **Associations Between Dimensions of Self-Consciousness and Attention to Social Comparison Information** | |
| Correlation between private self-consciousness and attention to social comparison information expected to be low and no difference expected between Japanese and Americans | Confirmed |
| Correlation between public self-consciousness and attention to social comparison information expected to be positive and high and no difference expected between Japanese and Americans | High correlations confirmed. Small difference found between Japanese and Americans |
| Correlation between social anxiety and attention to social comparison information expected to be positive and higher for Japanese than Americans | Positive correlation confirmed. Correlation actually higher for Americans |
| **Associations Between Dimensions of Self-Consciousness and Action Control** | |
| Correlation between private self-consciousness and action control expected to be unrelated or lowly related | Confirmed |
| Correlation between public self-consciousness and action control expected to correlate negatively and highly and no difference in correlations expected | Correlations are negative, but low, and higher for Japanese than Americans |
| Correlation between social anxiety and action control expected to be negative and high and greater in magnitude for Japanese than Americans | Confirmed |

attention to social comparison information although positive was greater for Americans than Japanese, opposite to predictions. We do not have a good explanation for this outcome. Perhaps Americans, who tend to be more privately self-conscious, find it difficult and even dissonant trying to attend to external pressures while being attuned to the inner self. With regard to the associations between dimensions of self-consciousness and action control, hypotheses were generally confirmed. The correlation between public self-consciousness and action control was found to be greater for Japanese than Americans, although no prediction was made here. As the correlations are relatively low and the difference small ($\Delta r = .08$), not much should be made of this finding.

Given that the nature of self-consciousness in Japan and the United States has been established in the two samples, it would be desirable to replicate the findings and to investigate implications of self-consciousness for consumption. Future research should bear in mind that the three components of self-consciousness are distinct. Interesting hypotheses of the mediating and moderating roles of self-consciousness and cultural differences open many possibilities for exploration.

## NOTES

1. Gudykunst, Yang, and Nishida (1987) examined self-consciousness in Japan, Korea, and the United States. Although they investigated a CFA model with three factors and each of the 23 items loading on its appropriate factor, none of the models fit satisfactorily. In addition, they did not formally compare structural parameters or factor means across groups. The comparisons that they did do are difficult to interpret because differences found could have been due to lack of invariance of key parameters and differential reliability, which they failed to examine.
2. The RNI is actually greater than 1.00, but using Bentler's (1990) bounded measure, the comparative fit index, the fit is 1.00.
3. Although the tests were performed on the covariance matrices, we present the correlations in this paragraph for ease of interpretation.

## REFERENCES

Anderson, J. C., & Gerbing, D. W. (1988). Structural equation modeling in practice: A review and recommended two-step approach. *Psychological Bulletin, 103*, 155-173.
Abrams, D. (1988). Self-consciousness scales for adults and children: Reliability, validity, and theoretical significance. *European Journal of Personality, 2*, 11-37.

Bagozzi, R. P., Baumgartner, H., & Yi, Y. (1992). State versus action orientation and the theory of reasoned action: An application to coupon usage. *Journal of Consumer Research, 18,* 505-518.

Bagozzi, R. P., & Heatherton, T. F. (1994). A general approach to representing multifaceted personality constructs: Application to state self-esteem. *Structural Equation Modeling, 1,* 35-67.

Bearden, W. O. & Rose, R. R. (1990). Attention to social comparison information: An individual difference factor affecting consumer conformity. *Journal of Consumer Research, 16,* 461-472.

Bentler, P. M. (1990). Comparative fit indexes in structural models. *Psychological Bulletin, 107,* 238-246.

Bentler, P. M., & Bonett, D. G. (1980). Significance tests and goodness of fit in the analysis of covariance structure models. *Psychological Bulletin, 88,* 588-606.

Brislin, R. W. (1986). The wording and translation of research instruments. In W. J. Lonner & J. W. Berry (Eds.), *Field methods in cross-cultural research* (pp. 137-164). Beverly Hills, CA: Sage.

Burnkrant, R. E., & Page, T. J. (1982). On the management of self-images in social situations: The role of public self-consciousness. In A. Mitchell (Ed.), *Advances in Consumer Research* Vol. 9 (pp. 452-455). Ann Arbor, MI: Association for Consumer Research.

Carver, C. S., & Glass, D. C. (1976). The self-consciousness scale: A discriminant validity study. *Journal of Personality Assessment, 40,* 169-172.

Carver, C. S., & Scheier, M. J. (1978). The self-focusing effects of dispositional self-consciousness, mirror presence and audience presence. *Journal of Personality and Social Psychology, 36,* 324-332.

Carver, C. S., & Scheier, M. J. (1987). The blind man and the elephant: Selective examination of the public-private literature gives rise to a faulty perception. *Journal of Personality, 55,* 525-541.

Cudeck, R. (1989). Analysis of correlation matrices using covariance structure models. *Psychological Bulletin, 105,* 317-327.

DeVos, G. (1985). Dimensions of the self in Japanese culture. In A. J. Marsella, G. DeVos, & F. L. K. Hsu (Eds)., *Culture and self: Asian and western perspectives* (pp. 141-184) New York: Tavistock.

Doi, T. (1986). *The Anatomy of Self: The Individual versus Society.* Tokyo: Kodansha.

Fenigstein, A. (1987). On the nature of public and private self-consciousness. *Journal of Personality, 55,* 543-554.

Fenigstein, A., Scheier, M. F., & Buss, A. H. (1975). Public and private self-consciousness: Assessment and theory. *Journal of Consulting and Clinical Psychology, 43*(4), 522-527.

Fleming, J. S., & Courtney, B. E. (1984). The dimensionality of self-esteem: II. Hierarchical facet model for revised measurement scales. *Journal of Personality and Social Psychology, 46,* 404-421.

Gerbing, D. W., & Anderson, J. C. (1992). Monte Carlo evaluations of goodness of fit indices for structural equation models. *Sociological Methods & Research, 21*, 132-160.

Gudykunst, W. B., Yang, S., & Nishida, T. (1987). Cultural differences in self-consciousness and self-monitoring. *Communication Research, 14*, 7-36.

Hamaguchi, E. (1985). A contextual model of the Japanese: Toward a methodological innovation in Japan studies. *Journal of Japanese Studies, 11*, 289-321.

Hattie, J. (1992). *Self-Concept*. Hillsdale, NJ: Erlbaum.

Heinemann, W. (1979). The assessment of private and public self-consciousness. A German replication. *European Journal of Social Psychology, 9*, 331-337.

Hull, J. G., Lehn, D. A., & Tedlie, J. C. (1991). A general approach to testing multifaceted personality constructs. *Journal of Personality and Social Psychology, 61*, 932-945.

James, W. (1890). *The Principles of Psychology* (2 vols.). New York: Holt.

Jöreskog, K. G., & Sörbom, D. (1989). *LISREL7: A guide to the program and applications*. 2nd ed. Chicago: SPSS.

Kuhl, J. (1985). Volitional mediators of cognition-behavior consistency: Self-regulatory processes and action versus state orientation. In J. Kuhl & J. Beckmann (Eds.), *Action control: From cognition to behavior* (pp. 101-128). New York: Springer.

Lebra, T. S. (1976). *Japanese Patterns of Behavior*. Honolulu: University of Hawaii Press.

Lennox, R. D., & Wolfe, R. N. (1984). Revision of the self-monitoring scale. *Journal of Personality and Social Psychology, 46*(6), 1349-1369.

Markus, H. (1977). Self-schemas and processing information about the self. *Journal of Personality and Social Psychology, 35*, 63-78.

Markus, H. R., & Kitayama, S. (1991). Culture and the self: Implications for cognition, emotion, and motivation. *Psychological Review, 98*, 224-253.

Markus, H., & Nurius, P. (1986). Possible selves. *American Psychologist, 41*, 954-969.

Markus, H., & Wurf, E. (1987). The dynamic self-concept: A social psychological perspective. *Annual Review of Psychology, 38*, 299-337.

Marsh, H. W. (1990). The structure of academic self-concept: The Marsh/Shavelson model. *Journal of Educational Psychology, 82*, 623-636.

Marsh, H. W. (1994). Confirmatory factor analysis models of factorial invariance: A multifaceted approach. *Structural Equation Modeling, 1*, 5-34.

Marsh, H. W., & Hocevar, D. (1985). Application of confirmatory factor analysis to the study of self-concept: First- and higher-order factor models and their invariance across groups. *Psychological Bulletin, 97*, 562-582.

McDonald, R. P., & Marsh, H. W. (1990). Choosing a multivariate model: Noncentrality and goodness of fit. *Psychological Bulletin, 107*, 247-255.

Nasby, W. (1989). Private and public self-consciousness and articulation of the self-schema. *Journal of Personality and Social Psychology, 56*, 117-123.

Poortinga, Y. H. (1975). Some implications of three different approaches to intercultural comparison. In J. W. Berry & W. J. Lonner (Eds.), *Applied cross-cultural psychology* (pp. 329-332). Amsterdam: Swets & Zeitlinger.

Smith, M. B. (1992). William James and the psychology of self. In M. E. Donnelly (Ed.), *Reinterpreting the Legacy of William James* (pp. 173-187). Washington, DC: American Psychological Association.

Solomon, M. R., & Schopler, J. (1982). Self-consciousness and clothing. *Personality and Social Psychology Bulletin, 8*(September), 508-514.

Stryker, S. (1987). Identity theory: Developments and extensions. In K. Yardley & T. Honess (Eds.), *Self and identity: Psychosocial perspectives* (pp. 83-103). New York: Wiley.

Triandis, H. C. (1989). The self and social behavior in differing cultural contexts. *Psychological Review, 96*, 506-520.

Turner, R. G., Carver, C. S., Scheier, M. F., & Ickes, W. (1978). Correlates of self-consciousness. *Journal of Personality Assessment, 42*, 285-289.

Weisz, J. R., Rothbaum, F. M., & Blackburn, T. C. (1984). Standing out and standing in: The psychology of control in America and Japan. *American Psychologist, 39*, 955-969.

Wicklund, R. A. & Gollwitzer, P. M. (1987). The fallacy of the private-public self-focus distinction. *Journal of Personality, 55*, 491-523.

# German and American Consumer Orientations to Information Technologies: Implications for Marketing and Public Policy

Norbert Mundorf
Ruby Roy Dholakia
Nikhilesh Dholakia
Stuart Westin

**SUMMARY.** Markets for the information technology industries are becoming global. The success of firms competing for a share of the global marketplace will increasingly depend on how well they understand and integrate consumer attitudes and behaviors toward these technologies. In order to contribute to that understanding, this paper reports a study of German and American consumers' attitudes toward and familiarity with new information technologies.

---

Norbert Mundorf is Associate Professor of Communication Studies; Ruby Roy Dholakia is Professor of Marketing; Nikhilesh Dholakia is Professor of Marketing; and Stuart Westin is Associate Professor of Management Science, The University of Rhode Island, Kingston, RI 02881.

The authors would like to acknowledge the data analysis assistance provided by David J. Cordeiro.

This research was supported by the Research Institute for Telecommunications and Information Marketing (RITIM), College of Business Administration, Ballentine Hall, University of Rhode Island.

[Haworth co-indexing entry note]: "German and American Consumer Orientations to Information Technologies: Implications for Marketing and Public Policy." Mundorf, Norbert et al. Co-published simultaneously in *Journal of International Consumer Marketing* (International Business Press, an imprint of The Haworth Press, Inc.) Vol. 8, No. 3/4, 1996, pp. 125-143; and: *Global Perspectives in Cross-Cultural and Cross-National Consumer Research* (ed: Lalita A. Manrai, and Ajay K. Manrai) International Business Press, an imprint of The Haworth Press, Inc., 1996, pp. 125-143. Single or multiple copies of this article are available from The Haworth Document Delivery Service [1-800-342-9678, 9:00 a.m - 5:00 p.m. (EST)].

© 1996 by The Haworth Press, Inc. All rights reserved.

In general, German consumers are found to be less familiar than Americans with a number of information technologies. They also tend to be more skeptical regarding the contributions of technology to society, medical care, the environment, and human life. These differences are more pronounced for college age respondents than for the older groups. College students in the U.S. show considerably greater familiarity with technology than older Americans, but this difference does not exist among Germans. The data also suggests that gender differences regarding attitudes toward technology are not as strong as expected.

Implications for intercultural marketing of information technologies are discussed. *[Article copies available from The Haworth Document Delivery Service: 1-800-342-9678.]*

## INTRODUCTION

Markets for information technology industries are becoming increasingly global. A number of factors contribute to this trend. The search for low-cost manufacturing bases by consumer electronic firms required production sites and markets beyond the American and European shores. Many firms start international operations at the same time they commence domestic operations because conventional internationalization patterns are no longer prevalent in high tech industries. Increasingly technologies respect no man-made boundaries. Satellite-based television networks, for example, are able to cross national boundaries easily. Deregulation is another factor that is ushering in global competition in telecommunications and broadcasting industries that were long protected as regulated monopolies. As deregulation proceeds further, it is expected that even local telecommunications in many countries will have to open up to some degree of competition, including perhaps international competitors.

In the information technology business, it is not just national boundaries that are being crossed–industry boundaries are being crossed as well. Because of integration of communication and computer technologies, computer, electronics, and telecommunications firms are now poised to invade each other's markets. While superior technology remains one of the key competitive weapons these firms employ, understanding the consumer and developing winning marketing strategies have also become very important issues in the globalizing information technology business. As the consumer electronics business has shown, the consumer is the ultimate arbiter of competitive success. In the integrated, multimedia technologies of the future, the success of the information technology firms that cater to household and small business markets worldwide will depend on how well they understand consumers' attitudes towards new technologies.

### Worldwide IT Markets

Market volume of Information Technology (IT) worldwide in 1989, including telecommunications services, was $1.4 trillion worldwide (CEC 1991; OECD 1989). OECD estimates that the share of information and communication technologies will double by the year 2,000 (OECD 1989). According to one estimate, revenues from computing alone will be about 12.5 percent of the U.S. GNP by 1990 (Fairley 1985). These are impressive figures when one considers that the U.S. automobile industry contributed only 2.3 percent to the American GNP in 1980.

ITs branch out into all areas of life. Two thirds of all workplaces are affected by IT directly or indirectly. Developers and producers of IT are influenced by visions and ideals of a future society such as the paperless office or factories without people. Despite the immense growth and volume of IT worldwide, projections may have been far more optimistic than the markets' ability to absorb the new technologies (Zoche 1993).

The study reported in this paper is part of a larger program of research that is investigating the consumer acceptance of new information technologies in North America, Europe, and Asia. In this particular study, attitudes and orientations towards technologies of German and American consumers are compared.

## RESEARCH OBJECTIVES

As the world's largest economy and the world's biggest market for information technology products and services, the United States is of interest not just to American companies, but to information technology firms worldwide. Similarly, as Europe's largest and the world's third largest economy, Germany is of interest not just to German and European firms, but to firms from other parts of the world, which want to tap into the German and European information technology markets. The attitudes and behaviors of consumers with respect to technology are of interest to anyone wishing to enter these markets. This study was undertaken to explore attitudes towards and familiarity with new information technologies in the United States and Germany. The findings from the study not only highlight the differences in these two giant markets separated by the Atlantic, they also provide useful insights for strategists in information technology firms and public policy makers grappling with the complex issues arising from the rapid proliferation of new information technologies (cf. Carey, 1992).

## Germany and the United States: Differences in Contexts

There are many similarities and differences between German and American consumers. In terms of per capita income, literacy or life expectancy, German and American consumers are more similar than dissimilar. As consumers of IT products and services, there are several differences. These differences arise from a variety of sources. Primary among these sources are the differences in context, i.e., the patterns of availability of various information technologies and differences in culture. In this section, we highlight some of the main differences in the availability and use of information technologies in Germany and the United States (see Table 1).

*Entertainment Technologies.* Like the U.S., virtually every household in Germany has at least one television set. Most of these sets are equipped with remote control. A survey by LINK Resources estimate cable subscribers to be 59% of German homes passed compared to 74% in the U.S. Fifty-four percent of German households have VCRs compared to 82 percent in the U.S. Compact Disc (CD) players have also achieved mass market levels and the German market penetration is higher than the U.S.

Until the mid-1980s, German TV viewing was limited to two major national networks and two/three, often part-time, regional services. The addition of two private broadcast networks, several cable services, and the increase in cable subscription, satellite, and home video has tremendously increased viewing options. Corresponding to expanded viewing options, average daily TV viewing by German adults has increased from 2.5 hours in 1986 to slightly over 3 hours in 1991 (Meyer and Schulze, 1993a, p. 236). Household viewing was 21% longer for cable compared to non-cable households (Meyer and Schulze, 1993a, p. 237). Despite this increase in German TV viewing, the levels are still much below the U.S., where the average adult watches close to 4 hours of TV daily (Nielsen Media Research 1993).

*Phone Based Technologies.* Customer equipment, mobile phone, satellite and data communications have been deregulated in Germany and are now offered by a number of competing companies. In the U.S., competition in the equipment market has been open and free from regulation for a longer period of time. As a result of these varied environments, U.S. consumers own a larger number of specific telephone devices such as answering machines and phone sets than German consumers as reported by Link Resources survey data in Table 1. Penetration of some of the newer telecom technologies such as cellular phones and fax machines, however, is comparable, across German and American consumers.

Basic telephone service is now available to almost all German households, having doubled since the 1970s. All telephone service is metered,

TABLE 1. Penetration of Entertainment and Information Technologies in American and German Households

| PRODUCTS & SERVICES | USA | GERMANY |
|---|---|---|
| TV set with remote | 83% | 85% |
| Cable TV subscription | 74% | 59% |
| Videocassette recorder (VCR) | 82% | 50% |
| Videodisc player | 6% | 1% |
| Hi-Fi Stereo System | 52% | 66% |
| CD Player | 31% | 53% |
| Multiple Telephones | 86% | 15% |
| Answering Machine | 43% | 14% |
| Cellular Telephones | 9% | 10% |
| Fax Machines | 4% | 5% |
| Computers | 26% | 13%* |

Source: LINK Resources Inc. 1992.
*Estimated by Meyer & Schulze 1993b.
(Sample = 300 in Germany; 2500 in USA)

which means phone customers pay for each local call. This may contribute to less frequent use of the telephone by Germans compared to Americans. Stransfeld and Seezen (1993) report that German females make an average of 12 private phone calls a week, compared to only 6 for males; also, female calls are about 2 minutes longer than males calls.

In the U.S. there are several telephone companies providing local and long distance service with a regulated service only at the local level. American consumers' use of the telephone network is extensive. In 1985, over 1.2 billion conversations occurred daily over the phone lines, 92 percent of which were calls in the local area (Statistical Abstracts 1992, p. 553). Number of overseas calls have increased from about 200 million calls in 1980 to over 1.2 billion calls in 1990 (Statistical Abstracts 1992, p. 552). Cellular systems and subscribers have seen a tremendous growth–from 32 systems in 1984 to 1,252 systems in 1991. Over 7.5 million subscribers had cellular service in 1991 (Statistical Abstracts 1992, p. 889).

*Computer Based Technologies.* Meyer and Schulze (1993b) report that

13% of all Germans and 31.5% of German middle class (white collar) households owned personal computers in 1990. The growth rate for personal computers is highest in household with school-age children. PC penetration is 39% in households with college-bound high-school students. LINK Resources estimate about 26 percent of U.S. households owned a PC in 1990 and this is expected to rise to 32.1 percent of all households by 1995. Demographic characteristics of the PC owning household suggests that 46 percent have at least one college degree and an average household income of $52,000 (LINK Resources, 1992).

## Responses to Information Technologies

Consumer responses to information technologies, in addition to their adoption, are influenced by a number of complex factors. Political and social trends play an important role. Germany, for instance, is very heavily ecology-oriented and the ecological movement plays a significant role in politics and society. The Social Democrats, one of the two major parties, just reaffirmed its rejection of nuclear power as an energy source. German consumers would be expected to be more sensitive towards the dangers of technologies. Also, fear of 'big brother' phenomena tends to be much greater, for reasons of undue government interventions in the past. This may be one factor explaining the reluctance of many Germans to use electronic mail networks (cf. Schmittler, 1992). Skepticism towards technology is more prevalent among younger Germans, although it often does not correspond to actual behavior. Meyer and Schulze (1993a) found that notably older German males are very much protechnology oriented; they tend to perform most repairs and they use technologies such as VCRs, CD players, and computers more than females do. Females use the telephone more frequently for social reasons.

Acceptance and use of information technologies is strongly influenced by the user's gender in Germany (Meyer and Schulze, 1993a) and in the U.S. (Mundorf, Westin, Brownell, and Dholakia, 1992). Computers, video games and other technologies tend to find greater acceptance among males compared to females (Kiesler, Sproull and Eccles 1985; Venkatesh and Vitalari, 1987). Although one might expect gender differences to be parallel for different countries, there is some indication that women began entering the professional workforce earlier in the U.S. compared to Germany (Brosius, Mundorf, and Staab, 1991). Cultural and historical roots play a role in such gender differentiation (Doerr, 1993). Gender might thus be an important indicator of cultural differences in addition to national origin.

Age is another important mediating factor in predicting attitudes towards technology. Individuals who are college age today were born into a world of computers and telecommunications, while those currently 50-60 years old were born prior to the 'Information Age.' Many of the older consumers were probably introduced to computers in their adult years, some time in the middle of their professional careers. Generational differences also emerge across cultures. Due to historical and economic factors, Americans experienced the introduction of many household and entertainment technologies sooner or faster than Germans. As a result of World War II, diffusion of technological advances into private homes in Germany was delayed up to two decades (Doerr, 1993). Also, younger Germans tend to be more skeptical of technical progress than young Americans. Even within Germany, the older generation tends to have a more positive attitude towards technology than the younger generation, while the pattern appears to be reversed among Americans (Meyer and Schulze, 1993a).

*Hypotheses*

The preceding discussion of the differences in availability of as well as consumer responses to information technology suggest the following:

H1: American consumers are more familiar with most information technologies than German consumers.
H2: Americans show a greater propensity to use information technologies than Germans.
H3: Germans tend to be more skeptical of the role of technology in society than Americans.
H4: Across cultures, college age consumers are more technology oriented than older consumers.
H5: Across cultures, men are more technology oriented than women.

## RESEARCH METHOD

*Sample Selection.* The research study was implemented among two groups of consumers in the U.S. and Germany. One group was composed of young students–212 American college students and 84 German college students. The second group was composed of different-aged non-students–244 in the U.S. and 50 in Germany.

The American and German samples are comparable along several dimensions. Non-students were selected from the middle class living in suburban areas and representing a variety of occupations including retired and homemakers. The college students in both countries were mostly

Communication and Journalism majors at mid-sized institutions with a similar age (20-22) and gender (about 50% male and 50% female) distribution. Since East Germans have lived in a market economy for only a few years, the German sample was composed only of West Germans to be comparable with the American sample.

Although college students as consumer samples are of limited utility, they are very significant for any research on information technologies. They can be considered as "lead users" (von Hippel 1990) of many of these new and emerging technologies. Typically, college students are heavy consumers of entertainment technologies. They are familiar with personal computers and have easy access to computer facilities on campuses. Families with college students or college bound students tend to have a higher personal computer penetration than the general population. Finally, as members of this group complete college education, enter the workforce, start new families and households, they represent the largest single market for marketers of information technologies. Thus, college-age samples were employed in this study not merely for reasons of convenience but because they constitute lead users of ITs.

*Questionnaire Development.* An instrument was developed to investigate familiarity with, attitudes towards and preferences for information technology. A resulting "Familiarity and Lifestyle Survey" was initially administered to 446 American consumers living in the northeastern United States. The questionnaire was then translated into German by a bilingual native speaker of German and verified by two scholars of German.

*Measures of Familiarity.* Respondent familiarity with a given list of information technologies was measured on a 5-point scale. The study focused on familiarity rather than ownership, mainly because college students are frequently familiar with technologies, although they may not own them. This allowed comparisons with older consumers. Four categories of information technologies were listed and included some technologies which are currently widespread (e.g., VCR, Cable TV, CD Player, Fax Machine, etc.), and others which represent new technologies not yet mass-marketed (CD-I, ISDN, Videophone, Multiple-Window TV, etc.). See Exhibit 1 for the list of technologies.

*Measures of Technology Seeking.* Nineteen pairs of forced-choice questions, each of which contained a pro-technology statement (e.g., "I like the convenience of Automatic Teller Machines") and a corresponding Anti-Technology statement ("I go to a bank only when it is open so I can deal with a teller") were designed as measures of technology seeking. Respondents were asked to circle one letter (A or B), which described their

EXHIBIT 1. Questionnaire Items

**Familiarity with Technology Items:**

1. <u>TV-based</u> including Cable TV, CD Player, VCR, Camcorder, Video Games, Multiple Window TV, and Programmable Remote Control.
2. <u>Personal Computing</u> including Personal Computer and PC with Modem.
3. <u>Phone-based</u> including Cellular Phone, Answering Machine and FAX machines.
4. <u>New communication technologies</u> including Caller ID, ISDN Telephone, CD-Interactive, and Videophone.

**Technology Seeking Scale (19 pairs of forced choice)**

For each of the following pairs of statements, CIRCLE the letter (A or B) that describes YOUR feelings best:

　　A. I would love to pay my bills through a convenient electronic system.
　　B. I wouldn't consider paying my bills by any means except checks that I write and mail personally.

　　A. I like to have as many channels as possible on my TV set.
　　B. I find that today's cable TV has too many channels.

**Technology in Society Scale (16 statements):**

Indicate how strongly you agree or disagree with the following statements by CIRCLING the appropriate number.

|  | Strongly Agree | | Neither Agree nor Disagree | | Strongly Disagree |
|---|---|---|---|---|---|
| Computerized databases invade people's privacy. | 1 | 2 | 3 | 4 | 5 |
| Technology improves our quality of life. | 1 | 2 | 3 | 4 | 5 |

feelings best regarding each pair of technology seeking statement. See Exhibit 1 for examples of this measure.

Care was taken to randomly label Pro- and Anti-technology statements. The statements were developed by three experts from different academic disciplines. The 19 pairs represent those on which all three agreed. A technology-seeking score (between 0.00 and 1.00) was computed for each respondent by adding the number of Pro-tech statements checked and dividing them by the total number of statements.

*Technology in Society.* A final set of 16 statements was developed to investigate general attitudes toward the role of technology in society. The statements represented a mix of statements skeptical of technology

("Computerized databases invade people's privacy"), and those in favor of technology ("Technology improves our quality of life"). Degree of agreement or disagreement with each statement was assessed on a 5-point scale.

*Intercultural Issues: Translation.* An effort was made to translate items on the scales literally, as far as possible. However, in several cases, literal translation did not seem meaningful. For the familiarity scale, only Multiple-Window TV was translated by a descriptive title, since no familiar term was available. All other terms were translated literally.

Several modifications were necessary for the technology seeking scale. For instance, one of the pairs of statements for the U.S. sample was:

A. I would love to vacation at Walt Disney World's futuristic EPCOT center.
B. I would love to vacation at Yosemite National Park.

Since both places are too removed from the average German's realm of experience, the location in (A) was replaced by Euro-Disney, and (B) was rephrased to "I like vacationing in nature."

Finally, no translation problems were encountered for the "Technology in Society" scale since statements were rather general in nature.

## RESULTS

Familiarity. Each of the four technology categories was subjected to MANOVA, using Country (U.S., Germany), Gender (M, F), and Age (Student, Nonstudent) as independent variables. For all three independent variables, MANOVA was significant at the 0.001-level: Country [$F (4, 576) = 52.68, p < 0.001$]; Age [$F (4, 576) = 9.90, p < 0.001$]; Gender [$F (4, 576) = 8.48, p < 0.001$]. Table 2 indicates the main effects and direction of means for the three independent variables.

In those cases where significant differences are found, they correspond to expectations for country, age, and gender differences. Table 2 confirms the expectation that Americans are more familiar with technologies than Germans, males tend to be more familiar with technologies than females, and younger subjects display greater familiarity than older ones.

The lack of a gender effect for phone technologies is probably due to the relatively greater level of comfort women feel with this compared to other technologies; the females' familiarity level is similar to males. For Personal Computing and Office technology, only an age effect materialized. Apparently, those of college-age are much more familiar with com-

TABLE 2. Familiarity with Information Technologies: Effect of Country, Age Group and Gender

|  | Country (U.S. > FRG) | Age Group (Students > Non-Students) | Gender (Males > Females) | Familiarity (4 = highest, 0 = lowest) |
|---|---|---|---|---|
| **INFORMATION TECHNOLOGIES:** | | | | |
| TV-related | *** | *** | *** | 2.58 |
| Phone-based | *** | ** | n.s. | 2.57 |
| Computing | n.s. | *** | n.s. | 2.27 |
| New Technologies | ** | n.s. | * | 0.77 |

Note: All means for the significant main effects follow the pattern listed above. Familiarity scores are averaged across all respondents, 4 = very familiar, 0 = not at all familiar.
$*p < 0.05$; $** p < 0.01$; $*** p < 0.001$.

puters and related technologies than older groups–regardless of country or gender. For New Communication Technologies, Americans show greater familiarity compared to Germans. The lack of an age effect and weak gender differences can be explained by two considerations: either the level of diffusion is roughly comparable for the groups compared, or there is a "floor effect," in that very few respondents are aware of a technology at all (e.g., CD-I).

MANOVA produced a two-way interaction for Country by Age Group [$F(4,576) = 4.06, p = 0.003$]. Univariate analyses proved significant for all four technology groups. The means and their comparisons are reported in Table 3.

Inspection of the means in Table 3 reveals that there is no significant difference between German students and older German respondents, while U.S. students reveal a greater level of familiarity with technologies than older Americans and both German groups. Also, for the more common types of technologies (TV and phone based), older Americans also show greater familiarity than the two German groups.

*Technology Seeking.* Analysis of Variance was performed using the Technology Seeking score (computed from the forced A/B binary choices) as the dependent variable and employing Country (U.S., Germany), Gender (M, F), and Age Group (Student, Non-Student) as independent variables. ANOVA was significant at the 0.001-level for Country [$F(1, 580) = 51.15, p < 0.001$] and Age Group [$F(1,580) = 74.8, p < 0.001$]. Americans displayed a greater degree of Technology Seeking ($M = 0.50$) compared to

TABLE 3. Familiarity with Information Technologies: A Function of Age Group and Country

|  | U.S. | | Germany | |
|---|---|---|---|---|
|  | Student | Non-Student | Student | Non-Student |
| TV-related | 3.17[1,2,3] | 2.39[1,4,5] | 2.02[2,4] | 1.94[3,5] |
| Phone-based | 3.10[1,2,3] | 2.49[1,4] | 1.98[2,4] | 1.86[3,5] |
| Computing | 2.61[1] | 1.95[1,4] | 2.38[4] | 2.20 |
| New Technologies | 0.90[2] | 0.76[4] | 0.49[2,4] | 0.73 |

Note: 4 = very familiar, 0 = not at all familiar. Comparisons of Mean values are by Duncan's test reported at p < .05.
[1] U.S.: Student-Non-Student comparison.
[2] Student: U.S.-Germany comparison.
[3] U.S. Student-German non-student comparison
[4] U.S. Non-Student-Germany student comparison.
[5] Non-student: U.S.-Germany comparison.

German respondents ($M = 0.40$). Also, students ($M = 0.54$) showed greater Technology Seeking than their older counterparts ($M = 0.42$). No significant gender differences emerged.

The significant effect of Age is apparently due to the high degree of technology seeking reported by American college students ($M = 0.59$) compared to all other groups (means around 0.40), as indicated by the Country by Age Group interaction [F $(1,580) = 15.74, p < 0.001$]. The former group showed significantly greater Technology Seeking ($p < 0.05$ by Duncan's test) compared to the other three groups, which were not significantly different from one another. Finally, a three-way interaction [F $(1,580) = 51.15, p = 0.003$) revealed that the only clear gender effect emerged for older Germans, where males ($M = 0.47$) displayed a greater degree of technology seeking than females ($M = 0.31$). Interestingly, older German males displayed a more positive attitude towards technology ($M = 0.47$) compared to their college-age counterparts ($M = 0.38$).

*Technology in Society.* The 16 statements developed to investigate attitudes towards the role of technology in society were also subjected to MANOVA, using Country (U.S., Germany), Gender (M, F), and Group/Age (Student, Non-Student) as independent variables. Main effects emerged for Country [F $(16,539) = 10.75, p < 0.001$], gender [F $(16, 539) = 2.72, p < 0.001$] and Age group [F $(16,539) = 1.72, p < 0.04$]. Summary results of univariate analysis of those statements associated with significant country differences are shown in Table 4.

As can be seen, Americans showed significantly stronger agreement with three general statements pertaining to the role of technology in life. They concede that it improves quality of life and gives control over nature. However, somewhat surprisingly, they also caution that, "With each technological innovation, we lose some US essential human quality." Germans revealed significantly greater concern than Americans did with specific technological advances, notably in the areas of the environment, medicine, human life, and society. However, they also agreed more strongly than the American respondents with the statement that "Compared to all past centuries, we live in the best of times."

A significant country by gender interaction [$F (16,539) = 2.15, p < 0.006$] emerged by MANOVA. Univariate analysis proved significant for two of the variables. Inspection of the means showed that older German women disagreed more strongly with the statement "Technology gives us control over nature" than the three other groups. In addition, German males disagreed less than all other groups with the statement "Technology is making our life impersonal."

## DISCUSSION

Findings in this study are generally consistent with predictions based on cultural, societal and economic differences between German and American consumers. Gender and in particular age were found to play a critical role as mediating factors.

The data support the view that American consumers are more familiar with most information technologies than German consumers. The difference between countries was most pronounced for TV and phone based technologies, i.e., those technologies most accessible to the mass market. For computing technologies, respondents' age group was the key predictor. College students are more familiar with computers than older groups of consumers. This may be due to the fact that high schools and colleges in both countries offer computer instruction, and that parents buy computers for college bound and college age children to give them a head start. Very few of the respondents in both countries were at all familiar with the group of new communication technologies included in the survey. American college students, however, showed a slightly higher level of familiarity compared to all groups of respondents.

The hypothesis that across cultures, college age consumers are more technology oriented than older consumers was *not* supported for the Ger-

TABLE 4. Attitudes Toward Technology in Society: Effect of Country, Age Group, and Gender

|  | Country | Age Group | Gender |
|---|---|---|---|
| **Significantly greater agreement by U.S. respondents** | | | |
| Technology improves our quality of life. | *** (U.S.) | * (Students) | - |
| Technology gives us control over nature. | *** (U.S.) | - | ** (Male) |
| With each technological innovation, we lose some essential human quality. | *** (U.S.) | - | - |
| **Significantly greater agreement by German respondents** | | | |
| Medical Technology has gone too far. | *** | - | ** (Females) |
| Society pays a high price for scientific and technological progress. | ** | - | - |
| Technological advances are gradually destroying our natural environment. | * | - | - |
| Technologies that affect human life and health should be strictly regulated. | * | - | - |
| Compared to all past centuries, we live in the best of times. | ** | - | *** (Males) |

Note: Only those items with significant country main effects are reported. For age and gender the group with the strongest agreement to the respective statement is indicated. The significance level for the effects is as follows:
* $p < 0.05$     ** $p < 0.01$     *** $p < 0.001$

man sample. German college students are far more conservative regarding the acceptance of technologies than their American counterparts. They are roughly at the same level as older Germans. This confirms the expectation that the younger generation of Germans is skeptical of technologies and is often not inclined to use many of them. The German students' orientation to technology also differed from the American students' orientation to technology which was particularly strong. As a 'window into the future' of societal attitudes towards technology, the responses of college-aged Germans suggest that differences between the U.S. and Germany are likely to persist rather than converge in the near future.

Based on research regarding repairs or 'playing' with technology (Meyer and Schulze 1993a), we had expected a strong gender effect. Although the study confirms that across cultures, men are more technology oriented than women, the gender effect is relatively weak. Because of greater telephone usage by women in both countries, gender effect did not exist for telephone-oriented technologies; women were as familiar as men with these technologies. Similarly, we found no gender difference in familiarity with computing technologies either. This may be an indicator that women are becoming relatively more comfortable with many technologies, particularly information technologies that are the focus of this research. As more and more women join the workforce, familiarity and experience with technology are probably contributing to the weakening of gender associations with these technologies. Several recent studies indicate that women tend to have a positive attitude towards technology if it is warranted by functional considerations and if the technologies and programs are easy to use (cf. Meyer and Schulze 1993b).

*Implications for Marketing Strategy*

Given the differences in the information technology contexts in Germany and the United States, the American sample was found to be more familiar with new information technologies, especially the technologies that are just emerging or anticipated in the near future. In Germany, new technologies–especially those dealing with telecommunications and computers–are not only launched first in the business arena but often tend to remain in the business arena. Familiarity with these technologies among the average household user is therefore limited. In the United States, not only are new technologies becoming available to the business and home markets simultaneously but there is also a gradual erasing of boundaries between work and home. This is happening in big organizations through growing use of telework and work-at-home, and in smaller entrepreneurial units through the direct merger of the householder and entrepreneur roles.

As expected, Germans are also skeptical about the benefits of new technologies and do not share the unbridled optimism that Americans seem to have for technologies. Although Americans in general exhibit less "techno-anxiety" than Germans, this study indicates that at a deeper level Americans may be disturbed about the fact that their simpler past is being rapidly eroded by hyper-technological culture endangering human relationships. This may be especially the case since technological change comes on top of the overall pace of social change (moving, job dislocations, family-life dislocations, etc.) in the United States. Thus, significantly more Americans than Germans agreed with the statement that "with each technological innovation, we lose some human quality."

The skepticism towards technology coupled with relative unfamiliarity with the technologies means that the German household market is likely to be less welcoming to new information products and services than the American market. An upbeat, techno-optimistic advertising campaign that works well in the United States may have to be recast as a tradition-supporting, low-key campaign in Germany. New technology marketers will also have to be more respectful of the boundaries between home and work in Germany than they are in the United States. In the U.S., in fact, many new technologies such as computers and fax machines celebrate the work-at-home ethic.

Even in the United States, the technology marketers will have to address the deeper level of anxiety about technology which is perceived to be destroying human qualities. Marketers will have to be sensitive to the human relationships that people value. This is already being attempted, for example, in the marketing of telecommunication services by companies like AT&T which advertise the joys of connecting across long distances. Advertising and promotion, however, are not enough to overcome the fundamental anxiety about the dehumanizing quality of technology. Ultimately, it is the developers of technological products and services who have to work on designs and distribution methods that make people preserve and even build human relationships.

## *Public Policy Implications*

This study implies that Germans are likely to keep a closer watch on the social impact of new technologies than Americans. At the same time, however, German government, businesses, and people in general are frustrated by the fact that the careful social monitoring of business and technology has made the high-technology sectors of German industry less competitive than the freewheeling American industry (BMFT 1993). Two valid but sometimes conflicting policy imperatives arise from this in Germany: (1) control the proliferation of new technologies, especially if they could potentially diminish the quality of life; and (2) promote the development of new technology, especially in those sectors where the global competitive initiative is in danger of being seized by American or Japanese firms. The simultaneous pursuit of these two policy objectives will strain the creativity of policy makers in Germany and the European Community.

In the United States, the generally techno-optimist attitudes found in this survey indicate that public policy makers can continue to pursue policies that favor high-tech industries. This only endorses what has been happening already at the Federal and State levels in the United States. There is, however, a deeper feeling of anxiety about the dehumanizing aspects of technology that policy makers will have to address. While it is difficult to establish causality, it is plausible that this deeper anxiety is because Americans do not see anyone–including their elected political representatives–as capable of keeping the growth of technology in check. It may be left to the media, with entertaining but alarming features like "Jurassic Park," to bring the debate about the social and political oversight of technology into sharper focus.

## CONCLUSION

This study provides a starting point for comparative cross-cultural research exploring consumer orientations to information technologies. It has tested key parameters which explain variations in usage and acceptance of these technologies. Future studies could expand this research in several directions. Comparable data could be collected from other countries, in particular those in advanced European and Asian markets. Other demographic variables, such as income and education could be introduced as predictors of technology acceptance. Finally, situational variables could be introduced to achieve more specific information regarding different circumstances and individual goals of technology use.

Most countries are currently developing visions of an "Information Superhighway." These highways will be connected bringing international and intercultural communication and marketing to a new level. While the technology is pushing ahead relentlessly, only users can make it succeed. Understanding user attitudes and behavior is thus critical for the success of the information society.

## REFERENCES

"Beim Satellitenempfang sind die neuen Laender vorn" [New Federal States Leading in Satellite Reception] (August 27, 1993). *VDI-Nachrichten,* 13.

BMFT (1993). Deutscher Delphi-Bericht zur Entwicklung von Wissenschaft und Technik. (German Delphi Report on the Development of Science and Technology). Bonn: Federal Ministry of Science and Technology.

Brosius, H. B., Mundorf, N., & Staab, J. F. (1991). The depiction of sex roles in American and German Magazine Advertisements. *International Journal of Public Opinion Research,* 366-384.

Bundesminister fuer Forschung und Technologie (1993). *Deutscher Delphi-Ber-*

icht zur Entwicklung von Wissenschaft und Technik. Bonn: Bundesminister fuer Forschung und Technologie.

Carey, J. (1992). Looking Back to the Future: How Communication Technologies enter the American Household. In: J. V. Pavlik and E. V. Dennis (ed.) *Demystifying Media Technology.* Mountain View, CA: Mayfield Publishing, 32-39.

CEC (1991). *Europa 2000–Ausblick auf die Entwicklung des Gemeinschaftsraumes* (Europe 2000–Perspectives on the Development of the Common Market). Brussels: European Commission.

Doerr, G. (1993). Frauen, Technik und Haushaltsproduktion: Zur weiblichen Aneignung der Haushaltstechnik [Women, Technology, and Household production: Female adoption of household technology]. In Meyer, S., & Schulze, E. (ed.). Technisiertes Familienleben: Blick zurueck und nach vorn [Technology and Family: A Look to the Past and the Future]. Berlin: Edition Sigma.

Elmer-Dewitt, P. (April 12, 1993). Take a Trip to the Future on the Electronic Superhighway. *Time,* 50-55.

"Ertragsdruck auf Informations- und Kommunikationsindustrie" [Performance pressure on Information and Communications Industry] (June 11, 1993). *VDI-News,* 1.

Fairley, R. (1985). *Software Engineering Concepts.* New York: McGraw Hill.

Katz, J. E. (February 4, 1991). Europeans like their privacy. *Telephony,* 22-25.

Kiesler, S., Sproull, L., & Eccles, J.S. (1985). Pool halls, chips, and war games: Women in the culture of computing. *Psychology of Women Quarterly,* 451-462.

Lafayette, J. (October 18, 1993). How Bell Atlantic is going interactive. *Electronic Media,* 4.

"Leading Global Telecommunications Carriers" (June 3, 1993). *Wall Street Journal,* 7.

LINK Resources (1992) Household Adoption of Information Technologies: A Multi-Country Survey. Unpublished document. New York.

Meyer, S., & Schulze, E. (1993a). *Projektergebnisse: Technikfolgen fuer Familien.* [Project results: Effects of technology for families]. Duesseldorf: VDI-Technologiezentrum.

Meyer, S., & Schulze, E. (1993b). Familie, Haushalt, Freizeit [Family, home, leisure]. In R. Stransfeld & J. Seetzen (ed.). *Anwendungen der Informationstechnik-Entwicklungen und Erwartungen* [Applications of Information Technology–Trends and Expectations]. Duesseldorf: VDI-Technologiezentrum.

Meyer, S., & Schulze, E. (1993c). Technisiertes Familienleben: Ergebnisse einer Laengsschnittuntersuchung [Technology and Family Life: Results of a Long-Term Study]. In Meyer, S., & Schulze, E. (ed.). Technisiertes Familienleben: Blick zurueck und nach vorn [Technology and Family: A Look to the Past and the Future]. Berlin: Edition Sigma.

Nielsen Media Research (1993). "TV Snapshot, Summer 1993" quoted in *Multichannel News.* October 4, 1993, p. 58.

OECD (1989). Policy Options for Promoting Growth through Information Technology. In *Information Technology and New Growth Opportunities. Information Computer Communications Policy.* Vol. 19, Paris: OECD, S133-201.

Schmittler, W. (1992). *Technikfolgenabschaetzung: Projekt- ergebnisse.* [Technology assessment: Project results]. Duesseldorf: VDI-Technologiezentrum.

Statistical Abstracts (1992) Selected Statistics. Washington, D.C. p. 552, 553, 889.

Stransfeld, R. & J. Seetzen (ed.). *Anwendungen der Informationstechnik-Entwicklungen und Erwartungen* [Applications of Information Technology–Trends and Expectations]. Duesseldorf: VDI-Technologiezentrum.

Venkatesh, A., & Vitalari, N.P. (1987). A post-adoption analysis of computing in the home. *Journal of Economic Psychology,* 161-180.

Vitalari, N.P. & Venkatesh, A. (1987). In-home computing and information services: A twenty year analysis of the technology and its impact. *Telecommunications Policy, 11,* 1, 65-81.

von Hippel, E. (1990). Predicting the Source of Commercially Valuable User Innovation via "Lead Users" in M.M. Saghafi, A.K. Gupta (ed.) *Advances in Telecommunications Management: Managing the R&D/Marketing Interface for Product Success: The Telecommunications Focus.* Vol. 1, Greenwich, CT: JAI Press, 131-145.

"Wir alle profitieren von ISDN" [We all benefit from ISDN]. (January 4, 1991). *VDI-Nachrichten, 1,* 9.

Zoche, P. (1993). *Trends in Telecommunications Technology: Germany.* Lecture presented at the University of Rhode Island, Kingston, R.I.

# Value Differences Between Polish and Romanian Consumers: A Caution Against Using a Regiocentric Marketing Orientation in Eastern Europe

Dana-Nicoleta Lascu
Lalita A. Manrai
Ajay K. Manrai

**SUMMARY.** The importance of values in understanding consumer behavior has been amply acknowledged in existing research. Many marketing practitioners planning to do business in Eastern Europe erroneously assume that the Eastern European market is relatively similar in terms of the value structure of consumers across different countries in that region. This paper argues that there are substantial differences between consumer segments in the various countries in the area, since their belief systems have been shaped by different environmental influences and cautions against the use of a regiocentric approach to marketing in Eastern Europe. To illustrate these differences, a cross-cultural study of instrumental and terminal values held by different demographic segments in two East European countries, Poland and Romania, was conducted. The findings sug-

---

Dana-Nicoleta Lascu is Assistant Professor of Marketing, University of Richmond, Richmond, VA 23173. Lalita A. Manrai is Associate Professor of Marketing and Ajay K. Manrai is Associate Professor of Marketing, University of Delaware, Newark, DE 19716.

[Haworth co-indexing entry note]: "Value Differences Between Polish and Romanian Consumers: A Caution Against Using a Regiocentric Marketing Orientation in Eastern Europe." Lascu, Dana-Nicoleta, Lalita A. Manrai, and Ajay K. Manrai. Co-published simultaneously in *Journal of International Consumer Marketing* (International Business Press, an imprint of The Haworth Press, Inc.) Vol. 8, No. 3/4, 1996, pp. 145-167; and: *Global Perspectives in Cross-Cultural and Cross-National Consumer Research* (ed: Lalita A. Manrai, and Ajay K. Manrai) International Business Press, an imprint of The Haworth Press, Inc., 1996, pp. 145-167. Single or multiple copies of this article are available from The Haworth Document Delivery Service [1-800-342-9678, 9:00 a.m - 5:00 p.m. (EST)].

© 1996 by The Haworth Press, Inc. All rights reserved.

gest that demographic segmentation can be effectively used for identifying and targeting consumers with different value structures in Poland, but, for Romania, demographic segmentation has practically no utility in this respect. Several managerial implications of the findings are discussed. *[Article copies available from The Haworth Document Delivery Service: 1-800-342-9678.]*

## INTRODUCTION

Culture instills in individuals norms and values that affect every aspect of their behavior as consumers. World cultures are set apart based on the relative importance or ranking of values (Rokeach 1973); that is, values are not held to the same degree by everyone, regardless of culture. Consequently, the identification of cultural values could have important implications for marketing strategy decisions (Spielvogel 1989; Vinson, Scott, and Lamont 1977). Another important characteristic of values is that they are derived from and modified through personal, social and cultural learning (Clawson and Vinson 1978). Kotler (1994) identifies consumer demographics, i.e., age, occupation, etc., as the personal factors influencing consumer behavior. Thus, a scrutiny of the relationship between consumer demographics and values is likely to provide marketing managers with valuable insights for market segmentation, product positioning and promotional decisions.

One region where this type of scrutiny may prove particularly useful is Eastern Europe, an area that is currently ripe for and open to foreign investment. Marketing managers planning to set up operations in this area frequently assume that this region is culturally similar and may target its consumers by using marketing strategies that strive for economies of scale, developing a standardized product and utilizing standardized marketing appeals–i.e., using a regiocentric marketing approach (Levitt 1983). Their philosophy may, in part, be supported by current practitioner-oriented publications which frequently refer to Eastern European consumers as an undifferentiated group, sharing, on one hand, an acquisition fever similar to the post-World War II American consumers' "yearning to acquire and consume" (Fox and Lears 1983, p.xii; Richins and Dawson 1992), and, on the other, a common recent history.

While concern with acquisition exists at the aggregate level in Eastern Europe, the differences between consumers in these countries warrant scrutiny and may suggest a caution against regiocentric marketing. Examples of such differences abound. For instance, some nationalities in the area–Bulgarians, Czechs, Poles, Russians, Slovaks, Serbs and others–share common slavic roots and languages, while others–Hungarians and

Romanians, who speak a Finno-Ugric language, Hungarian, and a Latin language, Romanian, respectively,–do not. National religions have various degrees of importance in these countries; for example, in countries like Poland, represented in the Vatican at the highest level, religion plays a crucial role, while in the other countries, it plays a lesser role. National religions themselves differ: Poland is a Catholic country, while the countries of the Balkans–Bulgaria, Romania, and the former Yugoslavia–are primarily Eastern Orthodox.

Aside from differences in these two principal elements of culture, language and religion, other differences are noted between the nations of Eastern Europe. For example, in the recent past which has substantially shaped generations, governments in Eastern Europe used different types of social control mechanisms, i.e., means that cultures use to control individual and group behavior. While the former Soviet Union, Bulgaria and Romania practiced very strict control of the population, using fear to keep in check deviance from the reigning communist ideology, Hungary, Poland and the former Czechoslovakia and Yugoslavia enjoyed more political and ideological freedom. In parallel, the countries which allowed more freedom were also permitted a certain degree of privatization that was unfathomable in the other countries of Eastern Europe (Naor 1986, 1990).

Such differences are bound to have an enduring relationship with the individually-held values in these countries: differences in historical, religious, politico-ideological and economic developments are likely to be indicative of value differences at the national level in Eastern Europe. Romania, a nationalistic, collectivist and traditional society (Naor 1990) has experienced isolation from the other countries in the region such that its value system is likely to be strongly affected by social traditions. Poland, however, has experienced–even during the communist regime– substantial exposure to Western media, tourism, urbanization as a consequence of the country's rapid industrialization; thus, Polish values are more likely to be shaped by individuals' personal experiences, rather than by tradition. Similarly, exposure to Western society, where individualism is an important societal value (Hofstede 1980), has instilled independence in Polish consumers.

This study examines differences between Polish and Romanian consumers in terms of their value orientation (terminal or instrumental) and explores how this orientation relates to demographics (age, education, and income) in the two cultures. The paper is organized into seven sections. The next section discusses the findings of the marketing and psychology literature on personal values. The third section further elaborates on the influence of different factors on personal values in Poland and Romania and offers hypotheses that address how these differences result in different value structures across demographic segments. The fourth section describes the methodology of the study, addressing the sample and site and the procedure employed for data collection. The fifth section describes the results of the study and the sixth section covers the conclusion and managerial implications of the study. The seventh section proposes directions for future research.

## *LITERATURE REVIEW: PERSONAL VALUES*

A review of the marketing literature reveals that little attention has been paid to date to the study of values. Helgeson et al. (1984) found that only 0.8 percent of the studies conducted between 1950 and 1981 deal with values and beliefs, while a review of the more recent literature, i.e., 1984 to 1991, revealed only seven consumer research articles that focused on values (Richins and Dawson 1992). Yet values represent enduring consumer characteristics whose examination may provide noteworthy insights on aggregate consumer behavior and justification for the extent to which marketing strategies can be standardized in different global regions.

Values have been defined as enduring beliefs that a specific mode of conduct or end-state of existence is personally or socially preferable to an opposite or converse mode of conduct or end-state of existence (Rokeach 1973, p. 5). An alternate definition describes values as centrally held cognitive elements which stimulate motivation for behavioral response and are responsible for the selection and maintenance of the ends or goals towards which individuals strive and regulate the methods and the manner in which this striving occurs (Vinson, Scott, and Lamont 1977, p. 45).

Values are thought to have a transcendental quality, guiding actions, attitudes, judgments, and comparisons across specific objects and situations and beyond immediate goals towards more ultimate goals (Rokeach 1973, p. 18). Typically, values have been measured using scales in which respondents evaluate behaviors and end states according to importance. Scales used to measure values include Kahle, Beatty and Homer (1986) and Munson and McQuarrie (1988) in marketing and Rokeach (1973), Braithwaite and Law (1985) and Levy (1985) in psychology. The scale most frequently used in both disciplines is the 36-item Rokeach (1973) scale which will also be used in the present study (see Table 1). This value scale has been deemed useful in identifying value configurations by revealing the various degrees of importance that individuals or cultural groups place on certain behaviors and end states (Richins and Dawson 1992).

TABLE 1. Instrumental and Terminal Values (Rokeach 1973)

| Instrumental Values | Terminal Values |
|---|---|
| Ambitious | A comfortable life |
| Broadminded | An exciting life |
| Capable | A sense of accomplishment |
| Cheerful | A world at peace |
| Clean | A world of beauty |
| Courageous | Equality |
| Forgiving | Family security |
| Helpful | Freedom |
| Honest | Happiness |
| Imaginative | Inner harmony |
| Independent | Mature love |
| Intellectual | National security |
| Logical | Pleasure |
| Loving | Salvation |
| Obedient | Self-respect |
| Polite | Social recognition |
| Responsible | True friendship |
| Self-controlled | Wisdom |

Among some of the characteristics of values are the following: similar values are widely held by most members of a culture or subculture; values are derived from and modified through personal, social and cultural learning; and a major role of values is that of a standard that individuals can use in formulating attitudes and guiding their own behavior (Clawson and Vinson 1978). Regarding the marketing applications of values, research suggests that values affect product preferences (Bozinoff and Cohen 1982; Henry 1976; Lessig 1975; Scott and Lamont 1974; Vinson, Scott and Lamont 1977) and are linked to consumers' perceptions of product attributes (Tse, Wong and Tan 1988). Values have been related to personal product benefits that consumers desire from the products they consume using a laddering approach based on association networks (Guttman 1990; Reynolds and Guttman 1988). Values have also been examined in relation to retail patronage (Mason, Durand and Taylor 1983), in relation to mass media (McCarty and Hattwick 1992; McCracken 1986; Reynolds and Craddock 1988), and deemed as useful in market analysis and segmentation (Spielvogel 1989; Vinson, Scott, and Lamont 1977), product planning, promotion, and public policy analysis (Vinson, Scott, and Lamont 1977).

Values have also been used in cross-cultural research in psychology (Bond 1988; Schwartz and Bilsky 1987, 1990), and in marketing (McCarty and Harrwick 1992; Tse, Wong and Tan 1988; Valencia 1989). Some of these studies (Belk and Pollay 1985; Pollay 1986), have used anthropological approaches, inferring values from observed behavior and developing value measures that apply only to specific consumption contexts. The marketing studies cited here may be classified into macro studies, which investigate how culturally-acquired values influence the consumption behavior of groups of consumers, and micro studies, which focus on how individually-held values affect consumers' behavior in the market place (Tse, Wong and Tan 1988).

The present article expands on the macro perspective. Rather than considering the influence of culture alone, we acknowledge that values are derived from and modified through personal, social and cultural learning (Clawson and Vinson 1978). For instance, with age, as learning occurs, these values are likely to change. And, as individuals transcend their social class as a consequence of education and changes in income, social learning is likely to, in turn, have an impact on their values. This study thus notes the role of personal and social influences in differentially shaping values across the two countries. The study proposes that personal factors such as age, education, and income are closely linked to values for Polish consumers. On the other hand, for Romanian consumers, these personal factors are not as closely linked to their value system; for them, values are more likely to be socially determined. The study, thus, proposes that, in Romania, the role of social factors such as traditionalism and collectivism are more closely linked to consumers' value system.

The study of value differences in Eastern Europe is important: once values are internalized, they become unconscious or conscious criteria in guiding behavior (Chusmir, Koberg and Mills 1989). Marketing practitioners need to be aware of value differences and the relationship between values and demographics in order to better understand and possibly predict both the behavior of industrial and individual consumers in the newly-opened marketplace, as well as that of channel members, facilitators and suppliers actively involved in the company's transactions in the region.

Identifying the particulars of the relationship between values and demographics will be especially useful for companies evaluating their marketing strategies in the respective countries: this information may be employed by companies attempting to segment the market for their products, in order to ensure accurate product and service positioning and targeting. Most companies rely on personal characteristics, such as demographic descriptors readily available from documents of reputable sources such as government, governmental and nongovernmental organizations. For segmentation purposes, therefore, they should be cautioned that, in Eastern Europe, demographics alone do not necessarily constitute the most relevant basis for segmentation; rather, demographics may prove to be more useful in segmentation when assessed in conjunction with consumer values.

Next, we examine the socio-cultural influences that Polish and Romanian consumers are exposed to and how these differences affect the values of demographic segments in these countries.

## DEMOGRAPHICS AND PERSONAL VALUES IN POLAND AND ROMANIA

Poland and Romania have been for half a century under Communist rule and are presently undergoing a process of transition from a planned to a market economy. Yet, the two countries' experiences before and after the iron curtain differ greatly. Historically, while Romanians pride themselves to be descendants of the Roman empire, officially changing their name in English language publications to further emphasize their Roman origin (Elvin 1990), Poles are a Slavic people and relative newcomers to the European continent, speaking a language similar to those of most Eastern Europe. During the course of centuries, however, both countries have had a long tradition of fighting foreign aggression and occupation to maintain national integrity and independence.

With regard to religion, most Romanians (80 percent) are Romanian Orthodox. Only 6 percent of Romanians are Roman Catholic, while 95 percent of Poles are Roman Catholic (*Country Reports* 1993). Religion is particularly important for Poland, having played a crucial role in the opposition to the Communist rule, while, in Romania, the high-ranking leaders of the church were also deputies to the Peoples's Grand National Assembly, as well as trusted informers of the Secret police.

One area that differentiates the two countries culturally is Romanians' strong feeling of nationalism and emphasis on present-day Romanians' links to their ancient Roman heritage (Naor 1990). This collectivist-nationalist general attitude was further strengthened by Romanians' isolation from their more developed Western neighbors due to the continued strong influence of traditional rural life, despite the Communist regime's drive towards industrialization and construction (Naor 1990). Romania's isolation and differentiation from its Western neighbors was further prompted by the Ceausescu policies of non-fraternization with Westerners, as well as those aimed at erasing all external debt by interdicting most imports, and exporting all consumer and industrial goods that international markets could absorb, thus causing a substantial decline in Romanians' standard of living (Ger, Belk, and Lascu 1993; Lascu, Manrai and Manrai 1993; Manrai, Lascu and Manrai 1993).

Poland, on the other hand, has experienced substantial growth and development even under Communism. Polish Communism encouraged a substantial amount of privatization. Moreover, Poland was not isolated from its Western neighbors; the accessibility of information in Poland was higher than in most Eastern European countries. Poland, unlike its neighbors, had an independent Catholic press, as well as numerous uncensored underground newspapers (Goszczynska, Tyszka and Slovic 1991). With regard to its industrial heritage, Poland, as well as the Czech Republic, Slovakia, Hungary and Slovenia, are frequently contrasted with Romania and Bulgaria where industrial growth is slow, but still ahead of the Commonwealth of Independent States, thus advancing the idea of a three-speed Eastern Europe (Lynn 1993).

The two countries also differ in terms of their standard of living: Poland is ahead of Romania in terms of GNP and GDP (Table 2). And, with regard to trading partners, Poland conducts most of its business with EC countries, whereas Romania's key partners remain the former members of the Council of Mutual Economic Assistance, i.e., the former communist bloc. Moreover, in terms of consumption, Poland distances itself from Romania in terms of percentage of leisure expenditure–an indicator of economic development: as income increases, individual consumers are more likely to spend a higher percentage of their income on leisure activities (see Table 3).

While culturally and economically Poland and Romania differ greatly, the two countries share a number of demographic similarities. First, the median age in the two countries is very close, 33 in Poland and 32.70 in Romania (Walden 1993). The level of literacy rate in the two countries is similar: in Poland, 98 percent continue to general secondary schools, and in Romania the literacy rate is a close equivalent of 98 percent (Walden 1993). In terms of income, however, the discrepancy is high: Poles average 2.9 million zloty ($180) per month (*Gazeta Wyborcza* 1993), while Romanians only earn 70,000 lei ($87) per month (Humphrey 1993).

The similarities in demographics and political-economic experience under Communism may erroneously lead marketers to assume that individual values are similar for the two countries. While this, on the surface, might be the case, it can only provide a superficial understanding of the market segments in these countries. A more useful approach to segmentation, targeting and positioning can be achieved if managers understand how personal and social factors differentially affect values in the two countries. This study argues that the relationship between demographics and values differs in the two countries, and suggests that companies use different marketing strategies in each country.

It has been mentioned earlier that individual values are derived from

TABLE 2. Country Profiles for Poland and Romania[1]

| | Poland | Romania |
|---|---|---|
| Population (Millions) | 38.3 | 23.5 |
| Urban | 62% | 52.7% |
| Ethnic Groups | Polish 99% | Romanian 89%<br>Hungarian 7.9%<br>Germans 1.6% |
| Religion | Catholic 95% | Eastern Orthodox 80%<br>Catholic 6% |
| Form of Government | Democratic Union | Parliamentary Republic |
| GDP Per Capita (in dollars) | 1,678 | 1,618 |
| GNP Per Capita (in dollars) | 1,800 | 1,618 |
| Imports Per Capita (in dollars) | 408 | 392 |
| Exports Per Capita (in dollars) | 392 | 253 |
| Per Capita Consumer Expenditure (in dollars) | 1,472 | 1,176 |
| Imports from/Exports to<br>Germany<br>EC<br>EFTA<br>CMEA | <br>26.5% / 18.3%<br>45.0% / 35.7%<br>10.1% / 8.7%<br>27.9% / 37.1% | <br>11.4% / 11.0%<br>19.6% / 31.4%<br>4.0% / 3.6%<br>35.9% / 34.7% |

[1] Source: *Euromonitor*, 1993

and modified through personal, social and cultural learning and subsequently used in formulating attitudes and guiding behavior (Clawson and Vinson 1978). It was also mentioned that Romanians are highly nationalistic, as well as a more collectivist society (Naor 1990)–and both traits were encouraged strongly by the communist regime, as well as by the current regime. Coupled with the strong influence of traditional rural life (Naor 1990), these characteristics have increased Romania's isolation and differentiation from its other Eastern European neighbors. As a result of this isolation, then, Romanians' value system is more likely to be influenced by society than by the individuals' life experiences.

On the other hand, Poland has tolerated the free flow of Western influence during the Communist regime, through media and tourism (Goszczynska, Tyszka and Slovic 1991), and has freely embraced an immediate transition to a market economy by welcoming foreign intervention after

TABLE 3. Consumer Expenditure by Product Category (in percentages)[2]

| | Food | Alcoholic Drinks | Tobacco | Clothing | Footwear | Housing | Household Fuels | Household Goods & Services | Health | Transport | Leisure | Others |
|---|---|---|---|---|---|---|---|---|---|---|---|---|
| Poland | 43.2 | 1.9 | 1.6 | 8.3 | 2.4 | 5.2 | 5.5 | 3.4 | 4.3 | 1.7 | 11.0 | 15.6 |
| Romania | 34.1 | 7.0 | 2.3 | 7.9 | 2.1 | 2.6 | 0.9 | 2.8 | 3.2 | 3.7 | 6.4 | 24.7 |

[2] Source: *Euromonitor* 1993.

the fall of Communism (Kolodko and Rutkowski 1991), becoming one of the most developed countries in Eastern Europe (Lynn 1993). These developments may have led to a situation where the Polish value system is more likely to be influenced by individuals' personal experiences–i.e., exposure to Western media, tourism, urbanization as a consequence of the country's rapid industrialization–rather than by social pressure.

At this stage, it should be mentioned that the collectivism-individualism dimensions should be interpreted as a continuum, in the sense prescribed by Hofstede (1980). Modern cultures, especially those of Western, highly developed, and more affluent countries tend to be more individualistic and exchange universalistic resources, such as money, information and products; traditional cultures, typically those of Eastern, less developed and less affluent countries tend to be more collectivistic and exchange particularistic resources such as love, status, and service (Foa and Foa 1974; Triandis et al. 1988). However, cultures (the Japanese culture, for instance) may exhibit both modern and traditional value systems and behaviors at the same time (Triandis et al. 1988). In the present study, the Polish and Romanian cultures, characterized by both individualism and collectivism, are assessed on these dimensions in comparison to each other, rather than in an absolute sense.

The differences in the emphasis that are given in Poland and Romania to individualism versus collectivism will lead to certain differences in the values held by the two peoples. In Western societies, where individualism is an important societal value, age has been shown to be significantly related to instrumental and terminal values. Chusmir, Koberg and Mills (1989) have shown that older individuals ranked terminal values such as national and family security and self-respect higher than younger respondents. Older respondents also ranked instrumental values such as cheerful, loving and imaginative higher than younger respondents (Chusmir, Koberg and Mills 1989). Similar findings are expected for Polish consumers who are more independent and less tied to tradition and nationalism than Romanian consumers, and for whom age is likely to further cement their values and belief systems. Consequently, with increase in age, Polish consumers are thought to give a higher importance to both terminal and instrumental values. For Romanian consumers, on the other hand, values are less likely to be related to age–their values mirror those of their community, rather than life experiences accumulated with age.

$H_{1A}$  Age will be positively correlated with instrumental values for Polish consumers, whereas, for Romanian consumers, age and instrumental values will not be correlated.

$H_{1B}$  Age will be positively correlated with terminal values for Polish consumers, whereas, for Romanian consumers, age and terminal values will not be correlated.

Education in both Poland and Romania is no longer linked to success and higher income under the new system. While, in the past, an advanced education guaranteed one's belonging to the intellectual class, and thus a higher standing in society, presently, some of the most successful entrepreneurs are former black market dealers, salespeople (Lascu, Manrai and Manrai 1993), and other talented service providers, such as hair dressers and technicians–who all held a lower status in the past. This status reversal, if anything, may lead individuals with a higher education but more limited means to express skepticism regarding societal values and have an overall cynical outlook. Thus, it is expected that, in Poland, more educated consumers are less likely to give a high importance to terminal values, since their achievement dreams, previously guaranteed by education, have collapsed with the fall of the Communist system. Also, the means for accomplishing these dreams–i.e., instrumental values–are less likely to be held as important during the new era when defining success is no longer within individuals' control.

On the other hand, Romanians' instrumental and terminal values are again not thought to be affected by their level of education, since their values are linked to those of their society.

$H_{2A}$  Education will be negatively correlated with instrumental values for Polish consumers, whereas, for Romanian consumers, education and instrumental values will not be correlated.

$H_{2B}$  Education will be negatively correlated with terminal values for Polish consumers, whereas, for Romanian consumers, education and terminal values will not be correlated.

Income demonstrates success and achievement in both societies. In the case of Polish consumers, those with higher incomes are likely to rate highly in importance both achievement goals–i.e., terminal values–and the path to reaching those goals–i.e., instrumental values. Polish consumers who have attained financial success have done so by being ambitious and capable, by taking risks, that is, by giving importance to the means of attaining success because they hold as important the end states of these accomplishments: a comfortable and exciting life, a sense of accomplishment, social recognition, financial security, etc.

Again, for Romanians, influenced more by collectivism and traditionalism, there is a diminished likelihood that income would significantly affect the importance they would give to instrumental and terminal values, which are collectively determined in this traditional society.

H$_{3A}$ Income will be positively correlated with instrumental values for Polish consumers, whereas, for Romanian consumers, income and instrumental values will not be correlated.

H$_{3B}$ Income will be positively correlated with terminal values for Polish consumers, whereas, for Romanian consumers, income and terminal values will not be correlated.

## METHOD

### Sample and Sites

The sample for this research study comprised of 123 Romanian subjects and 117 Polish subjects. The Romanian data were collected first and the Polish sample was subsequently matched in terms of demographics (gender and occupation, i.e., blue-collar versus white-collar) as closely as possible. Table 4 details the break-up of demographics for the Romanian and Polish samples. As can be seen, the income distribution for Romanian and Polish samples are different. This is expected and is consistent with the differences in the level of average income in two countries and its distribution. These samples are fairly representative of the urban population in Romania and Poland.

The data in Romania were collected in the capital city of Bucharest, population 2 million, by randomly contacting the passersby (residents and visitors) in two large apartment complex buildings with more than 500 apartments each. The data in Poland were collected in Wroclaw, a city of 700,000 inhabitants in Western Poland and the Polish sample was matched with Romanian sample on gender and occupation, as mentioned earlier.

### Research Instrument and Operationalization of Variables

The research instrument comprised of a two page questionnaire with three types of questions. The first two types of questions were the instrumental values and terminal values scales (Rokeach 1968). Each of these scales comprised of 18 items as given in Table 1. The participants were asked to respond to each of the 18 items in the instrumental and terminal value scales by indicating the extent to which the 18 listed instrumental values guided their daily lives and the extent to which the 18 listed terminal values influenced their long-term life objectives. These responses were sought on a 5-point scale by asking subjects to indicate the importance of values with 5 being "very important," 4 being "important," 3 being "of average importance," 2 being "of below average importance," and 1 being "of no importance." The third type of questions included information on demographics such as gender, occupation, age, education and income.

TABLE 4. Demographics of the Romanian and Polish Samples

| Demographic Variable | Romania (%) | Poland (%) |
|---|---|---|
| Gender: | | |
| Females | 50.4% | 51.3% |
| Males | 49.6% | 48.7% |
| Occupation: | | |
| Blue Collar Workers | 35.8% | 33.3% |
| White Collar Clerical | 8.1% | 8.5% |
| White Collar Professionals | 56.1% | 58.1% |
| Age: | | |
| ≤ 25 years | 8.9% | 12.3% |
| 26-35 years | 30.7% | 34.9% |
| 36-45 years | 28.1% | 40.7% |
| ≥ 46 years | 28.9% | 15.5% |
| Education: | | |
| Elementary School | 7.3% | 2.6% |
| High School | 18.7% | 7.7% |
| Some College | 31.7% | 41.0% |
| Completed College | 26.0% | 40.2% |
| Professional College | 15.4% | 7.7% |
| Post Graduate | 0.8% | 0.9% |
| Annual Income: | | |
| $ ≤ 499 | 5.7% | 3.9% |
| $ 500-999 | 21.1% | 2.6% |
| $ 1000-1499 | 30.9% | 7.9% |
| $ 1500-1999 | 30.1% | 10.5% |
| $ 2000-2999 | 11.4% | 26.3% |
| $ ≥ 3000 | 0.8% | 48.2% |

## Procedure and Response Rate

The data in both Romania and Poland were collected by two trained interviewers in each case. The Romanian interviewers approached the passersby near the stairwells of the apartment complex buildings, explained to them that the researchers were interested in measuring beliefs and attitudes of consumers and requested their participation. As many as 250 individuals in Romania were approached to get 123 subjects to agree for participation. The response rate was thus 49.2% for the Romanian sample. The Polish data were collected with a more focused target population in terms of gender and occupation. For Polish sample, 170 individuals were required to be approached to get 117 subjects to agree for participation thus giving a response rate of 68.8%. After the subjects agreed to participate in the study, the interviewers explained the questions in detail and recorded their responses to items in instrumental and terminal value scales as also the demographics.

## RESULTS

Subjects' responses to the 18 items of instrumental values scale were summed up to arrive at an overall instrumental value score. The Cronbach α reliability of the instrumental value scale was 0.91. Similarly, responses to the 18 items of terminal values scale were summed up to arrive at an overall terminal value score. The Cronbach α reliability of the terminal value scale was .87. The mean instrumental values scores for Romanian and Polish samples were 74.40 and 74.42 respectively. The mean terminal values score for Romanian and Polish samples were 74.43 and 77.01 respectively.

Hypothesis $H_1A$ through $H_3B$ predicted the nature of correlation between age, education and income with instrumental and terminal values for the two samples. Education was dichotomized (low versus high) since the data collected was categorical and the correlation of age, education and income with instrumental and terminal values was computed. Education was dichotomized by combining "elementary school," "high school" and "some college" as low-education group and "completed college," professional college," and "post graduate school" as high-education group. Next, a Pearson correlation was computed between each of these three demographics (age, education and income) and the instrumental and terminal values for the samples. Table 5 provides correlations for the Romanian sample and Table 6 provides correlations for the Polish sample.

Hypothesis $H_1A$ predicted that age will be positively correlated with instrumental values for Polish consumers whereas for Romanian consumers, age and instrumental values will not be correlated. As indicated in Table 6, the correlation between age and instrumental values for Polish consumers was 0.14, significant at $p = .07$ as predicted. Correlation between age and instrumental values for Romanian consumers (Table 5) was .04, not significant as predicted. Thus hypothesis $H_1A$ was supported.

Hypothesis $H_1B$ predicted that age will be positively correlated with terminal values for Polish consumers, whereas, for Romanian consumers, age and terminal values will not be correlated. As indicated in Table 6, the correlation between age and terminal values for Polish consumers was .10 and approached marginal significance ($p = .14$). The correlation between

TABLE 5. Pearson Correlations Between Demographics and Values for the Romanian Sample

|  | Age | Education | Income | Instrumental Values | Terminal Values |
|---|---|---|---|---|---|
| Age | 1.00 | −.04 | .16** | .04 | −.04 |
| Education | −.04 | 1.00 | .26* | .02 | .01 |
| Income | .16** | .26* | 1.00 | −.07 | −.03 |
| Instrumental Values | .04 | .02 | −.07 | 1.00 | .70* |
| Terminal Values | −.04 | .01 | −.03 | .70* | 1.00 |

TABLE 6. Pearson Correlations Between Demographics and Values for the Polish Sample

|  | Age | Education | Income | Instrumental Values | Terminal Values |
|---|---|---|---|---|---|
| Age | 1.00 | −.05 | .28* | .14*** | .10 |
| Education | −.05 | 1.00 | .11 | −.18** | −.15*** |
| Income | .28* | .11 | 1.00 | .13*** | .11 |
| Instrumental Values | .14*** | −.18** | .13*** | 1.00 | .69* |
| Terminal Values | .10 | −.15*** | .11 | .69* | 1.00 |

Notes.
*Significant at $p \leq .01$    **Significant at $p \leq .05$    ***Significant at $p \leq .10$

age and terminal values for Romanian consumers (Table 5) was −.04, not significant as predicted. Thus hypothesis $H_1B$ was partially supported.

Hypothesis $H_2A$ predicted that education will be negatively correlated with instrumental values for Polish consumers whereas for Romanian consumers, education and instrumental values will not be correlated. As indicated in Table 6, correlation between education and instrumental values for Polish consumers was −.18, significant at $p < .05$ as predicted. Correlation between education and instrumental values for Romanian consumers (Table 5) was .02, not significant as predicted. Thus hypothesis $H_2A$ was supported.

Hypothesis $H_2B$ predicted that education will be negatively correlated with terminal values whereas for Romanian consumers, education and terminal values will not be correlated. As indicated in Table 6, correlation between education and terminal values for Polish consumers was -.15, significant at p = .06 as predicted. Correlation between education and terminal values for Romanian consumers (Table 5) was .01, not significant as predicted. Thus hypothesis $H_2B$ was supported.

Hypothesis $H_3A$ predicted that income will be positively correlated with instrumental values for Polish consumers whereas Romanian consumers' income and instrumental values will not be correlated. As indicated (Table 6), correlation between income and instrumental values was 0.13, significant (p = .09), as predicted. Correlation between income and instrumental values for Romanian consumers (Table 5) was -0.7, not significant as predicted. Thus hypothesis $H_3A$ was supported.

Hypothesis $H_3B$ predicted that income will be positively correlated with terminal values for Polish consumers whereas for Romanian consumers income and terminal values will not be correlated. As indicated in Table 6, correlation between income and terminal values for Polish consumers was 0.11 and approached marginal significance (p = .13). Correlation between income and terminal values for Romanian consumers (Table 5) was -.03, not significant as predicted. Thus hypothesis $H_3B$ was partially supported.

## CONCLUSION AND MANAGERIAL IMPLICATIONS OF FINDINGS

Of the six hypotheses offered in the study, four were supported and two were partially supported-even for the partially supported hypotheses, the direction of results is as predicted. While, for Poland and Romania, instrumental and terminal values do not differ substantially, in order to better understand the differences in values of the segments, age, education, and income differences should be factored into the assessment of values. [The present study has also assessed the relationship between gender, another demographic variable, and, consistent with other studies-Beutell and Brenner (1986) and Powell, Posner and Schmidt (1984), among others,-no relationship was noted.] The assessment of values in conjunction with demographics was considered to be important, since values are derived from and modified through personal and social learning (Clawson and Vinson 1978), and are intrinsically related to the antecedents of such learning, i.e., demographics.

Some remarks are in order at this point on the evaluation of a number of other correlations noted in the study. A significant correlation was noted between age and income for both Romania and Poland–an expected result since, with age and increased expertise, earning potential increases. This is especially the case in Eastern Europe, where the opportunity for inherited wealth was minimal during Communism, which attempted to establish equality among the members of society.

A significant correlation was also noted between education and income for Romania but not for Poland. This may be explained by the fact that, in Romania, where entrepreneurship–which could ensure financial success in addition to or despite the level of one's education–has only been encouraged recently. A college education, however, guaranteed and continues to guarantee a higher income for the intellectual class in Romania. Such was the drive for a better education during the previous system in Romania that a large proportion of parents (intellectuals, workers or peasants) attempted to ensure that their children belonged to the intellectual class by hiring private tutors for their children in the key subject matters covered in school. In Poland, private entrepreneurs have surfaced and prospered long before the demise of the Communist system; as a result, Poles had the opportunity to improve their financial standing regardless of their level of education.

No correlation was noted between age and education for Poland or Romania. This is because our sample consisted of randomly selected adults and here, it is unusual for adults to attend school later in life–in fact, in both countries, the term "evening school" connotes lesser education despite similar instructional demands (this is becoming less the case as new universities are sprouting in these countries and as degrees of distinction are increasingly awarded to individuals later in life).

In conclusion, the study found age, education and income to play a significant role in the case of Poland but not in the case of Romania. These findings were consistent with the hypotheses that the values of Romanian consumers are shaped by their collectivist background, their historical isolation from their Western neighbors, and their strong influence of traditional rural life (Naor 1990), and derived to a lesser extent from personal factors such as demographics. On the other hand, Polish values, developed as a result of their interaction with Western neighbors and of the high accessibility of information relative to its Eastern European neighbors. As a result, age, education and income were significantly related to the learning processes they experienced due to this interaction.

These findings are important for companies planning to do business in these two countries. In the short term, marketing managers doing business in Romania and Poland should be cautioned against using a regiocentric approach: targeting segments of similar age, education, and income under the assumption that demographic characteristics of the respective groups have a similar relationships to individuals' instrumental and terminal values may result in failed marketing plans. For instance, television cigarette advertisements for Gauloises in Romania, stressing achievement–a middle-aged individual dressed in an expensive business suit driving in a Porsche with a blonde by his side and smoking this brand–was noted by the authors to elicit consistently negative comments regarding ostentatious display of wealth and the good life. In general, in Romania, individuals who are better off than their neighbors and friends attempt to downplay this fact. On the other hand, middle-aged Polish consumers appear to proudly display their new Western automobiles, attacking curbs at tremendous speeds in an attempt to attract attention. To summarize, then, demographic segmentation can be effectively used for identifying and targeting consumers with different value structures in Poland, while a similar attempt in Romania would be futile.

In the long term, as Romania advances industrially and further opens its doors to foreign investment, it is also likely to become more developed, such that the behavior patterns of consumer and channel members are going to increasingly approximate to those of other developed countries (Naor 1990). Then, the relationship between demographic characteristics and instrumental and terminal values in Romania is likely to become more similar to the equivalent relationship in Poland. Only at that point, a regiocentric strategy, where companies can afford to use marketing strategies that strive for economies of scale by developing a standardized product and utilizing standardized marketing appeals for regions that are culturally similar (Levitt 1983), would be justified.

## *FUTURE RESEARCH*

An area that warrants further scrutiny does not assume that rating highly in one type of value means a lower rating in another. This analysis of value is based on value *Quadrants*, i.e., instead of merely considering instrumental and terminal values, four groups are compared: (1) low ratings for both values, (2) high ratings for both values, (3) high rating of terminal values and low rating of instrumental values, and (4) high rating of instrumental values and low rating of terminal values.

Future research may also explore relationships between instrumental and terminal values and demographics for more countries and more consumers in the former Eastern Bloc. Of particular interest may be to explore peoples under domination–for instance Armenians under Azerbaijani rule,

Gypsies (the personae non-gratae of Eastern Europe) in the various countries which are anxious to dispatch them elsewhere. Marketers may find that these consumers differ vastly in their aspirations and ways of attaining these aspirations, consumption-related or otherwise.

Another demographic variable that merits further exploration is the urban versus rural differences in the instrumental and terminal values of the consumers in the two countries. It is expected that correlations would be lower for rural consumers, whose values are more likely to be dictated by tradition than for urban consumers. It would be interesting to note if any additional differences exist in this regard between rural and urban consumers in the two countries.

Compared to political, economic, and technological changes, the sociocultural environment evolves slowly: individuals who are raised with a system of values tend to carry those values with them throughout their lives. Radical transformations in the structure of society and its institutions, even in terms of the distribution of wealth, occur gradually even in the new democracies of Eastern Europe. Since these characteristics in fact determine consumer purchase decisions and competitive action, managers are well served to keep abreast of developments in the countries of Eastern Europe, and, at the same time, to familiarize themselves with the historical and cultural phenomena that have shaped the value system of these countries if they are planning to do business there. Understanding the relationship between the value system and consumer demographics and keeping current on such developments in the respective countries will enable marketing practitioners to:

a. better understand the socio-cultural environment in these countries and identify opportunities and threats that may differ from one Eastern European country to another;
b. segment the markets more effectively, and, consequently design products and marketing programs (market targeting and positioning) that are more successful in reaching specific groups of consumers;
c. overall, meet the needs of consumers in these countries better than competition.

## REFERENCES

Belk, R. and Pollay, R. (1985). Images of Ourselves: The Good Life in Twentieth Century Advertising, *Journal of Consumer Research,* 11, 887-897.

Beutell, N. and Brenner O. (1986). Sex Differences in Work Values, *Journal of Vocational Behavior,* 28, 29-41.

Bond, M. (1988). Finding Universal Dimensions of Individual Variation in Multi-Cultural Studies of Values: The Rokeach and Chinese Value Surveys, *Journal of Personality and Social Psychology,* 55, 1009-1015.

Bozinoff, L. and Cohen, R. (1982). The Effects of Personal Values and Usage Situations on Product Attribute Importance. In B. Walker et al. (eds.) *An Assessment of Marketing Thought and Practice*, Chicago: A.M.A., 25-29.

Braithwaite, V. and Law, H. (1985). Structure of Human Values: Testing the Adequacy of the Rokeach Value Survey, *Journal of Personality and Social Psychology*, 49, 250-263.

Chusmir, L., Koberg C. and Mills, J. (1989). Male-Female Differences in the Association of Managerial Style and Personal Values, *Journal of Social Psychology*, 129, 65-78.

Clawson, G. and Vinson, D. (1978). Human Values: A Historical and Interdisciplinary Analysis. In K. Hunt (ed.), *Advances in Consumer Research*, 5, 396-402.

*Country Reports* (1993), Walden Publishing, Ltd.

Elvin, J. (1990). Inside the Beltway, *The Washington Times*, February 5, p. A6.

*Euromonitor* (1993), European Data and Statistics, London.

Foa, V. and Foa, E. (1974), *Social Structures of the Mind*, Springfield, IL: Charles C. Thomas.

Fox, R. and Lears, T. (1983), *The Culture of Consumption: Critical Essays in American History 1880-1980*, New York, NY: Pantheon.

*Gazeta Wyborcza*, "GUS on Economy," 25, February 1, 21.

Ger, G., Russell B., and Lascu, D.-N. (1993). The Development of Consumer Desire in Marketizing and Developing Economies: The Cases of Romania and Turkey. In L. McAllister et al. (eds.) *Advances in Consumer Research*, 20.

Goszczynska, M., Tyszka, T., and Slovic, P. (1991). Risk Perception in Poland, *Journal of Behavioral Decision Making*, 4, 179-193.

Guttman, J. (1982). A Means-End Chain Model Based on Consumer Categorization Processes, *Journal of Marketing*, 46, 60-72.

Helgeson, J., Kluge E., Mager, J. and Taylor C. (1984). Trends in the Consumer Behavior Literature: A Content Analysis, *Journal of Consumer Research*, 10, 449-454.

Henry, W. (1976). Cultural Values Do Correlate with Consumer Behavior, *Journal of Marketing*, 13, 121-127.

Hofstede, G. (1980) *Culture's Consequences: International Differences in Work-Related Values*, Beverly Hills, CA: Sage.

Humphrey, P. (1993). Romania Gives Rail Strikers Three Hour Ultimatum, *The Reuter European Business Report*, BC Cycle, August 17.

Kahle, L., Beatty, S. and Homer, P. (1986). Alternative Measurement Approaches to Consumer Values: The List of Values (LOV) and Values and Life Styles (VALS), *Journal of Consumer Research*, 13, 405-409.

Kolodko, G. and Rutkowski, M. (1991). The Problem of Transition from a Socialist to a Free Market Economy: The Case of Poland, *Journal of Social, Political and Economic Studies*, 16, 159-179.

Kotler, P. (1994) *Marketing Management*, Englewood Cliffs, NJ: Prentice Hall.

Lascu, D.-N., Manrai, L. and Manrai, A. (1993). Status Concern and Product Consumption: A Cross-Cultural Study of Romanian and American Consumers, in *Proceedings of the European Marketing Academy Conference*.

Lessig, P. (1975). A Measurement of Dependencies Between Values and Other Levels of Consumer's Belief Space, *Journal of Business Research*, 3, 227-240.
Levitt, T. (1983). The Globalization of Markets, *Harvard Business Review*, 92-102.
Levy, S. (1985). Lawful Roles of Facets in Social Theories. In D. Canter (Ed.) *The Facet Approach to Social Research*, New York, NY: Springer-Verlag, 59-96.
Lynn, J. (1993) *The Reuter European Business Report*, BC Cycle, August 3.
Mason, J., Durand, R. and Taylor J. (1983). Retail Patronage: A Causal Analysis of Antecedent Factors. In W. Darden et al. (Eds.), *Patronage Behavior and Retail Management*, New York, NY: North Holland Elsevier.
McCarty, J. and Hattwick, P. (1992). Cultural Value Orientations: A Comparison of Magazine Advertisements from the United States and Mexico. In *Advances in Consumer Research*, 19, 34-38.
McCracken, G. (1986). Culture and Consumption: New Approaches to the Symbolic Character of Consumer Goods and Activities, *Journal of Consumer Research*, 13, 71-84.
Munson, M. and McQuarrie, F. (1988). Shortening the Rokeach Value Survey for Use in Consumer Research. In M. Houston (Ed.), *Advances in Consumer Research*, 15, 381-386.
Naor, J. (1990). Romania: Opportunities and Challenges. In V. Kirpalani (Ed.), *International Business Handbook*, New York, NY: The Haworth Press, Inc.
_____ (1986). Towards a Socialist Marketing Concept, *Journal of Marketing*, 50, pp. 28-39.
Pollay, R. (1986). The Distorted Mirror: Reflections on the Unintended Consequences of Advertising, *Journal of Marketing*, 50, 18-36.
Powell, G., Pozner, B. and Schmidt, W. (1984). Sex Effects on Managerial Value Systems, *Human Relations*, 37, 909-921.
Reynolds, T. and Craddock, A. (1988). An Application of the MECCAS Model to the Development and Assessment of Advertising Strategy, *Journal of Advertising Research*, 28, 43-54.
_____ and Gutman, J. (1988). Laddering Theory, Method, Analysis, and Interpretation, *Journal of Advertising Research*, 28, 11-31.
Richins, M., and Dawson, S. (1992). A Consumer Values Orientation for Materialism and Its Measurement, *Journal of Consumer Research*, 19, 303-316.
Rokeach, M. (1973) *The Nature of Human Values*, New York, NY: Free Press.
Schwartz, S., and Bilsky, W. (1987). Toward a Theory of the Universal Content and Structure of Values: Extensions and Cross-Cultural Replications, *Journal of Personality and Social Psychology*, 58, 878-891.
Scott, J., and Lamont, L. (1974). Relating Consumer Values to Consumer Behavior: A Model and Method for Investigation. In T. Greer (ed.), *Increasing Marketing Productivity and Conceptual and Methodological Foundations of Marketing*, Chicago, IL: A. M. A., 283-288.
Spielvogel, C. (1989). Global Consumer Segmentation Crosses National Lines, *Financier*, 37-40.
Triandis, H., Bontempo, R., Villareal, M., Asai, M., and Lucca N. (1988). Individ-

ualism vs. Collectivism: Cross-Cultural Perspectives on Self-Group Relationships, *Journal of Personality and Social Psychology*, 54, 323-338.

Tse, D., Wong, J. and Tan, C. (1988). Towards Some Standardized Cross-Cultural Consumption Values. In M. Houston (Ed.), *Advances in Consumer Research*, 15, 387-395.

Valencia, H. (1989). Hispanic Values and Subcultural Research, *Journal of the Academy of Marketing Science*, 17, 23-28.

Vinson, D., Scott, J. and Lamont, L. (1977). The Role of Personal Values in Marketing and Consumer Behavior, *Journal of Marketing*, 41, 44-50.

# Measuring Values
# in International Settings:
# Are Respondents Thinking "Real" Life
# or "Ideal" Life?

Suzanne C. Grunert
Thomas E. Muller

**SUMMARY.** Few studies have assessed how respondents, themselves, understand and evaluate the value measurement task in both national and cross-national surveys of personal values. This study, conducted in Canada and Denmark, aimed at a better understanding of respondents' reactions to value items. Alternate approaches to measuring people's value priorities were tested. This was achieved by explicitly distinguishing between respondents' day-to-day ("real") life and their "ideal" life. The predictive power of both value types was tested with the concept of product involvement. Results from both countries reveal some significant differences between "real" and "ideal" life values. Both were related to product involvement. The findings highlight the need for greater attention to the measurement methodology for obtaining value data, especially in cross-national research. *[Article copies available from The Haworth Document Delivery Service: 1-800-342-9678.]*

---

Suzanne C. Grunert is Associate Professor at the Department of Marketing, Odense University, Campusvej 55, DK 5230 Odense M, Denmark. Thomas E. Muller is Professor and Head, School of Marketing and Management, Griffith University, Queensland 4217, Australia.

[Haworth co-indexing entry note]: "Measuring Values in International Settings: Are Respondents Thinking 'Real' Life or 'Ideal' Life?" Grunert, Suzanne C., and Thomas E. Muller. Co-published simultaneously in *Journal of International Consumer Marketing* (International Business Press, an imprint of The Haworth Press, Inc.) Vol. 8, No. 3/4, 1996, pp. 169-185; and: *Global Perspectives in Cross-Cultural and Cross-National Consumer Research* (ed: Lalita A. Manrai, and Ajay K. Manrai) International Business Press, an imprint of The Haworth Press, Inc., 1996, pp. 169-185. Single or multiple copies of this article are available from The Haworth Document Delivery Service [1-800-342-9678, 9:00 a.m - 5:00 p.m. (EST)].

© 1996 by The Haworth Press, Inc. All rights reserved.

## RATIONALE FOR THE STUDY

This article addresses the problem of measuring people's value orientations. In particular, our focus is on the improvement of value-measurement methodology. With the growing application of the value concept in international marketing strategy, especially in segmentation efforts, ever increasing numbers of marketers are keen to collect data on their target consumers' values and to apply this information to advertising, product design, and positioning decisions. Clearly, standardized and validated procedures and instruments for measuring consumer values would be immensely useful in international marketing, and make survey research findings and benchmarks much more comparable.

## BACKGROUND

In a consumer behavioral context, values have been studied extensively and cross-nationally for about two decades and found to be relevant for a number of consumption related behaviors–though often in an indirect way. Examples are product ownership (Chéron & Muller, 1993), environmental concerns (Grunert & Juhl, 1991), touristic preferences (Muller, 1991), gift-giving behavior (Grunert & Wagner, 1989), criteria used for brand choice (Pitts & Woodside, 1983), media usage (Becker & Conner, 1981), or choice of leisure activities (Jackson, 1974).

The concept of values has received much attention in cross-cultural research because values are assumed to be shared by people within a culture, and can therefore be used to characterize the psychological similarities within–and differences across–cultures. Studying cross-cultural similarities and differences in values allows one to analyze and explain cultural differences in specific behaviors among a nation's consumers. Values are commonly regarded as the link between the individual and society because values help one to know and comprehend the interpersonal world and guide the individual's adaptation to surrounding conditions. That is, values are cognitive representations of various human needs, tempered by societal demands. People typically internalize a system of personal values, within which individual values have been prioritized or assigned a relative importance. It is a person's hierarchy of values that determines what activities, interests, and material goods are worth identifying with, cherishing, protecting, acquiring, or consuming. Indirectly, value priorities drive consumption behavior in the marketplace.

This said, one of the main problems recognized by many researchers, but rarely dealt with in practice, is the question of whether and how values and their influence on behavior can be verbalized and thus made accessible for measurement. A general model of the measurement process is shown in Figure 1 (see Grunert, Grunert & Kristensen, 1994).

On the right side, are the people whose values are to be measured. They have a value system. On the left side, is the researcher who usually starts with some theoretical basis, some catalogue of values, or other a priori notion about values: a value hypothesis. In trying to operationalize this hypothesis, the researcher develops a set of value indicators. The respondents, on the other hand, express their value system through their behavior, which also includes their speech behavior, or language. The core of the measurement process is trying to match respondents' behavior and the researcher's value indicators.

A convenient definition of values outlines their five main features: values are (1) concepts or beliefs (2) about *desirable* end-states or behaviors (3) that transcend specific situations, (4) guide the selection or evaluation of behavior and events, and (5) are ordered by relative importance (Schwartz & Bilsky, 1987).

The term "desirable" in this definition is crucial for understanding our study's purpose. "Desirable" can signify something which actually guides one's day-to-day life, as well as something which one wishes to have, but cannot attain, given present circumstances. These two meanings of desirability necessitate a distinction between what we have chosen to call "real" life values and "ideal" life values. Our notion of two distinct desirabilities and our terminology is similar to the distinction, in sociopsychological research, between self-image and self-concept. These latter terms have been applied to consumer behavior research problems as well

FIGURE 1. A General Model of Value Measurement

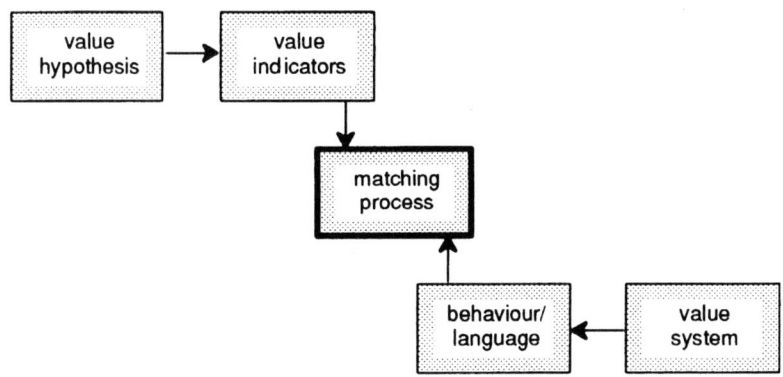

(cf. Dolich, 1969; Grubb & Grathwohl, 1967; Landon, 1974; Schenk & Holman, 1980; Sirgy & Danes, 1981).

"Real" life values reflect the current situation of an individual, i.e., the extent to which an individual actually achieves value fulfillment, given his or her daily life situation. By contrast, "ideal" life values are those which one would like to attain if no restraints at all were imposed on value fulfillment. The distinction between real and ideal values does not necessarily mean that a person would pursue one system of values in the current, "real" life–with its myriad demands, roles, and expectations–and a different set in an "ideal," unconstrained, unfettered life. What this conceptual disparity does suggest is that a person might attach different degrees of importance or priority to the same set of values under "real" life conditions, than would be the case under "ideal" life circumstances.

However, this remains an open empirical question. How are consumers prioritizing their values when asked to do so by value researchers? Are they thinking "ideal" life or are they thinking "real" life, i.e., subject to the realities and demands of everyday life?

Hence, this distinction between "real" and "ideal" values presents a methodological problem for any consumer researcher using the concept of values. Most of the published studies on consumer values used paper-and-pencil tests where respondents were asked to rank and/or rate the importance of a set of personal or social values. Two of the most commonly researched value inventories are the Rokeach Value Survey RVS (Rokeach, 1973) and the List of Values LOV (Beatty et al., 1985; Kahle, 1983). The value items on these inventories are, themselves, well grounded in theory. However, the tricky issue of how *survey respondents* understand and evaluate the value rating or ranking task has not been properly resolved.

For example, it is not known what thoughts or ideas respondents *associate* with the value prioritization task presented to them in a typical value survey. To our knowledge, only three exploratory studies have touched upon this value measurement problem–and, then, only tangentially. In Beatty and Talpade's study (1989), for each of the nine value items on LOV inventory, respondents were asked to describe the values in their own words, using either a word or a phrase. They found that five of the nine value were given a consistent synonym. However, several of the value items also showed a conceptual similarity that was difficult to differentiate. Similar results were obtained when Grunert (1990) asked West German respondents to write down the first three associations coming to their mind when hearing each value. When Grunert and Askegaard (in press) replicated the latter study with Danish respondents, each value on the LOV list had a multitude of connotations in respondents' minds. These findings, though tentative, signal that obtaining unambiguous value priority data from consumer surveys is a tricky task, given the abstract nature of human values.

Another way to frame this problem is to ask: In what *context* are respondents saying that one value has priority over another? The definitional issue raised earlier and the notion of values under "ideal" life conditions versus current life realities has not been empirically investigated. Do respondents in value surveys treat the value prioritization task as if they were completely free to pursue value attainment; or do they do the value rankings with their current life situation in mind, recognizing the many limitations to value fulfillment within day-to-day roles and demands? If the mode in which a consumer does the value ranking or rating task produces different value priorities, then our current value measurement procedures and instruments are flawed (cf. Muller, 1989, p. 62). In this study, we thus investigated whether respondents distinguish between values in "real" versus "ideal" life and whether these concepts could be made understandable.

If the notion of "ideal" and "real" life values is a genuine underlying concept, then one might also ask how the concept affects, or covaries with, value-driven attitudes and behaviors. A case in point: Does the distinction between "real" life and "ideal" life values imply that a different set of product ownership priorities (or product involvement) will result, depending upon which type of value is being visualized by the consumer and measured in the survey? A similar, though slightly different stance at this issue would be to follow McCrackens (1988, pp. 104-117) argument that consumer goods are used to cultivate what is otherwise beyond human being's grasp. Goods can help to recover this "displaced cultural meaning" by bridging the gap between one's reality and one's ideals. Hence, it may be assumed that the stronger this felt gap is, the more involved one is in products.

Hence, another goal of the present study was to test whether values measured under "real" life circumstances versus imagined "ideal" life conditions would produce different "versions" of product involvement–as detected by correlations between the two measures of value priorities and product involvement. For convenience, we chose the involvement construct to tap the relationship between attitude (or behavioral tendency) and the type of value construct measured–"real" life vs. "ideal" life.

Involvement has been a much-studied variable in consumer research. Zaichkowsky (1985) defines it as "A person's perceived relevance of the object based on inherent needs, values, and interests" (p. 342). If we specify involvement as product involvement, it signifies the relevance of a product to a consumer. Since Zaichkowsky's definition includes the aspect of values, it would be logical to hypothesize that consumers' values are predictors of product involvement. It then remains to determine whether product involvement correlates differently with measures of "ideal" life values than it does with measures of "real" life values.

Finally, if the notion of two separate value constructs (values measured with an "ideal" life in mind vs. values measured with "real" life limitations perceived by the respondent) is valid, then it should be detected in any culture, and would not be a culture-specific phenomenon. If this is the case, then the internationalization of value measurement can benefit from a refinement in the value measurement methodology. To test the value dichotomy in an international context, we carried out the same study in Canada and in Denmark and compared the findings in two ways: Did the distribution of value priorities change in both countries when respondents switched from a "real" life orientation to an "ideal" life mental set? Does the relationship between value priorities and product involvement (a by-product of value orientation) change in both countries, depending on how the values were measured ("real" life vs. "ideal" life)?

## STUDY DESIGN

Our study was designed to sort out the methodological issue of how the value prioritization task is construed in the consumer's mind and to determine whether the two views of personal values represent two different concepts that require separate measurement. Our goal was to better understand respondents' reactions to value measuring instruments.

The design represents a test of different questionnaire instructions for the rating of personal values and establishing a value hierarchy. This differentiation was achieved by explicitly distinguishing between respondents' "real" (day-to-day) life and their (imagined) "ideal" life. In order to assess the predictive power of both value types, the concept of product involvement was also employed. The study was performed first in Canada, then replicated in Denmark.

### The Questionnaire

Both Danish and Canadian questionnaires consisted of three main parts: value measures (nine items on the List of Values; Kahle, 1983), product involvement measures, and demographics. The original questionnaire used in Canada was in English. It was translated by a Danish native, with the values wording being based on previous uses of the List of Values (e.g., Grunert, 1990). This initial Danish translation was then translated back into English and both versions were compared for common meaning by two other bilinguals, who made the necessary changes.

The section on values was subdivided into two parts: a "real" life scenario, and an "ideal" life scenario. In both parts, respondents first chose their single most important value from the list, then rated each of the nine values on a 10-point importance scale. The interviewer read out the following instructions:

*"Real" life values.* "Here is a list of things that a person may strive for or want in their day-to-day life [SHOW RESPONDENT CARD AND READ OUT THE NINE VALUES]. Which *two* of these values do *you* feel you are striving for in your day-to-day life? [RECORD BOTH] And, of these two, which *one* is more important to you? [RECORD]. Since [READ MOST IMPORTANT VALUE] is most important to you, let's give it a score of 10. Now, let's rate the remaining items on a scale of 1 to 10, where "1" is not at all important and "10" is very important. How would you rate ... [SCORE REMAINING EIGHT VALUES, TOP TO BOTTOM]."

*"Ideal" life values.* "Now let's look at these same nine items from a different angle. Imagine an *ideal* life for yourself. In other words, a life where you were free to do and achieve anything you wanted; where you didn't need to worry about day-to-day concerns. Which *two* of these values are most important to you? [RECORD BOTH] And, of these two, which *one* is more important ... etc." (as before).

In the Canadian questionnaire, product involvement was measured by asking respondents to rate 26 widely different products on a 10-point scale, in terms of how interesting, important, or appealing each was to the individual. For the Danish survey, nine of these 26 products were selected on the grounds that a number of the products used in the Canadian study were culture-specific and were not commonly known to Danish consumers. Respondents had to rate the products on the same 10 point-scale, but separately for the three aspects "interesting," "important," and "appealing."

## The Canadian Sample

Data were collected in March, 1992, in Southern Ontario (English Canada) by sampling from five medium-sized cities: Hamilton, Burlington, Oakville, Mississauga, and Oshawa. Multi-stage cluster sampling was used to contact 351 female and male heads of households, and 183 valid questionnaires were obtained through in-home interviews (response rate: 52%). The sample's gender and age split: 55% female, 45% male; 18-24 (13%), 25-34 (26%), 35-44 (19%), 45-54 (19%), 55-65 (14%), 65+ (9%).

## The Danish Sample

Data were collected in September, 1992, in the city of Odense, Denmark's third largest city, and medium-sized by Danish standards. Using a combination of simple-random sampling and cluster sampling, 220 female and male respondents were contacted and 155 valid questionnaires were obtained through in-home interviews (response rate: 70%). The sample's gender and age split: 59.5% women, 40.5% men; 17-24 (35%), 25-34 (32%), 35-44 (9%), 45-54 (12%), 55- 65 (7%), 65+ (2%).

## RESULTS

The Canadian data are treated separately from the Danish data in the analyses which follow. Nonetheless, after looking at the findings in each country, cross-national comparisons are made at a conceptual level to establish the genuine differences between "real" life and "ideal" life value priorities, and their respective relationships to the concept of product involvement.

### "Real" versus "Ideal" Values

Table 1 shows what percentage of the respondents chose each of the nine values as being the single most important one in their lives. The data are broken down by "real" life and "ideal" life for Denmark and Canada.

The numbers reveal clear differences between "real" and "ideal" life values for both Danes and Canadians. Moreover, the direction of change in popularity of a value–as one moves from "real" conditions to "ideal" circumstances–is similar in both cultural groups. The exception is the value *being highly regarded and admired* which is less often chosen by Canadians as most important in the "ideal" life condition and more often

TABLE 1. Percentage of Canadian and Danish Respondents Choosing Each Value as Most Important Under "Real" Life and "Ideal" Life Scenarios

|  | Canada | | Denmark | | |
| --- | --- | --- | --- | --- | --- |
|  | "real" life | "ideal" life | "real" life | "ideal" life | |
| Security | 16.4 | 6.0 | 29.0 | 20.0 | Tryghed |
| Self-respect | 18.6 | 14.8 | 15.5 | 13.8 | Selvrespekt |
| Fun and enjoyment in life | 15.3 | 19.7 | 14.8 | 19.3 | Sjov og glæde i livet |
| Sense of accomplishment | 17.0 | 13.1 | 12.3 | 9.0 | Følelsen af at have udrettet noget |
| Self-fulfillment | 11.5 | 17.5 | 9.7 | 10.3 | Selvrealisering |
| An exciting life | 1.1 | 3.3 | 7.7 | 15.2 | Et spændende liv |
| Being highly regarded & admired | 3.3 | 2.2 | 4.5 | 6.2 | At blive respekteret af andre |
| Warm relationships with others | 12.6 | 21.9 | 3.9 | 4.1 | Nære relationer til andre |
| Sense of belonging | 4.4 | 2.2 | 2.6 | 2.1 | Følelsen af at høre til |

by Danes. This difference may be related to the slightly different wording in the two questionnaires: the Danish translation read *being well respected by others*.

The two values expressing hedonism (*fun and enjoyment in life* and *an exciting life*) and *self-fulfillment*, which is a value expressing an ego-orientation with a tendency towards hedonism, are chosen much more often as the most important value in the "ideal" life condition than in the "real" life condition. Those social values that signify a certain dependency on other persons' goodwill (*security* and *a sense of belonging*) are chosen less often in the "ideal" life condition. By contrast, *warm relationships with others*, which is both social and hedonistic oriented, was more popular in the "ideal" life condition. Finally, *self respect* and *sense of accomplishment*, which are individual values influenced by surrounding social conditions, are chosen less often in the "ideal" life condition than in the "real" life condition.

Values chosen more often in the "ideal" life condition than in the "real" life condition indicate a deficit in one's day-to-day life with regard to value fulfillment. We call these values "deficit values." Conversely, values chosen more often in the "real" life condition than in the "ideal" life condition can be thought of as "surplus values," i.e., their fulfillment is achieved to even a higher degree than one may feel necessary. Thus, it can be concluded from Table 1 that deficit values seem to reflect a longing for the brighter side of life, while surplus values indicate day-to-day constraints and realities.

This overall pattern of change in value priorities as one switches from a "real" life orientation to an "ideal" life mind-set is confirmed when examining the means of value importance ratings on 10-point scales (Figures 2 and 3). In the Canadian study, the only significant reversal is for *being highly regarded and admired*. This value receives a significantly higher mean rating in the "ideal" life condition, whereas it was less frequently chosen as a top-most "ideal" life value when the respondent's task was to choose one from among nine values.

Two noteworthy and interesting changes in importance of values can be seen in Figure 2. Apparently, when Canadian consumers visualize an "ideal" life, there is a strong downward shift in the importance of *security* and a correspondingly strong upward shift in the priority of *an exciting life*. In an ideal life, Canadians do not see that they would want more security; in fact, they seem to be saying that security should not be an important value in an ideal life. And they are more inclined to espouse excitement in such a life.

In the Danish study (Figure 3), seven of the nine values are rated significantly more important in the "ideal" life condition. Surprisingly, the mean importance of *security* increases among Danes in an ideal life. It is not clear why Danes would see themselves as espousing security even more in ideal circumstances, but this finding does point to a cultural difference in how security and an ideal life are viewed. Further research is needed to explore why *security* is a deficit value among Danes and a surplus value among Canadians.

The somewhat different results obtained with the two methods of measuring values (pick your top-most value vs. rate each value on an importance scale) are probably artifacts of the measurement or scaling problem. In forcing a respondent to choose one top-most value, we ignore one or more other values which may be very close in importance to the chosen one, since these other values do not appear in the comparative results. In the rating task, the value stimuli can be differentiated to a more subtle degree and all values figure in the comparative results.

## *Values and Product Involvement*

In order to assess how the priority (importance) given to a specific value (in "real" and "ideal" life situations) is related to level of product involvement, correlation matrices were generated so that the underlying interrelationships could be explored with the application of two-tailed significance tests. This analysis was possible because importance and involvement were both measured on interval scales. Assumptions about the direction of relationships (positive vs. negative correlations) were not made prior to testing, since these analyses were exploratory.

In the Danish study, twelve of the correlation coefficients were significant at $p < .01$ (two-tailed), as shown in Table 2. All were positive but weak. Neither the "real" nor the "ideal" versions of *fun and enjoyment, a sense of belonging, an exciting life,* and *being well respected* was related to product involvement. Out of the nine products assessed for relationships between value importance and product involvement, only long distance call and wrist watch seem to be important. In other words, values and product involvement were weakly related concepts in Danes' minds–at least for the few products that were tested.

Product selection-wise, the Canadian study was more extensive. The intercorrelations showed slightly stronger associations between product involvement and "real" and "ideal" life values, respectively. Correlations significant at the 1-percent level (two-tailed) are displayed in Table 3. All coefficients are positive.

In the "ideal" life condition, the values *self-respect* and *a sense of accomplishment* show no relationship to product involvement. In the

FIGURE 2. Canadian Study: Mean Value Importance Ratings When Measured Under "Real" Life and "Ideal" Life Scenarios

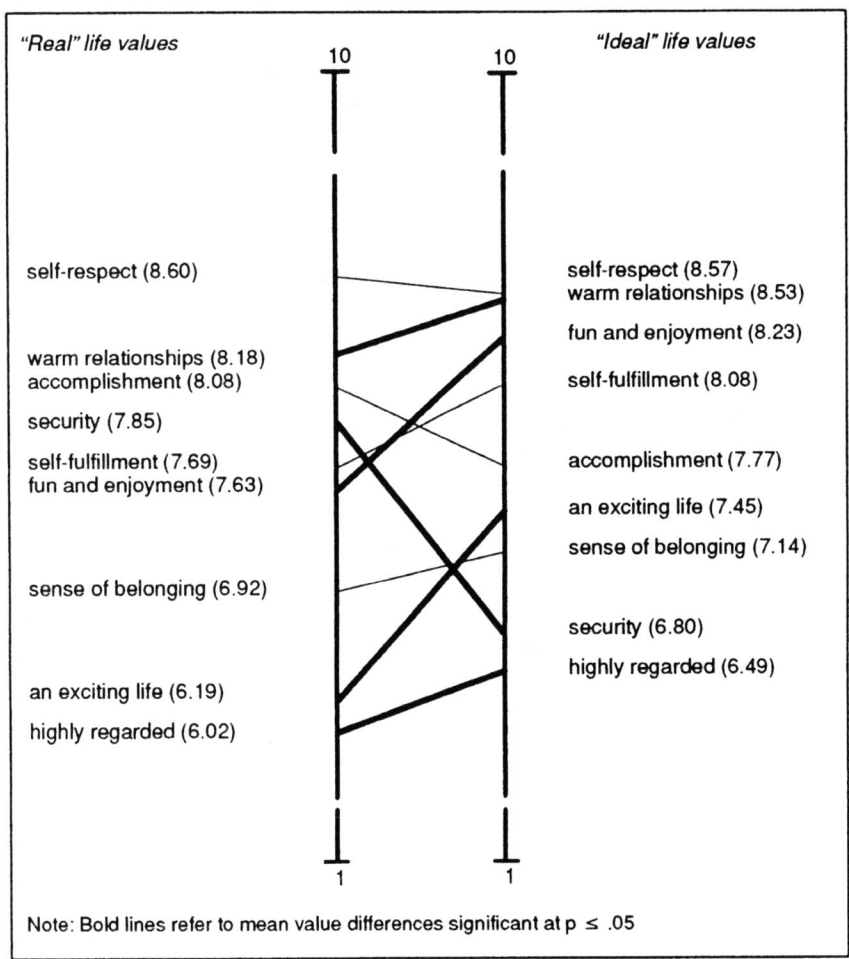

Note: Bold lines refer to mean value differences significant at $p \leq .05$

"real" life condition, neither *self-fulfillment, warm relationships with others,* nor *a sense of belonging* is significantly related to any of the 26 product involvement scores. This latter finding contradicts research that showed these values to be related to consumption decisions (Beatty et al., 1985; Muller, 1991; Muller, Kahle & Chéron, 1992). The disturbing implication is that our findings, when values are measured under "real" life conditions, are rebutting relationships reported when the distinction be-

FIGURE 3. Danish Study: Mean Value Importance Ratings When Measured Under "Real" Life and "Ideal" Life Scenarios

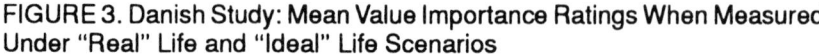

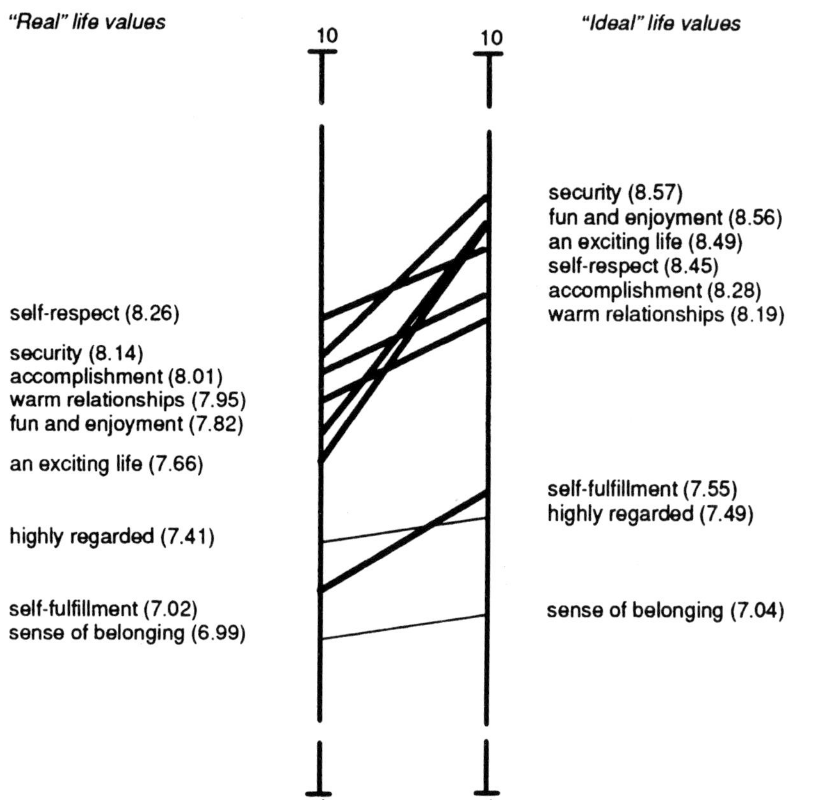


Note: Bold lines refer to mean value differences significant at $p \leq .05$

tween "ideal" and "real" values was ignored in earlier value surveys. Our finding tentatively suggests that researchers may have varying measurement problems when personal values are being tapped in consumer surveys and, thus, the conclusions they draw may be erroneous or misleading. In short, researchers cannot be sure how consumers are visualizing the value measurement task unless they explicitly construct the setting for the respondent.

There are obvious differences in the magnitudes of some correlation

TABLE 2. Danish Study: Significant Correlations Between Level of Product Involvement and Value Importance in "Real" Life and "Ideal" Life Scenarios

| Value | Product | "Real" life | "Ideal" life |
|---|---|---|---|
| Security | life insurance | .262 | - |
|  | long distance call | .250 | - |
|  | haircut | .241 | - |
| Self-respect | haircut | - | .235 |
| Fun and enjoyment in life | - | | |
| Sense of accomplishment | long distance call | - | .234 |
|  | greeting card | - | .230 |
|  | wrist watch | - | .226 |
| Self-fulfillment | wrist watch | .244 | .256 |
|  | Hawaii trip | .225 | - |
| An exciting life | - | | |
| Being well respected | - | | |
| Warm relationships with others | long distance call | .290 | .265 |
| Sense of belonging | - | | |

coefficients when one compares value importance under "ideal" life and under "real" life instructions to respondents. Examples: the priority given to *an exciting life* in "real" life correlates .401 with involvement with a fitness-club membership. The corresponding correlation under "ideal" life drops to .319 for the same product. *Fun and enjoyment* in "real" life correlates .270 with involvement with a luxury yacht; but the correlation is .347 when consumers think about this value in an "ideal" life context. *Being highly regarded and admired* as a "real" life value correlates .336 with involvement with a cellular car phone. The corresponding correlation with this product when consumers think of this value in an "ideal" life context is .212.

These discrepancies indicate that the value measurement method is critical to achieving reliability in inferences made about the *consequences* of values, e.g., product involvement, attitude, intention to buy, brand preference, or lifestyle orientation. These results underscore the fact that the existence of a value dichotomy in peoples' minds requires a more precise and valid measurement tool for capturing a segment's value orientations, especially if marketing strategies will be based on such value data.

## *DISCUSSION AND CONCLUSION*

What are the implications of our study's findings? The results indicate that the value measurement issue is a critical one. The inferred conse-

TABLE 3. Canadian Study: Significant Correlations Between Level of Product Involvement and Value Importance in "Real" Life and "Ideal" Life Scenarios

| Value | Product | "Real" life | "Ideal" life |
|---|---|---|---|
| Security | life insurance | .330 | - |
| | greeting card | - | .223 |
| | bottle of shampoo | - | .210 |
| | video movie | - | .202 |
| Self-respect | long distance call | .192 | - |
| | watercolour painting | .192 | - |
| Fun and enjoyment in life | Hawaii trip | .405 | .398 |
| | sports car | .302 | .361 |
| | luxury yacht | .270 | .347 |
| | swimming pool | .261 | .334 |
| | fitness club membership | - | .267 |
| | mountain bike | - | .239 |
| | fashion magazine | - | .231 |
| | cellular car phone | - | .229 |
| | private box seats | - | .207 |
| Sense of accomplishment | sports car | .242 | - |
| | dry cleaning | .159 | - |
| Self-fulfillment | fashion magazine | - | .218 |
| An exciting life | fitness club membership | .401 | .319 |
| | luxury yacht | .362 | .253 |
| | sports car | .298 | .270 |
| | Hawaii trip | .279 | .289 |
| | swimming pool | .266 | .207 |
| | cellular car phone | .262 | .225 |
| | fashion magazine | .242 | .291 |
| | mountain bike | .219 | .222 |
| | private box seats | - | .222 |
| Being highly regarded & admired | cellular car phone | .336 | .212 |
| | luxury yacht | .265 | - |
| | fitness club membership | .239 | .251 |
| | dry cleaning | .209 | .284 |
| | fashion magazine | - | .318 |
| | record or cd | - | .192 |
| | private box seats | - | .188 |
| Warm relationships with others | greeting card | - | .217 |
| | bottle of shampoo | - | .192 |
| Sense of belonging | haircut | - | .233 |

quences of value priorities on product preferences, involvement, attitudes, or behaviors in the marketplace will depend on how the value measuring approach is defined for consumers and how consumers are interpreting the task placed before them.

One of the objectives of this study was to discover whether respondents do distinguish in their minds between "real" and "ideal" life situations when rating value importance or expressing their value priorities. The answer is yes. In making this distinction, consumers reveal differing value priorities and value choices when required to express their value structures. Yet, the dichotomy of "real" versus "ideal" life values has never been addressed in consumer research which included measures of people's value priorities.

A disturbing thought is that our measurement of values under "real" and "ideal" life conditions has picked up significant differences in value hierarchy. Up to now, this was not an issue when value importance was measured through the standard approach of asking people to choose or rate values, without first explaining to them in what context they were making their priorities known. Moreover, when value priorities are measured in two different ways ("ideal" vs. "real"), the consequences of those value measurements show up differently when some criterion variable (e.g., product involvement) is measured at the same time. We found that the correlations between value priorities and one consequence of values–product involvement–depend on which type of value was captured in the measurement task. Thus, the connection between values and some predicted behavior will depend on how the value measures were obtained.

Our finding tentatively signals that the measurement problem in value surveys can lead to faulty conclusions by marketing managers who wish to apply value data to marketing decisions such as product design, segmentation, and the refinement of marketing communications. And we believe that our finding is just the tip of a methodological iceberg. The general issue of values and value measurement is a complex one and does not lend itself easily to scaled responses. We urge value researchers to continue to pursue this avenue of inquiry and to explore the definitional and contextual issues of value measurement.

Also, the studies done in Canada and Denmark foster the view that this measurement issue is not a culturally isolated problem. From an international research methodology standpoint, it is clear that instructions have to be given carefully in order to avoid different connotations and resulting differences in the interpretation of value priority data. This is especially true if conclusions will be drawn from comparative studies on values in the international setting. We recommend that a distinction be made between "ideal" life and "real" life when survey respondents are asked to reveal their value orientations.

A refinement to our exploratory study would be to use a monadic research design where one group of respondents expresses its value priorities under a "real" life scenario, and a second group is given the "ideal" life scenario. Moreover, the findings indicate some interesting aspects with regard to "surplus" and "deficit" values which suggest further exploration in studies of the "real" life-"ideal" life value dichotomy. Finally, further research is needed to investigate the relationship between "real" and "ideal" life value measures and other aspects of consumption behavior that are driven by value priorities.

## REFERENCES

Beatty, S. E., Kahle, L. R., Homer, P., & Misra, S. (1985). Alternative measurement approaches to consumer values: The List of Values and the Rokeach Value Survey. *Psychology and Marketing*, 2(Fall), 181-200.

Beatty, S. E., & Talpade, S. (1989). Value appeals in advertising. In: J. Childers, R. Bagozzi, & J.P. Peters (Eds.): *Marketing theory and practice,* Proceedings of the 1989 AMA Winter educators' Conference. Chicago, IL: AMA.

Becker, B. W., & Conner, P. E. (1981). Personal values and the heavy users of mass media. *Journal of Advertising Research*, 21, 37-41.

Chéron, E. J., & Muller, T. E. (1993). Relative importance of values as determinants of ownership patterns: Comparisons between the Canadian provinces of Ontario and Quebec. *Journal of International Consumer Marketing*, 5, 3, 37-53.

Dolich, I. J. (1969). Congruence relationships between self images and product brands. *Journal of Marketing Research*, 6, 80-84.

Grubb, E. L., & Grathwohl, H. L. (1967). Consumer self-concept, symbolism and market behavior: A theoretical approach. *Journal of Marketing*, 31, 22-27.

Grunert, S. C. (1990). Personal values of consumers: A cross-cultural comparison of underlying dimensions. Paper presented at the 22nd International Congress of Applied Psychology, Kyoto/Japan, 22.-27.07.1990.

Grunert, S. C., & Askegaard, S. (in press) "Seeing with the mind's eye": An exploratory study of the use of pictorial stimuli in value research. In: L. E. Kahle & L. Chiagouris (Eds.), *Values, lifestyles and psychographics*. Hillsdale, NJ: Lawrence Erlbaum.

Grunert, S. C., Grunert, K. G., & Kristensen, K. (1994). Une méthode d'estimation de la validité interculturelle des instruments de mesure: le cas de la mesure des valeurs des consommateurs par la liste des valeurs LOV. *Recherches et Applications en Marketing*, 8(4), 5-28.

Grunert, S. C., & Juhl, H. J. (1991). Values, environmental attitudes, and buying behavior of organic foods: Their relationships in a sample of Danish teachers. Working paper, Series H, No. 60. Århus: The Århus School of Business, Department of Information Science.

Grunert, S. C., & Wagner, E. (1989). Beziehungen zwischen Werthaltungen, Einstellungen, Schenken und Freizeit: Generationen- und Geschlechtsunterschiede im kulturellen Vergleich. Working paper. Stuttgart: Universität Hohenheim.

Jackson, R. G. (1974). A preliminary bicultural study of value orientations and leisure attitudes. *Journal of Leisure Research*, 5, 10-22.

Kahle, L. R. (Ed.). (1983). *Social values and social change: Adaptation to life in America.* New York: Praeger.

Landon, E. (1974). Self concept, ideal self concept, and consumer purchase intentions. *Journal of Consumer Research,* 1, 44-51.

McCracken, G. (1988). *Culture and consumption.* Bloomington, IN: Indiana University Press.

Muller, T. E. (1989). The Two Nations of Canada vs. The Nine Nations of North America: A cross-cultural analysis of consumers' personal values. *Journal of International Consumer Marketing,* 1, 4, 57-79.

Muller, T. E. (1991). Using personal values to define segments in an international tourism market. *International Marketing Review,* 8, 1, 57-70.

Muller, T. E., Kahle, L. R., & Chéron, E.J. (1992). Value trends and demand forecasts for Canada's aging Baby Boomers. *Canadian Journal of Administrative Sciences,* 9(4), 294-304.

Pitts, R. E., & Woodside, A. G. (1983). Personal value influences on consumer product class and brand preferences. *Journal of Social Psychology,* 119, 37-53.

Rokeach, M. J. (1973). *The nature of human values.* New York: Free Press.

Schenk, C. T., & Holman, R. H. (1980). A sociological approach to brand choice: The concept of situational self image. In: J.C. Olson (Ed.), *Advances in consumer research,* Vol. 7, pp. 610-614. Ann Arbor, MI: ACR.

Sirgy, M., & Danes, J.E. (1981). Self-image/product-image congruence models: Testing selected models. In: A. Mitchell (ed.), *Advances in consumer research,* Vol. 9, pp. 556-561. Ann Arbor, MI: ACR.

Schwartz, S. H., & Bilsky, W. (1987). Toward a universal psychological structure of human values. *Journal of Personality and Social Psychology,* 53, 550-562.

Zaichkowsky, J. L. (1985). Measuring the involvement construct. *Journal of Consumer Research,* 12, 341-352.

# The Search for Universal Symbols: The Case of Right and Left

Judy Cohen

**SUMMARY.** Symbols are potentially powerful communication devices in advertising, but many symbols are culture-specific. Advertisers whose targets are culturally diverse can benefit greatly by identifying symbols which are universal to mankind. One symbol which seems to transcend cultural boundaries is "right" versus "left." The preference for right over left has been evident cross-culturally and throughout history. This paper gives a cross-cultural overview of the symbolic meanings of right and left and then discusses possible reasons for the universality of the right-left phenomenon. With this background, several propositions are offered regarding the effect of right-left positioning in advertisements. Finally, suggestions for future research are given. *[Article copies available from The Haworth Document Delivery Service: 1-800-342-9678.]*

## INTRODUCTION

The issue of whether international advertising campaigns should be standardized has been debated for over 25 years. Some (including Elinder,

---

Judy Cohen is Associate Professor in the Marketing Department, Rider University, Lawrenceville, NJ 08648-3099. E-mail: JCohen@Rider. The author is left-handed, and proud of it.

The author would like to thank the anonymous reviewers and John Richardson for their helpful comments on this manuscript.

[Haworth co-indexing entry note]: "The Search for Universal Symbols: The Case of Right and Left." Cohen, Judy. Co-published simultaneously in *Journal of International Consumer Marketing* (International Business Press, an imprint of The Haworth Press, Inc.) Vol. 8, No. 3/4, 1996, pp. 187-210; and: *Global Perspectives in Cross-Cultural and Cross-National Consumer Research* (ed: Lalita A. Manrai, and Ajay K. Manrai) International Business Press, an imprint of The Haworth Press, Inc., 1996, pp. 187-210. Single or multiple copies of this article are available from The Haworth Document Delivery Service [1-800-342-9678, 9:00 a.m - 5:00 p.m. (EST)].

© 1996 by The Haworth Press, Inc. All rights reserved.

1965; Fatt, 1967; Levitt, 1983) have argued that international advertising strategies can be standardized globally. However, others (including Green, Cunningham, and Cunningham, 1975; Dunn, 1976; Ryans and Fry, 1976) argue that marketplace conditions, including cultural differences, preclude the successful use of standardized campaigns.

In his seminal work, Killough (1978) distinguished between standardization of the buying proposal (i.e., *what* is said in the advertisement) and standardization of the creative presentation (i.e., *how* that message is communicated). Both Killough and a more recent study by James and Hill (1991) found that buying proposals could be transferred internationally about half of the time; creative presentations could be transferred only about one third of the time. One reason why creative presentations are not readily transferable is because they often use symbols to communicate. Kanso (1992) found that managers who used a nonstandardized approach to international advertising agreed quite strongly with the statement "due to differences in traditions and customs, an advertiser must use symbols that are recognizable and meaningful to each market" (Kanso, 1992, p. 12). Because many symbols are culture-specific, the use of symbols in advertising can cause miscommunications. For example, the color purple symbolizes death in Latin America; black symbolizes death in Europe-America, and white symbolizes death in Asia (Ricks, 1983).

While standardization of advertising offers the benefits of cost savings and efficiency, these benefits are clearly outweighed by the results of miscommunications when inappropriate symbols are used. Advertisers whose targets are culturally diverse can benefit greatly by identifying symbols which are universal to mankind. Such symbols were suggested by Jung (1959) to be archetypes of the collective unconscious, i.e., ". . . universal images that have existed since the remotest times" (p. 288). One such archetype appears to be "right" versus "left." The preference for right over left has been evident cross-culturally and throughout history.

In order to increase our understanding of how left-right symbolism may impact upon international marketing communications, this paper gives a cross-cultural overview of the symbolic meanings of right and left and then discusses possible reasons for the universality of the right-left phenomenon. With this background, several propositions are offered regarding the effect of right-left positioning in advertisements. Finally, suggestions for future research are given.

## SYMBOLIC MEANINGS OF RIGHT AND LEFT

To gain understanding of the meaning of any word or concept, language can offer helpful clues. For example, in French, "gauche" means both "left" and "clumsy." In Spanish, "azurdas," meaning "go the wrong way," comes from the word "zurdo," for left. In Romany, "bongo" ("left") also means "crooked or evil" (Barsley, 1967).

In English, meanings of the phrase "left-handed" include "clumsy; awkward, insincere, dubious" (*Webster's New World Dictionary*, 1966); in addition to "awkward, dubious, insincere," *The American Heritage Dictionary of the English Language*, 1981 offers meanings such as "maladroit; obliquely derisive." The thesaurus in Microsoft Word (Soft-Art, Inc., 1984-90) includes the following meanings for "right": "just," "suitable," "correct," "sane," "rightful," and "rectitude." Synonyms for "right" include "fair," "equitable," "legitimate," "upright," "honest," "good," and "lawful." Interestingly, this thesaurus contains no negative connotations among meanings or synonyms for "left." However, the first meaning of "left" is given as "opposite to right." The meanings opposite to those given for "right" are certainly not positive ones. Roget's Thesaurus (1961) is more straightforward. Synonyms for "left" include "sinister." For left-handed, the Microsoft Word thesaurus includes "awkward, gawky, inept, bumbling, gauche, maladroit"; synonyms in Roget's Thesaurus include "awkward, backhanded, heavy-handed, clumsiness."

## GENERAL ASSOCIATIONS WITH "LEFT" AND "RIGHT"

The meanings associated with the left are not limited to denotative meaning. Other associations are abundant. Table 1 gives a variety of sources of information on left-right symbolism (described in Tables 2 and 3) and gives the methodological approaches used to analyze left-right symbolism. Table 2 gives a summary (by no means exhaustive) of general associations with "left" and "right," as perceived by a variety of populations. As Table 2 shows, negative associations for left, and the complementary positive connotations for right, are found among Europeans, Middle Easterners, Africans, Asians, Native Americans, and contemporary Americans.

On the most general level, "left" is associated with "bad" and "right" is associated with "good." Other associations can be placed into three categories. These categories form a continuum, from mundane existence to the supernatural. The first category deals with quality of life issues. These include (for left and right respectively): crime-righteousness; sickness-health; negative life principle-positive life principle; poverty-abundance; weak-strong; unclean/impure-clean/pure; passive-active; incorrect-correct; inferior-superior; low-high; bad luck-good luck; and bad omen-good omen.

The second category deals with issues of dark and light. In addition to the dark-light association itself, it also includes night-day and black-white

TABLE 1. Approaches for Studying Right/Left Symbolism

| Author (date) | Population | Approach |
|---|---|---|
| Barsley (1967) | various | primary and secondary sources |
| Burton (1982) | Atuot | ethnographic research |
| Chelhod (1973) | Arabs | text and linguistic analyses |
| Clark (1980) | W. Europe, middle ages | text analyses and secondary sources |
| Corballis and Beale (1976) | Gnostics (2nd Century) | secondary sources |
| | W. Europe (dream symbols) | secondary sources (Freud) |
| Coren (1992) | various | secondary sources |
| Domhoff (1973) | U.S. undergraduates | survey research |
| Du Boulay (1982) | Ambeli, Greece | ethnographic research |
| Evans-Pritchard (1953) | Nuer (Africa) | ethnographic research |
| Faron (1973) | Mapuche (Chile) | ethnographic research |
| Granet (1973) | Chinese | secondary sources |
| Hertz (1973) | Indo-European | linguistic analyses |
| | Native Americans | secondary sources |
| | Maori | secondary (ethnographic) sources |
| Holy (1983) | Berti (Muslim tribe in Sudan) | ethnographic research |
| Hori (1984) | Japanese undergraduates | survey research |
| Kruyt (1973) | Celebes | survey research |
| Littlejohn (1973) | Temne (Sri Lanka) | ethnographic research |
| Lloyd (1973) | ancient Greeks | primary and secondary sources |
| Miller (1982) | Native American | ethnographic and secondary sources |
| Mittwoch (1985) | ancient Greeks | primary sources (Pythagoras) |
| Needham (1973) | Nyoro (Africa) | secondary sources |
| TenHouten and Kaplan (1973) | W. Europe | primary sources (on Tarot cards) |
| | Chinese | primary sources (on yin-yang) |
| Wieschhoff (1973) | African | secondary sources |

and moon-sun. These associations are differentiated from quality of life issues because, although they are situations experienced in everyday life, they begin to address the boundary between the earthly and supernatural. Before the age of electricity, darkness was associated with the mystical and supernatural. The third category of left-right associations is concerned more specifically with the supernatural. This includes profane-sacred, earth-sky and death-life, hell-paradise; evil spirits-ancestral (good) spirits; earthly powers-heavenly powers and sorcerer-shaman.

Other associations with "left" and "right" include "female" and "male," respectively. An enlightened person might claim that, in this case, left-right positioning is not associated with any connotations of negative or positive, i.e., there are no negative associations with "female." However, the history of attitudes towards women, as well as the other associations with "left," would offer support for the notion that this positioning was not random; "female" is in fact in the inferior position.

TABLE 2. Associations with Left and Right

| LEFT | RIGHT | POPULATION | SOURCE |
|---|---|---|---|
| bad | good | U.S. undergraduates | Domhoff (1973) |
| | | Berti (Muslim tribe in Sudan) | Holy (1983) |
| | | Indo-European | Hertz (1973) |
| | | African | Wieschhoff (1973) |
| | | Mapuche (Chile) | Faron (1973) |
| | | Nyoro (Africa) | Needham (1973) |
| | | Gnostics (2nd century) | Corballis (1976) |
| | | Arabs | Chelhod (1973) |
| | | African | Wieschhoff (1973) |
| | | Nuer (Africa) | Evans-Pritchard (1953) |
| crime | righteousness | W. Europe | Corballis & Beale (1976) |
| sickness | health | Mapuche (Chile) | Faron (1973) |
| | | Nyoro (Africa) | Needham (1973) |
| negative life principle | positive life principle | W. Europe | TenHouten and Kaplan (1973) |
| poverty | abundance | Mapuche (Chile) | Faron (1973) |
| | | Nyoro (Africa) | Needham (1973) |
| weak | strong | U.S. undergraduates | Domhoff (1973) |
| | | Chinese | TenHouten and Kaplan (1973) |
| | | Nuer (Africa) | Evans-Pritchard (1953) |
| | | Atuot (Africa) | Burton (1982) |
| unclean, impure | clean, pure | U.S. undergraduates | Domhoff (1973) |
| | | Nyoro (Africa) | Needham (1973) |
| | | Celebes | Kruyt (1973) |
| | | Temne (Sri Lanka) | Littlejohn (1973) |
| passive | active | Chinese | TenHouten and Kaplan (1973) |
| incorrect | correct | U.S. undergraduates | Domhoff (1973) |
| | | western culture | Hertz (1973) |
| inferior | superior | African | Wieschhoff (1973) |
| low | high | U.S. undergraduates | Domhoff (1973) |
| bad luck | good luck | African | Wieschhoff (1973) |
| | | ancient Greeks | Lloyd (1973) |
| | | Arab | Chelhod (1973) |
| bad omen | good omen | Nyro (Africa) | Needham (1973) |
| | | African | Wieschhoff (1973) |
| | | ancient Greeks | Barsley (1967) |
| dark | light | U.S. undergraduates | Domhoff (1973) |
| | | Chinese | Barsley (1967) |
| night | day | U.S. undergraduates | Domhoff (1973) |
| | | Mapuche (Chile) | Faron (1973) |
| moon | sun | Japanese undergraduates | Hori (1984) |
| | | Atuot (Africa) | Burton (1982) |
| black | white | U.S. undergraduates | Domhoff (1973) |
| | | Nyoro (Africa) | Needham (1973) |
| profane | sacred | U.S. undergraduates | Domhoff (1973) |
| | | W. Europe (Tarot cards) | TenHouten and Kaplan (1973) |

## TABLE 2 (continued)

| LEFT | RIGHT | POPULATION | SOURCE |
|---|---|---|---|
| profane | sacred | Indo-European | Hertz (1973) |
| | | Maori | Hertz (1973) |
| | | Arabs | Chelhod (1973) |
| | | Celebes | Kruyt (1973) |
| | | Chinese | TenHouten and Kaplan (1973) |
| earth | sky | Chinese (yin yang) | Granet (1973) |
| death | life | U.S. undergraduates | Domhoff (1973) |
| | | Native Americans | Hertz (1909) |
| | | Chinese (yin yang) | Barsley (1967) |
| | | Mapuche (Chile) | Faron (1973) |
| | | Nyoro (Africa) | Needham (1973) |
| | | Celebes | Kruyt (1973) |
| | | Japanese undergraduates | Hori (1984) |
| | | Atuot (Africa) | Burton (1982) |
| hell | paradise | Maori | Hertz (1973) |
| | | Nyoro (Africa) | Needham (1973) |
| evil spirits | ancestral (good) spirits | Mapuche (Chile) | Faron (1973) |
| earthly powers | heavenly powers | Atuot (Africa) | Burton (1982) |
| sorcerer | Shaman | Mapuche (Chile) | Faron (1973) |
| | | Native American tribes in N. America | Miller (1982) |
| female | male | U.S. undergraduates | Domhoff (1973) |
| | | ancient Greeks - Pythagoras | Mittwoch (1985) |
| | | Western culture | Hertz (1973) |
| | | Native Americans | Hertz (1973) |
| | | African | Wieschhoff (1973) |
| | | Chinese (yin yang) | TenHouten and Kaplan (1973); Barsley (1967) |
| | | Nyoro (Africa) | Needham (1973) |
| | | Celebes | Kruyt (1973) |
| nature | culture | W. Europe (Tarot cards) | TenHouten and Kaplan (1973) |
| | | Native American tribes in N. America (bear - left handed - associated with nature) | Miller (1982) |
| | | Nyoro (Africa) | Needham (1973) |

In addition, "left" is associated with both "nature" and "art" and "right" is associated with "science" and "culture." In some cultures, these positioning may also have negative and positive connotations. In Northern European and United States cultures, stress is placed on the importance of being rational and scientific. However, other cultures place more emphasis on art. Similarly, in Judeo-Christian culture, since man (who is associated with culture) is supposed to have dominion over the earth (which is

TABLE 3. Beliefs and Behaviors that Instantiate General Left/Right Associations

| BELIEF OR BEHAVIOR | POPULATION | SOURCE |
|---|---|---|
| **BELIEFS** | | |
| right ear itching–someone speaking well of you; left ear itching–someone speaking poorly of you | W. Europe Caribbean | Brown (1979) Coren (1992) |
| right palm itching–will receive money; left palm itching–will lose money | Scotland Morocco Gypsies North American | Coren (1992) |
| positive influences enter through right side of body; negative influences through left | Maori | Coren (1992) |
| hand which the Devil uses | W. Europe | Coren (1992) |
| marks on left side of body considered to be made by the Devil; used to identify witches | W. Europe | Coren (1992) |
| road to Nirvana on right | Buddhism | Barsley (1967) |
| Judgment Day–those saved on Jesus' right; damned on his left | Christian | Matthew XXV (Barsley 1967) |
| penitent thief on Jesus' right; impenitent thief on his left | Christian | Barsley (1967) |
| Samael–Chief of Satans–same roots as "se'mol," meaning left | Jewish | Talmud (Barsley 1967) |
| good angel on right of person; bad angel on left of person | Jewish | Coren (1992) |
| Set, evil god, was "The Left Eye of the Sun"; Horus, god of life, was "The Right Eye of the Sun" | ancient Egypt | Coren (1992) |
| right hand sticking from ground shaking rattle gives shamanistic power; left hand means death. | Nootkins (Native American; North America) | Miller (1982) |
| Woman–created from Adam's left rib | Judeo-Christian | Barsley (1967) |

## TABLE 3 (continued)

| BELIEF OR BEHAVIOR | POPULATION | SOURCE |
|---|---|---|
| **BELIEFS** | | |
| right–male; left–female (cult of goddess Isis–priest holds image of a left hand) | ancient Egypt | Coren (1992) |
| "left-hand" Hindu sect worships Sakti, the female powers of deities | Hinduism | Coren (1992) |
| male embryos develop in left ovary; females in right | ancient Greece | Coren (1992) |
| right side–male principle; left side–female principle | Buddhism | Coren (1992) |
| **BEHAVIORS** | | |
| left hand–unclean, for personal hygiene; food eaten with right hand | Middle East N. Africa Chinese Nootkins (Native Americans) | Barsley (1967) Holy (1983) Granet (1973) Miller (1982) |
| sign of cross is made with right hand, even by left-handed persons | Christian | Coren (1992) |
| Whirling Dervishes–turn from left to right. Left hand pointed down; right hand pointed up. | Turkey | Barsley (1967) |
| Women summon djinn–evil spirit– by putting on veil with left hand and holding it up with left hand | Morocco | Barsley (1967) |
| swasitka–meant good luck or fortune–movement from left to right | Neolithic man, India, Egypt, Greece, Italy, Spain, America, Ireland, Brittany | Barsley (1967) |
| Buddhist prayer wheel–Wheel of Life–moves from left to right | Asia | Barsley (1967) |

associated with nature), one could argue that culture is superior to nature. However, other cultures (for example, some African groups) who have the same left-right associations do not believe in "man over nature" but rather in "man as part of nature." For these groups, there may be no positive or negative connotations with respect to left-nature/right-culture associations.

## INSTANTIATIONS OF LEFT-RIGHT ASSOCIATIONS

In addition to the left-right associations described above, a variety of different cultures also hold specific beliefs and engage in behaviors which instantiate the more general associations of left-right discussed above (Table 3). Beliefs are considered to be any notions which have not (and/or cannot) been substantiated, including legends regarding historical persons. Behaviors include activities which people engage in (e.g., in religious observance), and man-made symbols (e.g., the swastika). These beliefs and behaviors can also be placed into two of the categories described above, i.e., quality of life issues and the supernatural.

Some beliefs and behaviors follow directly from specific left-right associations. For example, as noted above, the right is generally associated with clean and pure; the left with unclean and impure. It should not be surprising to find that the right hand is used for eating, while the left hand is used for "unclean" bodily functions. Other instantiations reflect the more general left-bad/right-good dichotomy. In Western Europe, the left ear twitching meant someone was speaking ill of the person, while the same sensation in the right ear meant someone was speaking well of the person. In Christian iconography, the penitent thief was on Jesus' right; the impenitent thief was on his left. Another quality of life area symbol is the swastika, which moves from left to right. "Swastika" comes from the Sanskrit word "swasti," meaning well-being or good luck (*American Heritage Dictionary*, 1981). (Unfortunately, this ancient, cosmic symbol was given a profoundly negative new meaning by Nazi Germany.) Similarly, the Buddhist prayer wheel moves from left to right.

Most of the beliefs and behaviors associated with "left" deal with the supernatural. According to Christian beliefs, on Judgment Day, the damned will be on Jesus' left. Similarly, in Buddhism, the road to Nirvana is on the right. In Hebrew, "Smael," the Chief Satan, has the same three-letter root (s-m-l) as the word for "left." In Medieval Europe, it was believed that witches did everything inverted, e.g., were left-handed. In the Greek town of Ameli, a leftward funeral procession around the dead is believed to create a vampire. The behavior of throwing spilled salt over the left shoulder–in Satan's direction–to prevent bad luck has only recently lost favor. In some Native American cultures, a right hand sticking from the ground, shaking a rattle gives shamanistic powers; a left hand means death. Whirling Dervishes in Turkey turn from left to right, in their goal to achieve religious ecstasy. In Morocco, women are believed to summon evil spirits by holding up a veil with their left hand. In some cases, what is designated as "left" is subjective (e.g., the direction of a spinning wheel). What is important, however, is that, once a direction is defined as "left" or "right," the "left" has generally has negative associations, while the "right" has positive associations.

In addition to positive and negative beliefs and behaviors which are based on "right" and "left" is a belief which instantiates the association of "left" with "female." According to Judeo-Christian beliefs, woman was created from Adam's left rib.

## EXCEPTIONS TO THE LEFT-RIGHT DICHOTOMY

Of course, there are exceptions to these rules. For example, the early Romans associated "left" with good luck, until influenced by Greek methods of augury (Barsley, 1967). In Chinese culture, the "honorable side" is the left (Granet, 1973). For the Chinese, there are no absolutes. Rather, the Chinese believe that different forces alternate in nature, as do right and left. For example, when presenting gifts, the giver is to the left; the receiver is on the right.

In other cases, special consideration is given to the left, but these special considerations may not reflect a positive association. Among many Native American groups, bears (especially grizzlies) are considered healers (Miller, 1982). Bears are considered left-handed, to distinguish them from humans. However, bears are also considered unpredictable and dangerous, and reflect "the worst aspects of Nature" (Miller, 1982, p. 275). Among the Keres Pueblos, men are associated with left and women with right. However, this classification is not entirely at odds with the more common left-right dichotomy. Men are associated with left because they are killers, and therefore associated with death. Women are associated with right because they are associated with birth (Miller, 1982). Thus the death-life dichotomy still holds. Needham (1973) notes that in Nyoro symbolic classification, the moon is associated with right and the sun associated with left. However, for the Nyoro, the moon is considered beneficent, and the sun maleficent. Again, the good-right/bad-left dichotomy holds. Similarly, Burton (1982) argues that the Atuot saying that "God is left" does not mean that left is associated with good. Rather, it means that the left is associated with the unknowable. This includes death, which does not have a positive association.

We have seen that there are cases where the left seems to be on equal status to right, or actually higher status than the right. However, for some of these examples, the status of the left is not unequivocally positive. There are relatively few cases where the left is indisputably considered better than the right.

## ORIGINS OF RIGHT AND LEFT SYMBOLISM

We can better understand the constancy of right-left symbolism by examining its origins. Is right-left symbolism an artifact of culture, or is it physiologically based? In this section, we review a number of theories regarding the origins of right-left symbolism.

Attitudes towards the right as good and the left as bad no doubt developed due to the physiological fact that the majority of Homo Sapiens are right-handed. Therefore, two questions must be addressed: the origins of right-handedness, and the causes of left-handedness. We will consider those issues in this section, as well as the origins of other left-right associations.

Most animals tend to favor one paw, but they are split about equally on an aggregate level between right and left paws (Barsley, 1967; Brown, 1979). Hertz (1973) felt that if allowed to develop naturally, humans would also be about equally left-and right-handed, with perhaps a slight tendency towards right-handedness. The actual percentage of left-handers has been estimated at between one and 30 percent (Gardner, 1979). This percentage varies from culture to culture. In Japan, left-handed people comprise only two to three per cent of the population. Children are pressured to become right handed in order to write properly; characters can be written correctly only with the right hand (Katzenstein, 1989). In contrast, in the U.S., the percentage of left-handers has increased from 2 per cent in 1930 to 11 per cent in the 1970s (Brown, 1979). The fact that the number of left-handers tends to increase during "permissive" times supports Hertz' (1973) claim that it is nurture, not nature, which creates right-handedness. If this were completely true, however, we would expect different cultures to nurture different handedness. However, there is only one known culture which favors the left hand. The Taimyr natives of the Soviet Arctic are 75 per cent left-handed ("Southpaws of the North," 1990). Therefore, the question remains, why the right?

## ORIGINS OF RIGHT-HANDEDNESS

Origins of right-handedness in humans can be partially understood by the origins of same-handedness, i.e., the use of the same hand (either right or left) by all or almost all members of a society. One likely explanation for the development of same-handedness in humans concerns the creation of tools. When tools are not used, or used but not shared, handedness can be evenly split within a species. But when tools are shared, or made by one person for use by others, standardization is necessary (Corballis and Beale, 1976; Spennemann, 1985; TenHouten and Kaplan, 1973). Still, the question of why the right hand became the standard must be considered.

Many theories of varying levels of credibility have been proposed regarding the origins of right handedness. One explanation, developed in the nineteenth century, was that soldiers put their shields on their left side to protect their heart (since the heart is slightly to the left), leaving the right hand free for their swords. This theory has been discredited by Corballis and Beale (1979) and Spennemann (1985). They point out modern tribes which do not use shields (e.g., the Maori of New Zealand) are still right-handed. Corballis and Beale also note that women are not warriors, but are right-handed. An even less convincing theory is the "raising (sic) sun" theory (Spenneman, 1985). This theory, suggested by Von Meyer at a German anthropological society in 1873, suggested that early humans positioned themselves to the east, to face the rising sun. Thus, the right side of the body (facing south) was warmed by the rising sun, while the left side remained cold. As Spennemann notes, the problem with this theory is that one would expect people south of the equator to have their left sides (facing north) warmed by the sun, and thus be left-handed. This does not occur. Another theory, proposed by Jung, is that right-handedness is a part of human instinct, and a basic reflex (Jung, 1959). This theory does not explain how or why right-handedness became a basic reflex.

A more recent explanation deals with brain lateralization. The brain is split into two, seemingly symmetrical halves. Each half controls the activities of the opposite side of the body; hence, the right side is controlled by the left half of the brain. Each side also tends to specialize in certain skills. For the vast majority of humans, speech is located on the left side of the brain. Some feel that through the development of speech, man developed the left side of his brain more than the right; in turn, this led to use of the right hand as being the more able hand (TenHouten and Kaplan, 1973; Brown, 1979). In addition, the left side, being the verbal side, can "promote" itself more and downgrade the opposite side (Brown, 1979; Edwards, 1979).

Corballis and Beale (1979), however, support the idea that right-handedness *preceded* speech. As stated above, each side of the brain specialized in certain skills–but not in the sense of "a specific type of material" (Brown, 1979). Rather, the left side of the brain specializes in those activities which require sequential skills; the right side specializes in those activities requiring holistic skills. Tool use requires employment of sequential skills; thus it depends on the left side of the brain, which controls the right hand. Similarly, speech requires fine sequential motor skills. Perhaps man developed speech because his left brain, already developed through tool use, was capable of the necessary sequential motor skills.

Corballis and Beale also try to address the question of why sequential activities develop in the left side of the brain. At birth, both sides of the brain are capable of developing sequential skills. The side that starts to develop first is the side that develops sequential skills. Then other abilities are delegated to the other side. Ultimately the question must be asked–why does the left side develop first? Corballis and Beale (1979) reject genetic explanations, suggesting this positioning information is found in cytoplasm. They suggest that the universe has a bias towards the left. But were this true, we would expect all animals to be right-handed (Richardson, 1993). This is not the case. The possibility remains that the left side of the brain develops first in humans (with its sequential skills) precisely because humans are right handed! Further research is needed to truly understand where this positioning information is located and how it works.

We can summarize several theories which help shed light regarding positive associations with the right and negative associations with the left, bearing in mind that there is at present no definitive explanation. Favoring of the right and downgrading of the left developed as a result of the overwhelming human tendency towards right-handedness. Right-handedness resulted from the need for same-handedness. Same-handedness itself developed from tool use and thus a need for standardization. Right-handedness is correlated with the left hemisphere of the brain, which, as the side to begin development first, specializes in sequential functions such as tool use. Why the left side begins development first is open to speculation and research. In any case, the fact that the right hand is favored in all cultures (with one known exception) cannot be ignored.

## CAUSES OF LEFT-HANDEDNESS

Since right-handedness is the norm, we should further investigate whether left-handedness is downgraded simply because it is different, or whether there are in fact negative qualities associated with left-handedness. Contrary to Hertz's (1973) proposition that left-handedness would be almost as common as right-handedness if society allowed nature to take its course, Coren (1992) offers striking evidence to support his theory that left-handedness (as well as mixed-handedness) is a result of birth stress-related injuries to the brain (including stresses such as premature birth, prolonged labor, breathing difficulty, low birth weight, breech birth, RH incompatibility, instrument birth, Caesarian delivery, and multiple births). Furthermore, he points out that the same birth-related injuries or pathologies may cause other psychological and neurological problems. These problems are therefore likely to be associated with left-handedness. Thus left-handedness does not cause these problems, but can serve as a marker for the existence of such problems. Research does in fact show that groups with certain psychological and neurological problems have a higher incidence of left-handedness than the general population. These problems include: alcoholism, poor spatial and verbal ability, criminality, drug abuse, emotionality, juvenile delinquency, predisposition towards aggression, psychosis, schizophrenia, school failure, and slow physical development (Coren, 1992). Of course, not all left-handed people exhibit these traits. However, the higher incidence of left-handedness among people with such undesirable traits can strengthen the association of left with bad.

## ORIGINS OF OTHER LEFT-RIGHT ASSOCIATIONS

As Table 2 indicates, associations of right with male and left with female is common in both Eastern and Western cultures. There are several possible explanations for this. The male-female dichotomy may be related to the art-science dichotomy as well as the culture-nature dichotomy. Both of these dichotomies are traced to hemisphere lateralization of the brain. Each hemisphere controls the *opposite* side of the body. The right side (the left hemisphere) is associated with science; the left side (the right hemisphere) is associated with art. "Its ["right's"] beauties are those of geometry and taut implication. Reaching for knowledge with the right hand is science" (Bruner, 1965, p. 2). Science supposedly comes from the left hemisphere of the brain (and thus through the right hand) due to the need for logical sequential thinking (although scientists may first develop their theories holistically). The right hemisphere of the brain is important for artists. Dancers and musicians, for example, must perform holistically (a right brain activity). Edwards (1979) teaches students to draw by quieting the left side of their brain. Since women's activities have been directed more towards the arts rather than towards science, one would expect women to be associated with "left."

Culture is associated with the left hemisphere (and thus right-handedness) due to the relationship between the left hemisphere and tool use (as well as other cultural behaviors such as writing). The right hemisphere is therefore the realm of nature. Women are associated with nature due to childbirth, lactation and menstruation (Brain, 1982). Thus women are also associated with the right hemisphere, and the left hand. Women may also be associated with the right hemisphere because they are more likely to use both hemispheres when processing information, while males are more strongly lateralized (Meyers-Levy, 1989). Meyers-Levy found that when males were "primed" with a task that required right-hemisphere use, they performed relatively poorly on the categorization task which followed. When they were "primed" with a task that required left-hemisphere use, they performed relatively well on the subsequent task. Women, however performed equally well, regardless of which hemisphere was active on the priming task. For the tasks studied in this experiment, at least, men appeared to be more dependent on the left hemisphere for successful information processing.

While hemisphere lateralization appears to be a possible explanation for left-female, right-male associations, it has some drawbacks. Coren (1992) points out that women are actually more *right* side oriented on three of four measures of sidedness (right-footedness, right-earedness, and the all important right-handedness). The one area where women are more likely to be left-oriented than men is eyedness. (The definition for earedness and eyedness is which eye a person prefers to use, when they can use only one. For example, a person using a camera must choose one eye to use.) Thus, perhaps the best explanations for the relationship between women and left are based on nonscientific reasons. One such explanation for associating women with the left side is the concept that the right dominates the left just as males, in many traditional societies, have dominated women (Mittwoch, 1985).

## *CONCLUSIONS REGARDING ORIGINS OF RIGHT-LEFT SYMBOLISM*

It appears that, while right-left symbolism manifests itself through culture, it originates in physiology, rather than in culture itself. Therefore, this symbolism is extremely deep rooted. While culture is difficult to change, physiology is impossible to change. By recognizing the enduring nature of right-left symbolism, marketers can avoid making major blunders in their international communications.

## *PROPOSITIONS*

Although there is a deep physiological basis for right-left symbolism, its application to advertising may be subtle. In this section, propositions will be offered regarding the implications of right-left symbolism for international advertisers.

The apparently universal symbolic meanings of right and left may have important consequences for international advertisers, who can benefit by being able to standardize certain aspects of their creative presentations. While many of right-left associations are specific, the most general association is that good behaviors and states of being are associated with the right; bad behaviors and states of being are associated with the left. These meanings may affect consumer response to right-left positioning of products in advertisements. Advertisers must decide where to position visuals of "good" products (i.e., the advertised product) or good situations (e.g., the consequences of using a "good" product, or a pleasant situation which the advertiser wants associated with his product). The first proposition to be offered is:

> *Proposition 1:* For all cultures and subcultures, consumer response is more favorable to advertisements in which the good product or situation is placed to the right, and the bad product or situation is placed to the left, than when the positioning is reversed.

Several types of advertisements use placement of "good" versus "bad" products or situations. In comparative advertising, when the competitor's product is shown, the advertised product would be the "good" product and the competitor's product the "bad" product. A good versus bad situation would include the effects of using the advertised product versus the effects of not using the advertised product or of using the competitor's product. Advertisements showing visuals of before product use/after product use should also have a left-right orientation. One could argue that this orientation is due to the fact that most languages are written from left to right. However, this proposition should also be applicable to cultures and individuals who are nonliterate. Perhaps the most interesting test would involve literate people in cultures where language is written from right to left, as in Hebrew. As Table 3 notes, Jewish tradition does support the general left-bad/right-good dichotomy.

An extension of Proposition 1 regards positioning when a model is used in the advertisement. The proposition would be as follows:

> *Proposition 2:* When a model appears in the advertisement, consumer response is more favorable when the good product or situation is positioned to the *model's* right and the bad product or situation is positioned to the *model's* left, than when positioning is reversed.

In this situation, the good product or situation would be on the *viewers'* left and the bad product or situation would be on the *viewers'* right. However, several (miscellaneous) examples indicate that, in the United States at least, viewers may not use the model as the point of reference, and so may not make the switch in orientation. For example, in an article on gifts made over the years to the President of the United States, Groskinsky (1990) notes that a pair of appliquéd Western boots (given to Eisenhower) included an eagle holding the olive branch in its left hand (which is on the viewer's right); arrows are held in its right hand (on the viewer's left), rather than the correct reversed positioning.

A similar mistake was made by persons whose educational level was probably higher than the artist of the Western boots. A display of folk art at the National Museum of American Art in Washington, D. C. includes the sculpture *The Throne of the Third Heaven of the Nations' Millennium General Assembly*. Gould (1987) noted that the Old Testament figures were to the viewer's left, but to Jesus's right; the New Testament figures were to the viewer's right, but Jesus's left. This was the reverse of the traditional positioning. Gould found, upon an inquiry to the curator, that the mistake was not made by the artist, but was made by the museum staff.

On a more popular level, in the Walt Disney movie, "The Devil and Max Devlin," the picture on the cover of the videocassette shows the devil to the viewer's left, but talking in Max Devlin's right ear. Yet, we know from the widespread Western behavior of throwing salt over one's left shoulder that the devil is located over one's left shoulder.

It appears that in some cultures, the point of left-right orientation may have to be the viewer's rather than the models. Advertisers should be careful to pretest to identify which is most appropriate for each culture. In cultures where the left hand is considered the unclean hand, for example, viewers should have no problems orienting themselves towards the model's right and left.

More specific associations of right and left, discussed above, lead to other propositions. In many cultures, "left" is associated with female, while "right" is associated with male. We would therefore expect:

*Proposition 3:* Consumer responses are more favorable to advertisements in which the product meant for male use or the male model is positioned to the right, and the product meant for female use or the female model is positioned to the left, than when the positioning is reversed.

The positioning of products is not problematic. For example, an advertisement showing personal care products developed specifically for male and female use would be placed to the right and left, respectively. However, the positioning of male and female models is subject to the same issues as described in Proposition 2. When there is both a male and female model in the advertisement who are somehow interacting with each other (as opposed to two separate scenes, as in a before-after advertisement), problems may arise. When the female model is to the male model's left (theoretically the correct positioning), she will be to the viewer's right. It is not clear that viewers will make the switch. Again, further testing in specific cultures is necessary to determine specific target market's reactions.

Right has also been associated with science and left with art (Brown, 1979). We would therefore expect:

*Proposition 4:* Consumer response is more positive to emotional appeals when the advertised product is placed on the left than on the right; consumer response is more positive to rational appeals when the advertised product is placed on the right than on the left.

Proposition 4 reflects the fact that artists are considered to be oriented towards emotions, while scientists are considered rational. In fact, research using EEGs to measure brain activity does show that advertisements with emotional appeals are processed mostly in the right side of the brain, while advertisements with rational appeals are processed primarily in the left part of the brain (McCarthy, 1991). This reflects the fact that stimuli in the viewer's left visual field are processed in the right side of the brain, and vice versa.

The last, specific left-right dichotomy discussed above relates to nature-culture. We would expect:

*Proposition 5:* Consumer response is more positive when situations or products associated with nature are positioned to the left and situations or products associated with culture are positioned to the right in advertisements, rather than the opposite.

Theoretically, products which are promoted as "all natural" would be positioned to the left; products positioned as high-technology or scientifically developed would be positioned to the right. This could cause a conflict with respect to the basic proposition that the advertised (good) product should always be positioned to the right. On closer inspection, however, most products promoted as "all natural" are in some way processed (e.g., ice cream) and thus are not really in their natural state. Such product processing makes positioning to the right more appropriate (with truly natural products such as the raw cream positioned to the left.) Some products are truly all natural, such as organic produce. Whether the good-right/bad-left positioning or the culture-right/nature-left processing takes precedent would need to be examined through research.

Other propositions regarding left-right positioning are more general. When we discuss positioning, we can distinguish between positioning of two products/situations/models with respect to each other, or with respect to their positioning within the picture frame. We would expect:

*Proposition 6:* For all of the above propositions, consumer response is stronger when there are at least two products/situations/models side by side (thus having left and right positions with respect to each other), rather than when there is just one product/situation/model positioned only in the left or the right side of the picture frame.

For left-right associations to be meaningful, the viewer must have a frame of reference to indicate that a position is actually to the right or left. Therefore, meaningful comparisons are necessary, rather than simply positioning in the picture frame. For example, positioning only one product targeted towards males on the right side of the picture frame is not as compelling as showing that the product meant for males is to the right of the product meant for females. This is because the picture frame is itself only a small portion of what the viewer knows intuitively to be a larger picture. Because the "real" scene pictured extends both to the left and right of the picture frame, placement within the picture frame does not constitute an absolute right or left positioning. When the male product-female product, high-technology product-all natural product, or good product-bad product are juxtaposed with respect to each other, however, positioning becomes clear. Indeed, with the exception of emotion-rational appeals, which are processed in different parts of the brain, it should not matter what part of the picture plane the two products/situations/models are placed; the important positioning is only with respect to each other.

The above propositions and, in fact, the universality of right-left symbolism, is based upon the assumption that traditional beliefs are still held in contemporary cultures. The extent to which this is true depends on the extent to which cultures retain their traditional beliefs. We would therefore expect:

*Proposition 7:* Cultures which retain traditional beliefs are more likely to have strong left-right associations; cultures which have lost or rejected their traditional beliefs will have weak left-right associations.

For example, the United States has a culture which, for the most part, values innovation and change. Traditions are not revered. This contrasts with some Middle East countries such as Saudi Arabia or Iran, where traditions are strong. To the extent that traditions have been lost, and right-left associations have weakened, we would expect that Propositions 1 through 3 are less applicable than in areas where traditions are strong. (Proposition 4 will still hold, however, due to the physiological basis for the left-right associations.) Indeed, it is perhaps surprising that Domhoff

(1973) still found as many traditional left-right associations as he did with United States undergraduates, especially when the research was done during a time period of strong rejection of traditional values.

In order to determine the strength of left-right associations, it is also possible to look at a more specific measure within individual cultures, i.e., the extent to which left-handedness is present in a population. We can expect:

*Proposition 8:* The *fewer* left-handed people in a population, the *stronger* the left-right associations.

As discussed above, the extent of left-handedness varies among different populations. This may in part be due to differences in birth stresses (if, for example, motherhood tends to occur at a younger age in some societies than others). However, the extent of left-handedness is also determined by cultural pressures. In some cultures, the pressure to be right-handed is very strong. For example, in Japan, the system of writing is dependent on right handedness (Katzenstein, 1989). Similar pressure to eat and write with one's right hand is found in mainland China (Coren, 1992). When societies become more permissive regarding left-handedness, this should reflect a weaker association between the left and all things that are bad.

## CONCLUSION: POSSIBLE EMPIRICAL RESEARCH

Exploratory studies should be done to determine whether "left" holds negative, gender, and/or nature (versus culture) or art (versus science) associations in each culture studied. To some extent, this preliminary research has been conducted in many cultures, as indicated in Tables 2 and 3. However, it should be updated, especially in cultures which have undergone modernizing changes since the research was originally conducted. Cultures to be tested should range from very traditional to very modern. In addition, both nonliterate persons and literate persons should be tested. Among literate persons, cultures whose writing goes from left to right as well as from right to left and vertically should be tested. This will help identify whether before/after (left-right) situations reflect writing conventions as opposed to symbolic meanings.

Several of the issues discussed above are rather straightforward. For these issues, empirical testing should also be simple. For example, Proposition 1 (positioning of products/situations to the left and right of each other) can be tested using an experimental design. The testing of Propositions 7 and 8 (which are concerned with the extent to which cultures have retained their traditional left-right associations) are important to determine whether traditional beliefs are still held. However, when traditions have weakened, advertisers can at least do no harm by following the general right-left associations discussed above. While the right-left positioning may not have the impact desired, at least no messages unfavorable to the advertised product will be communicated.

Other issues are more complicated. For example, while strong left-right associations may be present in a culture, exploratory research will be necessary to determine what actually constitutes "right" versus "left" in visuals. For example, the placement of pictures around the border of the advertisement might show the gradual improvement in the user's situation after using a certain product (such as hair coloring which is applied in a series of steps to create a gradual change). While *Webster's New World Dictionary* (1968) equates "left-handed" with "counterclockwise motion," this does not necessarily hold for all cultures. Similarly, the propositions dealing with positioning with respect to model(s) in advertisements deal with uncertainties in applying the general right-left associations to specific situations. To recognize the basic right-left dichotomy is insufficient in these cases; it is also necessary to understand how "right" and "left" are actually identified in each culture. To fail to identify which side is right versus left in these more complicated situations could lead to extremely negative results. For example, in cultures which identify the left hand as the unclean hand, positioning the advertised product to the viewers' right, but the model's left, could create very negative associations with the advertised product.

Right-left symbolism appears to be a universal symbol, deeply rooted in human consciousness. As such, it may have important implications for international advertisers. More empirical research relating right-left symbolism to advertising is necessary. The basic concept of right-left symbolism is relatively simple. However, understanding how to apply these symbols to advertising is more complex. These complexities of implementation offer important opportunities for research but also possible risks for international advertisers. In any case, international advertisers need to be aware of the possible ramifications of right and left.

## REFERENCES

*American Heritage Dictionary of the English Language* (1981). Boston: Houghton Mifflin Company.

Barsley, M. (1967). *The Other Hand: An Investigation into the Sinister History of Left Handedness,* New York: Hawthorn Books.

Brain, J. L. (1982). Witchcraft and Development, *African Affairs* (July), 81 (324), 371-384.
Brown, M. (1979). *Left Handed: Right Handed*, North Pomfret, Vermont: David and Charles.
Bruner, J. S. (1965). *On Knowing: Essays for the Left Hand*, New York: Atheneum.
Burton, J. W. (1982). Lateral Symbolism and Atuot Cosmology, *Africa*, 52 (1), 69-80.
Chelhod J. (1973). A Contribution to the Problem of the Pre-eminence of the Right, Based upon Arabic Evidence. In R. Needham (Ed.) J. J. Fox (Trans). *Right and Left* (pp. 239-262). Chicago: University of Chicago Press. (Reprinted from *Anthropos*, 1964, 59, 529-545.
Clark, S. (1980). Inversion, Misrule and the Meaning of Witchcraft, *Past and Present*, 87, 98-127.
Corballis, M. C. & Beale, I. L. (1976). *The Psychology of Left and Right*, Hillsdale, New Jersey: Lawrence Erlbaum Associates.
Coren, S. (1992). *The Left-Hander Syndrome*, New York: The Free Press.
Domhoff, W. (1973). But Why Did They Sit on the King's Right in the First Place? In R. E. Ornstein (Ed.) *The Nature of Human Consciousness* (pp. 143-147). San Francisco: W. H. Freeman and Co. (Reprinted from *Psychoanalytic Review*, 1969-70, 56, 596.)
Du Boulay, J. (1982). The Greek Vampire: A Study of Cyclic Symbolism in Marriage and Death, *Man* (June), 17 (2), 219-238.
Dunn, S. W. (1976). Effects of National Identity on Multinational Promotional Strategy in Europe, *Journal of Marketing* (Fall), 40 (4), 50-57.
Edwards, B. (1979). *Drawing on the Right Side of the Brain*, Los Angeles: J. B. Tarcher.
Elinder, E. (1975). How International Can European Advertising Be? *Journal of Marketing* (Spring), 28 (2), 7-11.
Evans-Pritchard, E. E. (1953). Nuer Spear Symbolism. In R. Needham (Ed.) *Right and left* (pp. 92-107). Chicago: University of Chicago Press. (Reprinted from *Anthropological Quarterly*, 26, 1-19.)
Faron, L. C. (1973). Symbolic Values and the Integration of Society among the Mapuche of Chile. In R. Needham (Ed.) *Right and left* (pp. 187-203). Chicago: University of Chicago Press. (Reprinted from *American Anthropologist*, 1962, 64, 1151-1164.
Fatt, A. C. (1967). The Danger of "Local" International Advertising, *Journal of Marketing*(Winter), 31 (1), 60-62.
Gardner, M. (1979). *The Ambidextrous Universe*, New York: Charles Scribner's Sons.
Gould, S. J. (1987). *Time's Arrow. Time's Cycle*, Cambridge, MA: Harvard University Press.
Granet, M. (1953). Right and Left in China. In R. Needham (Ed. and Trans.) *Right and left* (pp. 43-58). Chicago: University of Chicago Press. (Reprinted from *Etudes sociologiques sur la Chine*. Paris: Presses Universitaires de France, 1953, 261-278.

Emel gelmiş akşam yemeği ... ...
hastaliklari uzmani ayagimiza geldi.Cigerini cok kotu bulmadigini soyledi
umarim dogrudur.sigarayi azaltti ama tamamen birakamadi.Gelme meselesi
hakkinda bir sey yazmadin..Tatiliniz ne zaman? Simdilik bu kadar..
Gelismeleri yaz.
OPtum
AYLA

___

Get 100% FREE Internet Access powered by Excite
Visit http://freelane.excite.com/freeisp

aylabaysal@excite.com on 05/17/2000 02:15:05 AM

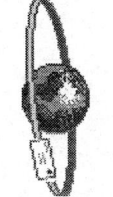

To: Isil M. Clark/GP/RPCO
cc:
Subject Emekli Sandigi
:
Fax to:

Dostcagizim;
naber?Yine cok yogunsun degilmi? Dun yine emkli sandigindan aradilar ve paranin bankadan geri gonderildigini ve benim nicin cekmedigini sordular? Ben de senin artik Amerika'da yasadigini soyledim.Maasin tamamen kesilmesi icin en az bir sene gecmesi gerekliymis.Kadin daha sonra tekrar aradi ve eger mumkunse senin onu aramani gerekirse parayi oraya transfer edceklerini soyledi ama bana kalirsa sakin oyle birsey yapma eninde sonunda ilerde bunlar faiziyle sana geri odettirirler.Ona evii oldugunu soylemedim.Yine de sana telefonunu ve ismini vereyim de bir ara ve kestirmeye calis. en son 98 de cekmistik herhalde bankaya bakarmisin daha yeni gonderiyor parayi.Bu nasil bir ulke anlayamdim....Odemeler subesinden Sema YILDIZ tel:312-414 44

Green, R. T., Cunningham, W. H. & Cunningham, I. C. M. (1975). The Effectiveness of Standardized Global Advertising, *Journal of Advertising*, 4 (3), 25-30.
Groskinsky, H. (1990). A Little Something for the President, *Smithsonian* 21 (December), 82-89.
Hertz, R. (1973). The Pre-eminence of the Right hand: A Study in Religious Polarity. In R. Needham (Ed. and Trans.) *Right and Left* (pp. 3-31). Chicago: University of Chicago Press. (Reprinted from *Revue Philosophique*, 68, 1909, 553-580.
Holy, L. (1983). Symbolic and Non-symbolic Aspects of Berti space, *Man* (June) 18 (2), 269-288.
Hori, T. (1984). Dual Symbolic Classification of Opposed Concepts, *Japanese Psychological Research*, 26 (4), 235-239.
James, W. L. & Hill, J. S. (1991). International Advertising Messages: To Adapt or Not to Adapt (That Is the Question), *Journal of Advertising Research* (June/July), 31 (3), 65-71.
Jung, C. G. (1959). *The Basic Writings of C. G. Jung.* (V. S. de Laszlo, Ed.) New York: The Modern Library.
Kanso, A. (1992). International Advertising Strategies: Global Commitment to Local Vision, *Journal of Advertising Research* (January/February), 31, 10-14.
Katzenstein, G. (1989). *Funny Business*, New York: Prentice-Hall.
Killough, J. (1978). Improved Payoffs from Transnational Advertising, *Harvard Business Review* (May-June), 61 (3), 92-103.
Kruyt, A. C. (1973) Right and Left in Central Celebes. In R. Needham (Ed. and Trans.) *Right and left* (pp. 74-91). Chicago: University of Chicago Press. (Reprinted from *Bijdragen tot de Taal-, Land- en Volkenkunde van Nederlansch-Indie*, 100, 1941, 339-356.
Levitt, T. (1983). The Globalization of Markets, *Harvard Business Review* (May-June) 61 (3), 92-103.
Littlejohn, J. (1973). Temne Right and Left: An Essay in the Choreography of Everyday Life. In R. Needham (Ed.) *Right and left* (pp. 289-298). Chicago: University of Chicago Press.
Lloyd, G. (1973). Right and Left in Greek Philosophy. In R. Needham (Ed.) *Right and left* (pp. 167-186). Chicago: University of Chicago Press.
McCarthy, M. J. (1991, March 22). What Makes an Ad Memorable? Recent Brain Research Yields Surprising Answers, *Wall Street Journal*, p. B3.
Meyers-Levy, J. (1989). Priming Effects on Product Judgments: A Hemispheric Interpretation. *Journal of Consumer Research* (June), 16 (1), 76-86.
Miller, J. (1982). People, Berdaches, and Left-handed Bears: Human Variation in Native America, *Journal of Anthropological Research* (Fall), 38 (3), 274-287.
Mittwoch, U. (1985) Lateralization and Sex, *The Behavioral and Brain Sciences*, 8(4), 644.
Needham, R. (1973). Right and Left in Nyoro Symbolic Classification. In R. Needham (Ed.) *Right and Left* (pp. 299-341). Chicago: University of Chicago Press. (Reprinted from *Africa*, 37, 1967, 425-451.
Richardson, J. (1993), personal communication.

Ricks, D. (1983). *Big Business Blunders,* Homewood, IL: Dow-Jones Irwin.

*Roget's Thesaurus* (1961). Garden City, NY: Garden City Books.

Ryans, Jr., J. K. & Fry, C. (1976). Some European Attitudes on the Advertising Transference Question: A Research Note, *Journal of Advertising,* 5 (2), 11-13.

"Southpaws of the North" (1990, September 25), *Toronto Globe and Mail.*

Soft-Art, Inc. (1984-1990). *Thesaurus* [Computer Program]. Redmond, WA: Microsoft Corporation.

Spennemann, D. H. R. (1985). On the Origins and Development of Handedness in Humans, *Homo,* 36 (3), 121-141.

TenHouten, W. D. & Kaplan, C. D. (1973). *Science and its Mirror Image,* Los Angeles: University of California Press.

*Webster's New World Dictionary of the American Language, College Edition* (1966). Cleveland: The World Publishing Company.

Wieschhoff, H. A. (1973). Concepts of Right and Left in African Cultures. In R. Needham (Ed.) *Right and Left* (pp. 59-73). Chicago: University of Chicago Press. (Reprinted from the *Journal of the American Oriental Society,* 58, 1938, 202-217.)

# Consumer Advertising in Germany and the United States: A Study of Sexual Explicitness and Cross-Gender Contact

Francis Piron
Murray Young

**SUMMARY.** This study investigates the pervasiveness of seven sexual advertising elements in selected German and U.S. magazines targeted toward upscale female readers. Results indicate a trend between 1986 and 1992: sexual-oriented visual stimuli were used 60% more in the United States than in the German magazines; advertisements depicting suggestively clad models appeared almost twice as often, while ads with partially clad models declined fifty percent during the period studied. The use of more sexually explicit messages, such as nudity and sexual contact(s) between male(s) and female(s), was limited but stable over the periods studied. Representative advertisements and analytical procedures are included to foster further studies in other media and countries. *[Article copies available from The Haworth Document Delivery Service: 1-800-342-9678.]*

---

Francis Piron and Murray Young are Lecturers in International Business at The Chinese University of Hong Kong, Shatin, NT, Hong Kong.

The authors acknowledge the assistance of Bernice Wong and Amy Mak of The Chinese University of Hong Kong on various aspects of the research and thank two anonymous reviewers for their insightful suggestions.

[Haworth co-indexing entry note]: "Consumer Advertising in Germany and the United States: A Study of Sexual Explicitness and Cross-Gender Contact." Piron, Francis, and Murray Young. Co-published simultaneously in *Journal of International Consumer Marketing* (International Business Press, an imprint of The Haworth Press, Inc.) Vol. 8, No. 3/4, 1996, pp. 211-228; and: *Global Perspectives in Cross-Cultural and Cross-National Consumer Research* (ed: Lalita A. Manrai, and Ajay K. Manrai) International Business Press, an imprint of The Haworth Press, Inc., 1996, pp. 211-228. Single or multiple copies of this article are available from The Haworth Document Delivery Service [1-800-342-9678, 9:00 a.m - 5:00 p.m. (EST)].

© 1996 by The Haworth Press, Inc. All rights reserved.

A binational study on the use of sexual components in printed advertisements is discussed in three sections. Following a review of prior research, the study's research design and method are described. Results of the analysis are then presented and implications of the findings are provided. Suggestions for future research are also provided.

## PRIOR RESEARCH

Evidence of an inverse relationship between the use of sexually explicit advertising and the impact of such advertising (measured in terms of brand names recall) has existed for decades (Baron 1982). Specifically, brand names were recalled less faithfully when the ad contained sexual (Alexander and Judd 1978; Steadman 1969) or erotic (Weller, Roberts and Neuhaus 1978) components. Also, Belch, Belch, Holgerson and Koppman (1982) noted that ads using nudity were perceived as more offensive than those that did not, even though partial nudity was deemed attractive. Examining the relationship between explicit sexual components and the processing of verbal information, Severn, Belch and Belch (1990), conclude that

> the use of a sexual appeal does interfere with message comprehension, particularly when there is substantial information available for processing. (p. 21)

While the use of sex in advertising is not a recent occurrence, within the last decade, sexual components in advertising may have increased both in frequency (Sciglimpaglia, Belch and Cain 1979) and explicitness (Soley and Kurzbard 1986). Some researchers (Gould 1990; Dichter 1990) contend that the symbolic representations of sexuality in marketing and consumer behavior themes have developed into an "imagery [that] reflects the importance of sexuality as an essential consumption element" (Stern 1991, p. 384).

The pervasiveness and nature of sex in advertising suggest the importance of distinguishing sexual appeals, and sex or gender roles. Sexual appeals allude to the mechanism through which the use of sexual components entreat the viewer to respond to the advertising message. These may be through attention, allure, recall enhancement or emotional involvement (Shimp 1993, p. 344). Sex or gender roles describe the "culturally constructed category which goes beyond but encompasses the biological category of sex, the social-psychological category of sex role, the psychological category of masculine/feminine identity, and the psycho-behavioral category of sexuality" (Artz and Venkatesh 1991).

In a review of gender differences in art and advertising, Schroeder (1993) compares male and female models in Victoria's Secret advertisements, and concludes that female models' implicit message is "I am available," while it is "I am in control" for males, and that models' artistic reference is "the reclining nude" for females and "portraits of leaders" for males. But, Lipman (1992) observes that the general perception of women sexuality in advertising may be changing as "advertisers are finding their portrayals of women just aren't 'politically correct' anymore. They've been pummelled by public outcry over bimbos in beer commercials and fashion ads."

The issue of gender also relates to the gender of the audience targeted by advertisers in print media. Klassen, Jasper and Schwartz's (1993) analyzed advertisements in *Playboy, Ms.* and *Newsweek,* publications targeting distinct audiences (male readers, female readers and readers of both genders, respectively). Their study of subtle visual cues in ads involving female-male relationships revealed a complex set of relationships between the sexes. Ferguson, Kreshel and Tinkham's (1990) studied advertising in *Ms.,* a publication targeting a single gender audience with an interest in the "non-sexist portrayal of women," found that advertising in the magazine depicting women as sexual objects had increased over the period under study.

From this body of research, several issues emerged. First, most of these studies, were conducted in North America and focused on North American consumers. This is understandable, given the size of the American advertising market. But, media targeted to specific gender audiences are available in many countries, and multinational studies could be conducted. The need for cross-cultural studies in advertising is important since one of the "major causes for international advertising mistakes has traditionally been the neglect of cultural attitudes of consumers in foreign countries" Jeannet and Hennessey 1992, p. 504). In addition, cross-cultural advertising studies provide a richer understanding of the globalization-customization debate (Levitt 1983; *Journal of International Consumer Marketing* 1991).

A second issue concerns the use of sexually explicit messages in media targeting women. Considering the evidence put forth above (i.e., the consensus that sexual components tend to distract from a message's claims), and the desire by some women's groups to implement a "new feminism," where advertising campaigns would depict women as real people rather than "sex objects," it may be instructive to determine if and how advertising has changed. To do so, we investigate whether the number of advertisements using sexually explicit visuals in magazines targeting women has increased or decreased, and whether types of sexual appeal used have changed.

The study, though, does not address the issues of gender representation or of sexual stereotyping in advertising, an issue on which there is considerable debate and research. The former is summarized by Buttle (1989). Examples of the latter include Sciglimpaglia, Lunstron and Vanier (1979) and DeYoung and Crane (1992) report on attitudes of American and Canadian women respectively toward sexual stereotypes in advertising. (For very readable reviews of the history of sex stereotyping and gender representation in advertising, see Courtney and Whipple (1983) and Artz and Venkatesh (1991), respectively.) Also, the focus of this research is not on advertising as a vehicle for social communication (Goldman 1992), but on the utilization of more obvious sexual components (i.e., the degrees of (un)dress and the levels of physical contact). For a comprehensive review of less obvious, nonverbal, gender cues, see Schroeder (1993).[1]

To address the issues of sexual explicitness and gender relationship in a cross-cultural context, a study comparing printed advertisements in two countries over three periods of time was developed. Precedents for aspects of such an approach are numerous. Venkatesan and Losco (1975), and Ferguson, Kreshel and Tinkham (1990) examined advertisements in print media over a period of years. Classification of dress/undress and physical contacts have been employed by Soley and Kurzbard (1986). Research examining media targeted to upscale females include Lysonski (1985), Ruggiero and Weston (1985). Research examining changes in gender-relevant messages in advertising over time includes Lysonski's (1985) and Mitchell and Taylor's (1990) studies of advertising stereotypes in British print media. But, examination of the aforementioned variables in an integrated research design is without direct precedent and represents one of the contributions of this study.

## RESEARCH DESIGN AND METHOD

The method employed draws on the conceptual framework of gender display developed by Goffman (1976). Specifically, the nature of physical contact between men and women is examined, and the level of overt sexual display is addressed. Treatment of other aspects of Goffman's typology for gender relations in print ads (e.g., proportionate size of male and female actors, and ritualized subordination with implied ranking of functions shown in face-to-face portrayals of men and women) is provided by Klassen, Jasper and Schwartz (1993), and Schroeder (1993). Visual elements have been found to be of particular importance in advertisements for clothing and cosmetics (Mitchell and Taylor 1990), product categories prominent in women's magazines.

Four levels of dress/undress are employed. These measures, developed by Reid, Salmon and Soley (1984), were found useful in understanding the nature of sexual content of television advertisements. Three categories of physical contact (Soley and Reid 1985) are also utilized to help determine the extent and nature of potential changes in the sexual content of consumer advertisements. Soley and Reid (1985) found that over one third of print ads for television programs contained sexual elements. Using such measures, Soley and Kurzbard (1986) found that, while the percentage of advertisements with sexual content had not increased between 1964 and 1984, sexual depictions did change, becoming more overt with a greater reliance on visual than verbal sexual elements. Inclusion of contact categories may also be important because of a "reverse sexism" phenomenon in advertising, wherein males are depicted as sexual objects for women (Coleman 1989).

The study compares measures using German and American fashion magazines. Germany and the U.S.A. were chosen because of general similarities in economic development (*Book of Vital World Statistics* 1990), lifestyles and expenditures (*The World Factbook* 1992), and sophistication of the advertising industry. Such a selection is in keeping with the findings of Boddewyn and Kunz (1991) that cultural, religious and economic characteristics of countries are the dominant factors in explaining national patterns of decency in advertising.[2]

The years 1986, 1989 and 1992 were selected for study to help investigate potential rapid changes in the number and types of sexually explicit advertisements. These years represent the period within which a growing awareness of the need for more responsible sexual behaviors was promoted through the media. For example, public service announcements and direct mail campaigns described the consequences of sexual promiscuity. Advertisements in print and electronic media advocated the use of condoms to reduce the spread of sexually transmitted diseases.

*Sample Selection and Procedure*

The sample consisted of 1,475 full-page and larger advertisements that appeared in four leading magazines targeting women in 1986, 1989 and 1992. For each of the three years, the March, June, September and December issues were inspected. The two German magazines were *Petra* and *Vogue* (German language edition), and the two American magazines were *Mademoiselle* and *Vogue* (U.S. edition). *Petra* and *Mademoiselle* were selected for their editorial and audience similarities.[3] Inclusion of the

German language edition and the American edition of *Vogue* enhances the prospect of reducing a random error. That is, by selecting two versions of the same magazine, and two unrelated magazines, we attempt to reduce random variations and to capture a systematic effect. In addition, because of its many editions in foreign languages, *Vogue* is seen as a global magazine while *Petra* and *Mademoiselle* are published only at a national level. In other words the global and national natures of the media selected should enhance the possibility of identifying a robust rather than random effect.

Procedures employed the method used by Soley and Kurzbard (1986) in their comparative study of 1964 and 1984 magazine advertisements. That is, two persons were trained in coding advertisements. The two coders were native German speakers who had graduate level training in consumer behavior and had lived in the United States for a number of years. Consequently, they were both culturally and linguistically competent to evaluate the advertisements from the countries under study. In the pretest stage, the coders assigned sample advertisements to given categories and discussed problems to understand existing differences in category assignments.

In the actual study, the coders' initial agreement coefficient reached 78%. As reported by Soley and Kurzbard (1986):

> Agreement coefficients range from +1.0 to −1.0, where +1.0 indicates perfect agreement and 0.0 indicates agreement due to chance alone. A coefficient of 0.75 indicates inter-coder reliability is 75% above the level expected by chance. Agreement coefficients above 0.80 are considered unconditionally reliable; items with coefficients between 0.60 and 0.80 are accepted as conditionally reliable; items below 0.60 are considered to be unreliable. (p. 47)

Thus, a coders' agreement coefficient of .78 indicated acceptable reliability. To resolve differences in coding, each coder expressed his/her reasons for the coding categorization. Discussion continued until a mutually agreed classification was reached.

### *Coding Units*

The coding of the advertisements followed the method identified in Soley and Kurzbard (1986). Specifically, only full page or larger size photographs with visible adult models were studied. Ads depicting undiscernible adult models as well as ads depicting only part(s) of a body (e.g., a leg, an arm, a foot or a hand) were not included in the study. Also, advertisements consisting of drawings, sketches, and/or verbal sexual elements were not retained for consideration. The advertisements selected for the study were then grouped into four degrees of dress/undress of the model(s) and according to the presence and type of cross-gender physical contact. (Definitions for each of the variables are provided in a subsequent section, and sample advertisements are available from the authors upon request.)

The use of dress and contact categories across cultures is not without difficulties. For example, while a visual suggesting intercourse is likely to be regarded as a provocative sexual element in most cultures, an open blouse, while commonly perceived as a sexual statement, may be deemed more or less alluring according to one's culture. In this research, the countries studied share many historical and cultural bonds that would tend to generate similar interpretations of the degree of sexual explicitness. (See Terpstra and David (1991) for discussion of numerous aspects of common heritage between the U.S. and Germany.)[4] The degree of dress/ undress, purported to assess increased levels of sexual stimulation from sensual mouth (i.e., moderate) to nudity (i.e., high), was assessed utilizing a classification developed by Reid, Salmon and Soley (1984). Ads showing slightly opened or opened lips with lipstick were categorized as "Sexy Lips." Ads depicting models wearing open blouses, shirts or gowns (which exposed chest area), full-length lingerie, mini-skirts, "muscle shirts," "short-skirts," tight clothing which enhances the figure, hiked skirts that expose the thigh constituted the category "Suggestively Clad." Ads wherein models show underapparel, three-quarter length or shorter lingerie, bodysuits, bikinis, or models showing bare backs, shoulders, and/or thighs were classified as "Partially Clad." Finally, in the category "Nudity," were ads depicting bare bodies, including silhouettes, the wearing of translucent underapparel or lingerie, as well as poses where the model wears only a towel. The distinction made between nudity and suggestiveness is the base for Shimp's (1993) discussion of varying levels of sex appeal in advertising.

Physical contact between male and female models utilized the categories developed by Soley and Reid (1985). They are: (1) Simple contact, referring to holding hands and nonintimate touching; (2) Other contact, defined as more intimate touching such as kissing, hugging, embracing, and "playful wrestling"; (3) Suggestion of intercourse, defined as males and females embracing in a prone position, or while semi-clad or naked, or together in bed or bathroom, or depiction of other bedroom scenes.

Clearly, the degree of dress/undress and the degree of cross-gender contact are not independent. Therefore, a particular advertisement could be coded twice. For example, an ad depicting a woman wearing lingerie, showing bare shoulders, and embracing a fully clothed man was coded twice: once as "partially clad" and once as "other contact." However, within the dress/undress and within the contact categories, each classification (e.g., sexy lips for the former, other contact for the latter) exhibits the characteristic of a good classification schema: clear, exhaustive and exclusive. For enhanced comparability, and in an effort to provide some form of standardization across years and magazines, the number of elements coded was expressed relative to the total number of pages in the issues studied and translated on a "per 100 pages" basis.

## RESULTS

The results are presented on the basis of the research design, an approach utilized in many of the studies cited earlier. Changes in the extent and nature of sexual components in advertising can be viewed from a number of perspectives. This section presents findings at four units of analysis: country, year and country, a composite profile, and specific stimuli in magazines.

### Country

Use of the four levels of (un)dress stimuli in the German and American publications were found to be similar. Changes reflecting increases or decreases in the use of specific stimuli remained generally close to the proportions observed in 1986. Only the variable "suggestively clad" differed significantly ($F = 17.07$, $p < .01$). As illustrated in Figure 1, the use of suggestively clad models was almost twice as frequent in American as in German magazines. Another variable, "nudity," approached statistical significance ($F = 4.2$, $p = .06$).

### Year and Country

Longitudinal changes in the visual message elements were investigated within each country, and none of the variables were found to have had statistically significant changes over the years. The data indicates that the total number of sexual components used in German and U.S. advertisements in magazines targeting upscale, female readers neither increased nor decreased significantly during the 1986-1992 time period. A closer examination of the data, however, revealed that within each country one of the two magazines may have offset the effect attributed to the other. This issue is examined later in more detail.

FIGURE 1. Use of Suggestively Clad Models

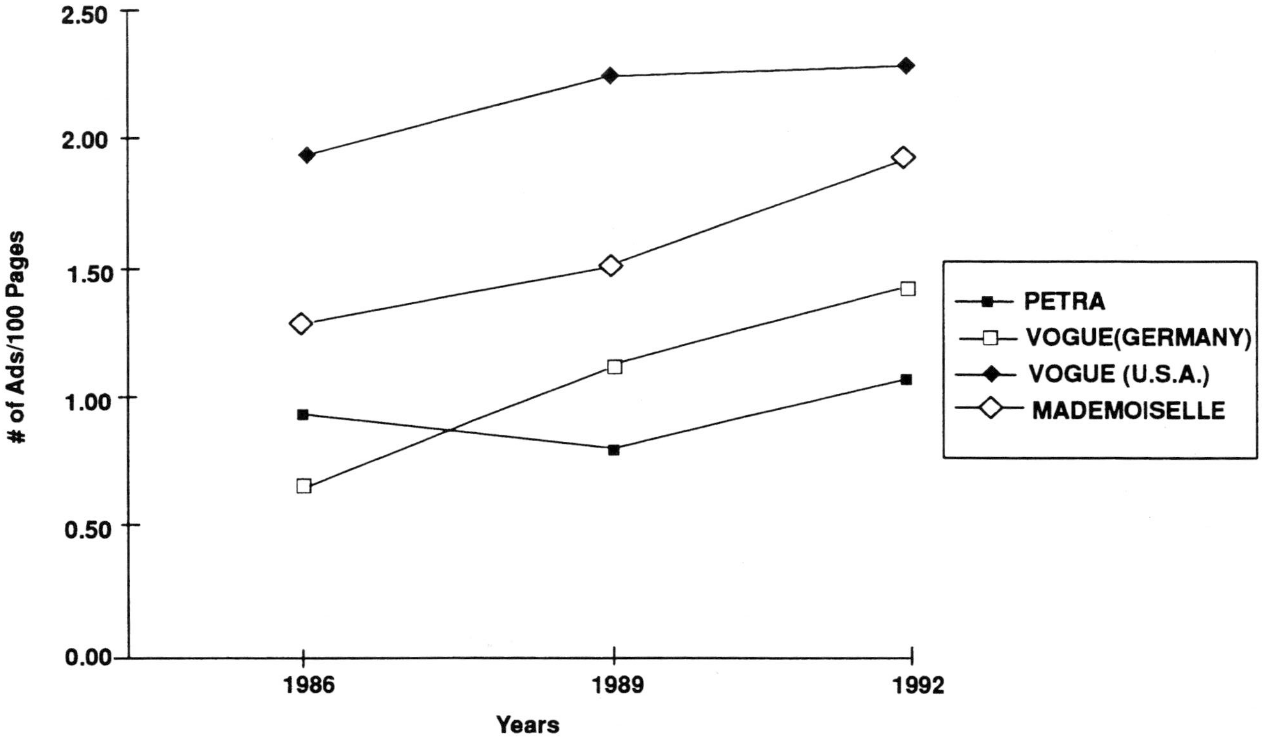

## Composite Profile

In an attempt to gain a richer understanding of the data, and to investigate whether changes may have occurred on a more general than specific basis, the four measures of the degree of dress/undress were summed to form an index. The three measures of the level of cross-gender contact were also summed to form an index. The results indicate that in the United States, the use of sexual components was significantly higher over the three time periods than in Germany ($F = 11.73$, $p < .01$). Specifically, the U.S. magazines used an average of 3 pages per 100 with models in different degrees of dress/undress. The German magazines had only 2.2 pages per hundred. The second index, measuring cross-gender contact occurrences, differed significantly neither across time nor across countries.

## Specific Sexual Components

The objective of this part of the analysis was to assess the specific contribution of any of the seven variables in the four magazines. Both visual and statistical analyses are reported.

Initially, a plot was created for each of the variables, by magazine. The results, as shown in Figure 2, evidenced two trends during the 1986-1992 period: (1) the use of suggestively clad models, already twice as frequent in the U.S. magazines as in the German magazines, increased by 50% (from 0.82 to 1.28 occurrences and from 1.62 to 2.20 occurrences per 100 pages in the German and U.S. magazines respectively); (2) the use of partially clad models was reduced by one half (from 0.69 to 0.32 occurrences and from 0.71 to 0.36 occurrences per 100 pages in the German and U.S. magazines respectively). Nudity and suggestion of intercourse were infrequently observed, and the use of other sexual elements was generally stable.

Contrary to expectations, the two national editions of *Vogue* magazine differed in the frequency of sexual components used. While the proportion of ads depicting various levels of (un)dress and physical contact is similar in both editions, the German edition contains about 60% of the total sexual components found in the American edition.

Advertisements using more provocative stimuli such as nudity or suggestion of intercourse were rare. For example, even the highest number of advertisements containing nudity (*Petra*, 1992) was .28 occurrences per 100 pages published. That is, assuming a 100 page issue of the magazine and four issues per year, a reader might be exposed to one ad containing nudity during the course of a year. Also, while not differing at statistically significant levels, suggestion of intercourse, as a visual tool, has evolved

FIGURE 2. Suggestively vs. Partially Clad Models

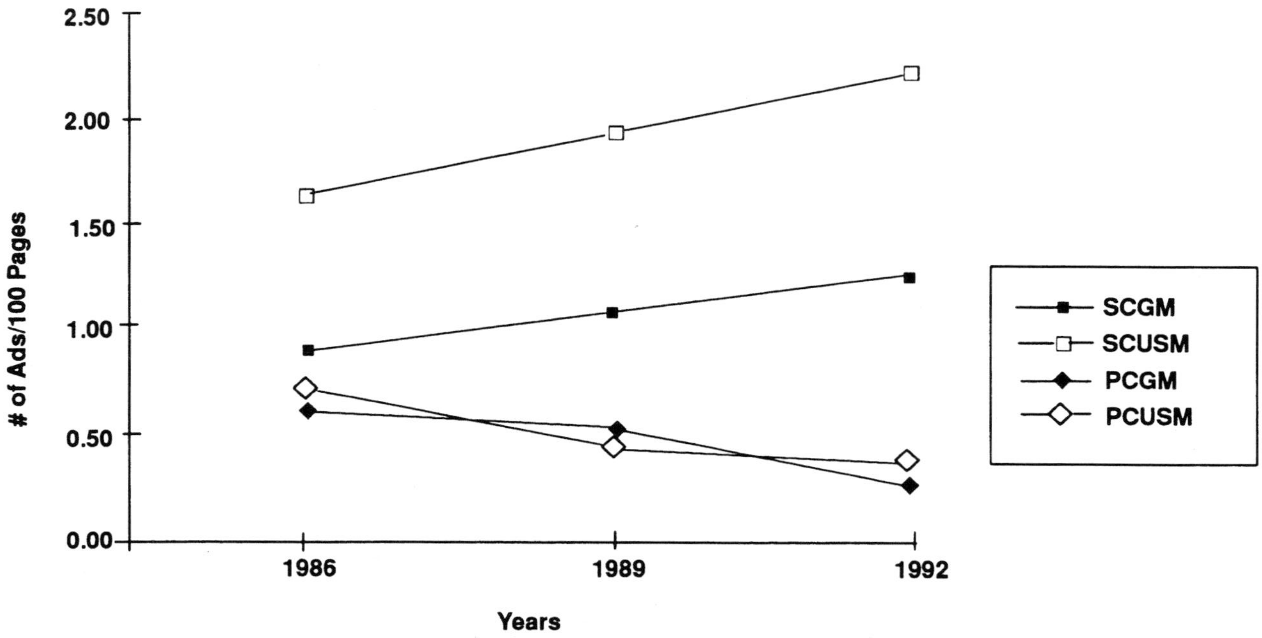

SCGM: Suggestively Clad German Magazines; SCUS: Suggestively Clad U.S. Magazines; PCGM: Partially Clad German Magazines; PCUS: Partially Clad U.S. Magazines

differently. Use in German magazines was observed in 1986 *(Vogue)*, but not until 1989 was it observed in the United States *(Vogue)*. However, while frequency of use stabilized or declined in Germany, it increased somewhat in the American magazines studied.

## DISCUSSION

The sample of German and U.S. advertisements in women's magazines revealed a shift from the use of partially to suggestively clad models. Also, more obvious or blatant sexual elements, such as suggestion of intercourse or total nudity, were rare and utilized less often than other categories of sexual appeal. This is, perhaps, surprising as the popular consensus might assume that publications targeting middle-income females would feature products (like perfume, body oil, soaps, lingerie, and vacations) traditionally prone to more visual, sexual components.

Overall, the research lends partial support to Ferguson, Kreshel and Tinkham (1990) who detected an increase over time in the portrayal of women in advertising as alluring sexual objects. Specifically, while our findings indicate consistency, rather than an increase, in the frequency of sexual components over the period investigated, the observed shift from partially to suggestively clad models could be viewed as maintaining or even bolstering the depiction of women as alluring sexual objects. Finally, for the same reasons, earlier findings by Sciglimpaglia et al. (1979) on the increase in frequency, and by Soley and Kurzbard (1986) on the explicitness of sexual components in advertising were not corroborated. The disparity between this study using magazine advertisements and previous research findings using television ads may be attributed to the differences in media investigated. That is, conveying evocative messages may be more easily accomplished through the use of sight, sound and motion than is possible in a medium such as magazines.

In spite of the overall consistency mentioned above, differences were observed across magazines in terms of the number of advertising pages containing elements of sexual appeal. *Mademoiselle* (American) and *Petra* (German) carried a mid-range of such advertisements with a low of 2.23 ads per 100 pages (*Petra* 1989) and a high of 3.12 ads per 100 pages (*Mademoiselle* 1992). However, during the period studied, the number of ads depicting sexual components increased by 50% in *Mademoiselle* and decreased by 20% in *Petra*. Stated operationally, by 1992, *Mademoiselle* showed one more ad containing sexual material per 100 pages than *Petra*.

The German and U.S. editions of *Vogue* represented both extremes of the sample, with the German edition always featuring less than two pages of ads depicting levels of dress/undress, and the U.S. edition always offering more than three occurrences on a per 100 page basis. Both editions of *Vogue* magazine are targeted to similar audiences with respect to age (64% of the U.S. readers and 55% of the German readers are between 18 and 34 years old) and income (30% of the U.S. readers and 40% of the German readers have household incomes of US$60,000 or more). The disparity noted in this study (i.e., the German edition shows 60% of ads containing sexual appeal vs. 100% for the U.S. version) may be attributed to advertisers' strategies and/or to differences in target audiences' perception of the appropriateness or relevance of sexual appeal to the product(s) involved. While we cannot discuss advertisers' specific and intended strategies, given the secrecy that traditionally surrounds such decisions at both the agency and client levels. Thus, it may be more helpful for the discussion to consider consumers' attitude toward the use of sexual components in advertising.

That German female readers be less favorably inclined towards sexual appeals in advertising and, by extension, that advertisers would use less of them may seem counterintuitive, given Shimp's (1993) position that "sexual explicitness is more prevalent and more overt elsewhere, for example, in Brazil and Western Europe" (p. 343). It may be that the observed disparity in the number of sexually explicit advertisements between the United States and German editions of *Vogue* reflects the targeted audiences' cultural differences, possibly attributable to consumers' habituation.

Habituation is a simple and pervasive form of learning (Leaton and Tighe 1976) where repeated exposures to a novel conditional stimulus (e.g., sexual appeals) eventually diminishes the investigating reflex (e.g., consumers' positive affect). For example, the pervasiveness of partial nudity (e.g., topless bathing on public beaches and swimming pools) in Western Europe may have rendered German audiences less sensitive to its sexual appeal. Given advertising agency research on which stimuli generate attentional lure, enhance recall and evoke emotional responses (Shimp 1993, p. 344), German audiences' habituation to different forms of nudity may account for the shift as German consumers may react less positively to sexual components in advertising. Conversely, U.S. audiences, because of the lesser exposure to public nudity, may perceive sexual appeal as a more novel stimulus.

## *LIMITATIONS*

A number of factors serve as delimiters in the present study. They may, though, serve as guideposts for further research.

Advertising in the six-year period from 1986-1992 was influenced by well-publicized campaigns regarding sexual behavior and/or abstinence in light of the dangers of AIDS. Studies spanning longer time frames may more clearly reflect efforts made by the advertising industry to modify print appeals in response to client and or societal pressures.

The study did not attempt to address a common criticism of advertising, the "gratuitous" use of sexual elements. That is, use of suggestively clad models (either male or female) for products that are not inherently sexual– for example alcohol or automotive supplies. Such "blatant" use of visual sexual elements may be particularly prone to elicit criticism from persons both without and within the advertising community.

While the focus of this study was on visual elements, sexual content of advertisements is also found in the words (headlines and text) of print ads. Such techniques, often less obvious to the casual reader, may be no less influential (either positively or negatively, according to the reader's perspective). Future research should document changes in the frequency and nature of such techniques.

Additionally, the use of print magazines as the focal medium may be a limit in itself. That is, one could advance that the use of sexual elements is more pronounced in television, outdoor advertising (such as billboards), and direct mail. Fortunately, the categorization and comparative techniques employed in this study are easily employed in such research.

This longitudinal study spanning a six-year period detects a significant change away from partially to suggestively clad models. It may be that, as audiences mature, advertisers recognize that women appreciate more subdued sex appeals. This trend may also reflect a desire for greater aesthetic or artistic expressions in advertising since partial nudity may be perceived as similar to pornography (Stern 1992). Future studies could investigate attitude changes which may take longer periods of time to emerge.

## *CONCLUSION*

The purpose of the research was to examine the pervasiveness and nature of visual sexual components in consumer print magazines. Selected German and U.S. women's magazines from 1986, 1989 and 1992 formed the sample. The four magazines were: the German and the U.S. editions of *Vogue* magazine, *Petra* (German language) and *Mademoiselle* (English language). Two types of visual sexual components were examined: degrees of dress/ undress (four levels) and cross-gender contacts (three levels). The frequency of advertisements containing visual sexual components was expressed in a standardized form of occurrences per 100 pages of magazine content.

The findings indicate a shift in the use of visual sexual components in advertisements in magazines targeting upscale women between 1986 and 1992. The trend appears to have been away from more explicit stimuli, such as partially clad or nude models, to more subdued messages, such as suggestively clad models. Similarly, cross-gender contacts were few altogether, and more intimate contacts as those suggesting intercourse were very scarce. This tendency toward less overtly sexual message elements has been noted in advertising in general, as creative directors and some agency clients seek to avoid depictions that could be construed as anti-feminist (Berger 1992). An issue for future research is whether the changes in advertising in print media targeting women are also present in media targeted toward other demographic or psychographic groups.

Numerous factors may have contributed to the changes observed in this study. For example, by using less blatant visual sexual components, advertisers may be responding to increased awareness in the more developed nations towards safer sexual behaviors. Also, it may be that the advertising industry has responded favorably to some groups' call for a depiction of women as real persons, rather than sexual objects. Efforts to measure and document such a development across both countries and media are to be encouraged.

Changes in advertising may also be related to increased awareness of gender issues in organizations that do advertising. While a few multinational firms have begun to educate their managers about gender issues (Castor 1992), no progress has been documented at the level of advertising agencies. It is important that all levels of the communications chain–producers, retailers, facilitating intermediaries, and consumers–become increasingly sensitive to this significant issue.

It would be interesting to continue to monitor such phenomena across time and countries, and to assess consumers' response, in terms of purchases, to the changes evidenced in this study. To assist in such efforts, representative advertisements, graphical displays of selected data and discussion of statistically significant differences have been included in this paper. The methodology employed here could also be easily adapted to investigate the phenomenon of interest in other media and countries. By so doing, researchers can work toward the betterment of a variety of constituencies.

## NOTES

1. While not the focus of the current research, issues such as the feminist view of sexual ideologies in general and of sex in advertising in particular, and gender roles and gender portrayals in culture are discussed in scholarly symposia (such as the Association for Consumer Research's "Gender and Consumer Behavior Conferences," 1991 and 1993) and in specific editions of scholarly publications (such as *Journal of Consumer Research*, Vol. 19, 1993 and, *Advances in Consumer Research*, Vol. 18, R. Holman and M. Solomon, eds., 1991).

2. Aspects of similarity include GDP per capita, household size, literacy rates,

religious affiliation tendencies, newspaper readership, and other variables. Details are available from the authors.

3. *Petra* reaches 4.4% and *Mademoiselle* 4.3% of German and American women respectively. Sixty-seven percent of *Petra* readers and 53% of *Mademoiselle* readers belong to the 20 to 49 year-old group. Also, each magazine allocates about 40% of its pages to coverage of fashion, cosmetics and hairstyles. Likewise, each devotes 10% of their content to topics related to health, relationships and sex, cartoons, science and nature.

4. The authors acknowledge the contribution of an anonymous reviewer for this point.

## REFERENCES

Alexander, M. & Judd, B. (1978). Do Nudes in Advertisements Enhance Brand Recall? *Journal of Advertising Research,* 18, 47-50.

Artz, N. & Venkatesh A. (1991). Gender Representation in Advertising. In R. Holman and M. Soloman (Eds.), *Advances in Consumer Research,* Association for Consumer Research, 18, 618-623.

Baron, R. (1982). Sexual Content and Advertising Effectiveness: Comments on Belch et al. (1981) and Caccavale et al. (1981). In A. Mitchell (Ed.) *Advances in Consumer Research,* Association for Consumer Research, 9, 428-430.

Belch, M., Belch, G., Holgerson, B. & Koppman, J. (1982). Psychological and Cognitive Responses to Sex in Advertising. In A. Mitchell (Ed.), *Advances in Consumer Research,* Association for Consumer Research, 9, 424-427.

Berger W. (1992, October 5). No Sex Please, We're Skittish. *Advertising Age,* p. 12C-17C.

Boddewyn, J. & Kunz, H. (1991). Sex and Decency Issues in Advertising: General and International Dimensions. *Business Horizons,* 34(5) 13-20.

Buttle F. (1989). Sex-Role Stereotyping in Advertising: Social and Public Policy Issues. *Quarterly Review of Marketing,* 14(4) 9-14.

Castro, L. (1992, January 2). More Firms 'Gender Train' to Bridge the Chasms that Still Divide the Sexes. *The Wall Street Journal,* p. 11, 14.

Coleman, L. (1989). What Do People Really Lust After in Ads? *Marketing News,* 23(23) 12.

Courtney, A. & Whipple, T. (1983). *Sex Stereotyping in Advertising.* Lexington, MA: Lexington.

DeYoung, S. & Crane, F. (1992). Females' Attitudes Toward the Portrayal of Women in Advertising: A Canadian Study. *International Journal of Advertising,* 11(3) 249-255.

Dichter, E. (1990). Examples of Sexual Signification in Consumption. In R. Holman & M. Solomon (Ed.) *Advances in Consumer Research,* Association for Consumer Research, 17.

Ferguson, J., Kreshel, P. & Tinkham, S. (1990). In the Pages of *Ms.*: Sex Role Portrayals of Women in Advertising. *Journal of Advertising,* 19(1) 40-51.

Goffman, E. (1976). *Gender Advertisements.* New York: Colophon Books.

Goldman, R. (1992). *Reading Ads Socially.* New York: Routledge.
Gould, S. (1991). Toward a Theory of Sexuality and Consumption: Consumer Lovemaps. In R. Holman and M. Solomon (Ed.) *Advances in Consumer Research,* Association for Consumer Research, 18, 381-383.
Jeannet, J. & Hennessey H. (1992). *Global Marketing Strategies.* Boston: MA. Houghton Mifflin.
*Journal of International Consumer Marketing* (1991). Special Issue on Global Marketing, 3(4).
Klassen, M., Jasper, C. & Schwartz, A. (1993). Men and Women: Images of Their Relationships in Magazine Advertisements. *Journal of Advertising Research,* 33, 30-39.
Leaton, R. & Tighe, T. (1976). *Habituation: Perspectives from Child Development, Animal Behavior and Neurophysiology.* Hillsdale, NJ: Erlbaum.
Leiss, W., Kline, S. & Jhally, S. (1990). *Social Communication in Advertising.* Scarborough, ON: Nelson Canada.
Levitt, T. (1983). The Globalization of Markets. *Harvard Business Review,* (May-June) 92-102.
Lipman, J. (1992, January 31). Finally, Some Marketers Seem Ready to Give Bimbo Ads a Rest. *The Wall Street Journal,* p. B1.
Lysonski, S. (1985). Role Portrayals in British Advertisements. *European Journal of Marketing,* 19(7) 37-55.
Mitchell, P. & Taylor, W. (1990). Polarizing Trends in Female Role Portrayals in UK Advertising. *European Journal of Advertising,* 24(5) 41-49.
Reid, L., Salmon, C., & Soley, L. (1984). The Nature of Sexual Content in Television Advertising. In R. Belk, et al. (Ed.), *Proceedings of the American Marketing Association,* American Marketing Association, 214-216.
Ruggiero, J. & Weston, L. (1985). Work Options for Women in Women's Magazines: The Medium and the Message. *Sex Roles,* 12(5/6) 535-47.
Schroeder, J. (1993). Visualizing Gender: Interpreting Nonverbal Sex Differences in Advertising. In A. Joy and F. Firat (Ed.) *New Visions in a Time of Transition.* Kingston, RI: University of Rhode Island.
Sciglimpaglia, D., Belch, M. & Cain, R. Jr. (1979). Demographic and Cognitive Factors Influencing Viewers' Evaluations of 'Sexy' Advertisement. In W. Wilkie (Ed.), *Advances in Consumer Research,* Association for Consumer Research, 6, 62-65.
Sciglimpaglia, D., Lunstron, W. & Vanier, D. (1979), Women's Role Orientation and Their Attitudes Toward Sex Role Portrayals in Advertising. In J. Leigh and C. Martin (Ed.) *Current Issues and Research in Advertising,* University of Michigan, 163-175.
Severn, J., Belch, G. & Belch, M. (1990). The Effect of Sexual and Non-Sexual Advertising Appeals. *Journal of Advertising,* 19(1) 14-22.
Shimp, T. (1993). *Promotion Management & Marketing Communications,* 3rd ed. Orlando, FL: Dryden Press, Harcourt Brace Jovanovich.
Soley, L. & Kurzbard, G. (1986), Sex in Advertising: A Comparison of 1964 and 1984 Magazine Advertisements. *Journal of Advertising,* 15(3) 46-54.

Soley, L. & Reid, L. (1985). Baiting Viewers: Violence and Sex in Television Program Advertisements. *Journalism Quarterly*, 62, 105-110, 113. Steadman, M. (1969). How Sexy Illustrations Affect Rand Recall. *Journal of Advertising Research*, 9, 15-19.

Stern, B. (1991). Two Pornographies: A Feminist View of Sex in Advertising. In R. Holman and M. Soloman (Ed.) *Advances in Consumer Research*, Association for Consumer Research, 18, 384-391.

Terpstra, V. & David, K. (1991). *The Cultural Environment of International Business*. 3d ed. Cincinnati, OH: Southwestern.

Venkatesan, M. & Losco, J. (1975). Women in Magazine Ads: 1957-1971. *Journal of Advertising Research*, 15(5) 49-54.

Weller, R., Roberts, C. & Neuhaus, C. (1979). A Longitudinal Study of the Effect of Erotic Content Upon Advertising Brand Recall. In *Current Issues and Research in Advertising 1979*, J. Leigh and C. Martin, Jr. eds. Ann Arbor, MI.

# Reviewers

Pat Anderson, Quinnipiac College
Rick Andrews, University of Delaware
Nancy Artz, University of Southern Maine
Soren Askegaard, Odense University, Denmark
George Avlonitis, The Athens University of Economics & Business, Greece
Hans Baumgartner, Pennsylvania State University
Michelle Bergadaa, Groupe ESSEC, France
Dominique Bouchet, Odense University, Denmark
Frank Bradley, University College Dublin, Ireland
Carter Broach, University of Delaware
Ray Burke, Harvard University
Victor Cordell, George Mason University
Janeen Costa, University of Utah
Sheng Deng, University of Saskatchewan, Canada
Luiz Dominguez, INCAE, Costa Rica
Dogan Eroglu, Georgia State University
Sevign Eroglu, Georgia State University
Guliz Ger, Bilkent University, Turkey
Flemming Hansen, Copenhagen Business School, Denmark
Deborah Heisley, University of California at Los Angeles
Kristiaan Helsen, University of Chicago
Donna Hoffman, Vanderbilt University
Easwar Iyer, University of Massachusetts at Amherst
Sharan Jagpal, Rutgers University
Dipak Jain, Northwestern University
Carol Kaufman, Rutgers University
Robert Kent, University of Delaware
Paul Lane, Western Michigan State University
Dana Lascu, University of Richmond
Gilles Laurent, Groupe HEC, France
Steve Lysonski, Marquette University
Mary Ann McGrath, Loyola University at Chicago
Joan Meyers-Levy, University of Chicago

Luis Moutinho, University of Wales College of Cardiff, U.K.
Michael Munson, Santa Clara University
Noel Murray, University of Delaware
Per Ostergaard, Odense University, Denmark
Arvind Rangaswamy, Pennsylvania State University
Pradeep Rau, George Washington University
William Ross, University of Pennsylvania
Dominique Rouzies, Groupe ESSEC, France
Mohan Sawhney, Northwestern University
Jonathan Schroeder, University of Rhode Island
Sudi Seshadri, University of Maryland
John Sherry, Northwestern University
Ronald Tuninga, Open University, The Netherlands
Berend Wierenga, Erasmus University, The Netherlands

# Index

Page numbers followed by n. indicate note.

Advertising
  buying proposals in, 188
  of cigarettes, 26,163
  creative presentation in, 188
  in European Union countries,
    58-59,61,62
  hyperreality of, 31
  in Japan, 77
  right-left symbolism in,
    7,19,188-207
    art associations of, 192
    beliefs and behaviors
      associated with,
      193-194,195-196
    cultural associations of,
      192,194,201,204,205-206
    dark/light associations of,
      189-190,191
    exceptions to, 196
    gender associations of,
      190,192,193,194,196,
      200-201,203-204
    implications for international
      advertising, 201-207
    quality-of-life associations of,
      189,191
    relationship to brain
      lateralization, 198,
      200-201,204
    relationship to left-handedness,
      197,199-200,206
    relationship to
      right-handedness, 197-199,
      206
    relationship to traditional
      beliefs, 205-207
    supernatural associations of,
      190,191-192,193-194,195
  sexually-explicit, 7-8,19,211-228
    of brand name products, 212
    consumers' message
      comprehension in, 212
    cross-gender physical contact
      measures of, 215,217-218,
      220,225
    dress/undress measures of,
      215,217-218,219,220,221,
      224-225
    "gratuitous," 224
    habituation effect in, 223
    longitudinal changes in,
      213,215,218,222,223-224
    sex/gender roles in,
      212,214,215
    women as sexual objects in,
      8,213-214,222,225
  standardization of, 7,19,187-188
  on television, 58,59,61,222,224
African culture, right-left symbolism
  of, 189,190,191,192,194,
  196
*American Heritage Dictionary of the
  American Language*, 189
Answering machines, German-U.S.
  ownership pattern
  comparison, 128,129
Arab culture, right-left symbolism
  of, 190,191,192
Archetypes, of collective
  unconsciousness, 188
Armenians, 163-164
Attitudes, cultural influence on, 12-13

Banalization, 31,32,53
Bangladesh, sales of foreign brand cigarettes in, 25-26
Belgium
 advertising in, 59
 consumer expenditures, 47
 consumption per capita, 49
 grocery shops, 57
 personal value survey, 51,52
Belize, American television programs in, 28
Beverages, European Union consumption patterns of, 47,48,49
Big Bird (television character), 25
Brand choice, value measures for, 170
Brand equity, in European Union countries, 65
Brand name products
 in cross-national markets, 29
 marketing policies for, 2
 registration of, in European Union countries, 60
 sexually-explicit advertising of, 212
Brand strategies, in European Union countries, 65
Buddhism, right-left symbolism of, 193,194,195
Bulgarians, 146-147

Cable television, German-U.S. subscription pattern comparison, 128,129
Canada
 consumer complaining behavior in, 71
 consumer values prioritization in, 174-184
 product involvement correlation, 178-181,182
 of "real" versus "ideal" values, 6,18,175,176-181,182,183
Catholicism, in Poland, 147,151,152,153

CD players, German-U.S. ownership pattern comparison, 128,129,130
Cellular telephones, German-U.S. ownership pattern comparison, 128,129
Change agents, cultural, 2,25
Channel Tunnel, 61
China
 consumer complaining behavior in, 71-72
 right-left symbolism in, 190,191, 192,194,196
Christianity, right-left symbolism of, 193,194,195,203
Cigarettes
 advertising of, 26,163
 Western brands, popularity of, 25-26
Coca-Cola, 2,29,30,33
Collective unconscious, 188
Collectivism, of consumer behavior, 15-16
Collectivist cultures, 15-16
 characteristics of, 73,74,75
 concept of self in, 73,74,75,99
 consumer complaining behavior in, 91-92
 blame attribution in, 84,86-87
 economic development and, 79-80
 environmental attributes in, 80,82
 management implications of, 91-92
 perception of suppliers and, 80-81,82,84,85,86
 personal norms and, 85,89
 personal and social attributes in, 83
 self-enhancing bias in, 86-87
 situational attributes in, 82-83
 social class and, 85,88-89
 social ties and, 88
 social norms and, 85,89

in-groups of, 3-4
  membership in, 76-77
  social interactions of, 74,75-76
  Italy as, 76
  Japan as, 74,75-77
  Romania as, 5-6,147,151,
    153,155,162
College students, attitudes towards
    information technology,
    131-141
  towards new technologies,
    135,139,140
  towards telephone-based
    technologies, 134,135,
    137,139
  towards television-based
    technologies, 134,135,137
Colonel Sanders, 24,25
Colors, symbolic meaning of, 188
Communism
  collapse of, 1-2,28
  in Poland, 151-152,153
Competition, global, 40
Computer-based industries
  consumer attitudes towards,
    129-130,134-135,136,
    137-138
  revenue of, as percentage of GNP,
    127
Consumer behavior, effect of culture
    on, 9-21
  abstract elements of, 11-12,13
  conceptual model of, 13-14,
    15,17,19,20-21
  definitional elements of, 10,11-13
  material elements of, 11-12,13
  theories of, 19-20
Consumer complaining behavior,
    69-96
  antecedents, 79,80,82-83
  attitudes towards, 71-72
  brand loyalty and, 70,71
  in collectivist versus individualist
    cultures, 17,79-80
  blame attribution in, 84,86-87

economic development and,
  79-80
environmental attributes in,
  80,82
management implications of,
  91-92
perception of suppliers and,
  80-81,82,84,85,86
personal norms and, 85,89
personal and social attributes
  in, 83
self-enhancing bias and, 86-87
situational attributes in, 82-83
social class and, 85,88-89
social ties and, 88
social norms and, 85,89
consumer repurchase intentions
  and, 71
exit behavior in, 3,71,78-79
  antecedents, 79,80
  effect of collectivism on, 79,
    80-81,84,86,87
  culturally-determined rates of,
    91
  perception of suppliers and,
    80-81
incidence rates, 78-79
macromarketing and, 71
negative word-of-mouth behavior
  in, 3,71,78-79
  antecedents, 79,80
  effect of collectivism on,
    79,80-81,84,87
  culturally-determined rates of,
    91
  perception of suppliers and,
    80-81
  effect of social ties on, 80,
    87-88
private responses in, 78-79
research issues in, 77-78
third-party responses in, 78
U.S.-based focus of, 71
voice behavior in, 3,78-79
  antecedents, 79,80

effect of collectivism on, 79,80-81,85,86,87
culturally-determined rates of, 90-91
perception of suppliers and, 80-81
personal attitudes towards complaining and, 85,89
rates of, 71
relationship to exit behavior, 92-93n.
social class and, 85,88-89
social norms and, 85,89
Consumer decision process
culture and, 44,45,46
Engel and Blackwell model of, 42,44,45-46
family and, 44,46,48
information environment of, 45
lifestyle and, 44,45-46,51,53
motives in, 44,45
need recognition in, 44,45
reference groups and, 44,46,64-65
in retailing environment, 44,46
social factors in, 44,45
values and, 44,45,46,48,51,52
Consumer expenditures, in European Union countries, 46,47
Consumer products
consumer attitudes towards, 81
as cultural artifacts, 12,13
international marketing of, 3
Western, global popularity of, 25-26
Consumer research
cross-cultural/cross-national, 9-22
consumer behavior domains in, 15,20-21
definitional aspects of, 10-13
framework of, 13
methodological issues in, 20
theory development and validation in, 19-20
subcultural, 10-11

Consumption, universal homogeneity of, 2
"Consumption communities," 28
Consumption patterns, of European Union countries, 47,48,49
Council of Mutual Economic Assistance, 152
Country image, relationship to product image, 65
Cultural artifacts, 12,13
Cultural differences, effect of globalized hyperreactivity on, 32
Cultural universals, 11
Culture
effect on consumer behavior, 12-13
abstract elements of, 11-12,13
conceptual model of, 13-14, 15,17,10,20-21
definitional elements of, 10,11-13
material elements of, 11-12,13
effect on consumer decision process, 44,45,46
globalization of, 27
Marxist theory of, 11-12
subjective, 12
Cultures, value differences among, 146
Customer relations, of Japanese firms, 77
Customer satisfaction/dissatisfaction, 3-4,70. *See also* Consumer complaining behavior
Customization, standardization versus, 40-41
Czechs, 146-147

"Dallas" (television program), 26,28
Denmark
advertising in, 58,59
consumer expenditures, 47
consumers' lifestyles, 53
consumer values prioritization in, 51,52,174-184

product involvement
correlation, 175,178-181
of "real" versus "ideal"
values, 6,18,175,
176-181,183
consumption per capita, 49
grocery shops, 57
Deregulation, of
telecommunications, 126
"Devil and Max Devlin, The"
(motion picture), 203
Disney, 2,26,29,33
Disneyland, 26,28,29,30,32
Distribution networks, European
Union marketing
regulations for, 60-61,64
Donald Duck (cartoon character), 26
"Dynasty" (television program), 26


Eastern Europe. *See also* specific
Eastern European countries
cultural heterogeneity, 5
ethnogenesis in, 28
national differences among, 146
regiocentric market strategies for,
5,6,18,146
Eastern Orthodox Church, 147,153
Eisenhower, Dwight D., 202-203
Engel and Blackwell model, of
consumer decision process,
42,44,45-46
Entrepreneurship, in Eastern Europe,
162
Environmental issues, value
measures for, 170
Ethnogenesis, 27,28,29
EuroDisneyland, 26
European Common Market
countries. *See also* specific
European Common Market
countries
consumer complaining behavior
in, 71

European Economic Community. *See
also* specific European
Economic Community
countries
globalization of, 27
European Union, 39-67. *See also*
specific European Union
countries
advertising in, 58-59,61,62
brand strategies in, 65
consumer markets, 40
consumers' language abilities,
50,54
consumption patterns, 2,47,48,49
income allocation patterns,
46,47,48
income levels, 2
marketing infrastructures,
41,56-61,64
distribution networks,
60-61,64
internationalization of
companies and, 61-63,64
media and advertising
environment of, 58-59
price effects of, 60
product policies and, 59-60
of retail industry, 56-58
market similarity in, 41-56
consumer values and lifestyles
factors in, 48,51,54,64-65
Engel and Blackwell model of,
42,44,45-46
expenditures and income
allocation patterns and, 46-48
family and household structure
factors in, 48,50,64-65
homogenization process in,
2-3,54-56,64
European Value Systems Group, 51

Family
effect on consumer behavior, 13
effect on consumer decision
process, 44,46,48

Fax machines, German-U.S.
    ownership pattern
    comparison, 128,129,140
Flesh, Ben (literary character), 27
Food products
    European Union consumption
        patterns of, 47,48,49
    European Union marketing
        regulations for, 60
    international marketing of, 3
Fordism, 33
France
    advertising in, 58,59
    consumer expenditures, 47
    consumers' lifestyles, 53
    consumption patterns, 47,48,49
    grocery shops, 57
    personal value survey, 51,52


Gainsborough, Thomas, 31
Garage sales, 33
German consumers
    complaining behavior, 71
    information technology acceptance
        by, 5,17-18,127-141
        age factors in, 130-131,
            134-135,136,137-138
        attitudes towards technology's
            social role and, 133-134,
            136-137,138,139-141
        of computer-based
            technologies, 129-130,
            134,135,137
        cultural factors in, 130
        gender factors in, 130,134,
            135,138,139
        of new technologies, 135,
            139,140
        political factors in, 130,
            140-141
        public policy implications of,
            140-141
        social factors in,
            130,138,139-140,141
        technology-seeking attitudes
            and, 132-133,135-136,138
        of telephone-based
            technologies, 128-129,
            134,135,137,139
        of television-based
            technologies, 128,135,137
Germany
    advertising in, 58,59
    beer purity law, 59-60
    consumer expenditures, 46,47
    consumers' lifestyles, 53
    consumption per capita, 49
    grocery shops, 57
    income allocation patterns, 47,48
    personal values survey, 51,52
    sexually-explicit advertising in,
        211,215-225
        dress/undress measures of,
            218,219,220,221
        habituation effect in, 223
        longitudinal changes in,
            218,221,222,223-224
Gift-giving behavior, value measures
    for, 170
Globalization
    adaptation versus, 20
    commerce and, 24-27
    of culture, 27
    hyperreactivity in, 2,14,17,
        27,29-33
    local resistance to, 27-29
*Great Victorian Collection, The*
    (Moore), 31
Greece
    advertising in, 58,59
    consumer expenditures, 47
    consumption per capita, 49
    grocery shops, 57
Grocery shops, of European Union
    countries, 56-58
Gross National Product (GNP)
    comparison with transnational
        corporations' revenues,
        24-25

computing-related revenue as percentage of, 127
Gypsies, 163-164
  right-left symbolism of, 189,193

Hinduism, right-left symbolism of, 194
Honda, 30
Hungarians, 146-147
Hyperreactivity, globalized, 2,14,17,27,29-33
  consumers' resistance to, 33
  course and effects of, 31-33

Imperialism, 27
Income allocation patterns, of European Union countries, 46,47,48
Individual, culturally-influenced concepts of, 72-73. *See also* Self-concept; Self-consciousness
Individualism, of consumer behavior, 3,15,16
Individualist cultures
  characteristics of, 74,75
  concept of self in, 72-73,74-75,98-99
  consumer complaining behavior in
    blame attribution in, 86-87
    environmental attributes in, 82
    perception of suppliers and, 81,82
    personal and social attributes in, 83
    self-enhancing bias in, 86-87
    situational attributes in, 82
    social class and, 85,88-89
    social norms and, 89
    social ties and, 87-88
  Poland as, 5-6,147,155

Industrial products, international marketing of, 3
Information Superhighway, 141
Information technology, consumer acceptance of, German-U.S. comparison, 5,17-18, 125-143
  age factors in, 130-131,134-135, 136,137-138
  attitudes towards technology's social role and, 133-134, 136-137,138,139-140
  of computer-based technologies, 129-130,134,135,137
  cultural factors in, 130
  gender factors in, 130,134, 135,138,139
  of new technologies, 135,139,140
  political factors in, 130,140-141
  public policy implications of, 140-141
  social factors in, 130,138, 139-140,141
  technology-seeking attitudes and, 132-133,135-136,138
  of telephone-based technologies, 128-129,134,135,137,139
  of television-based technologies, 128,135,137
Information technology industry
  internationalization of, 126
  marketing strategies of, 126
  market value of, 127
Infrastructure
  cultural, 12
  marketing, 56-61,64
Innovations, diffusion of, 81
Ireland
  advertising in, 58,59
  consumer expenditures, 47
  consumption patterns, 47,48,49
  grocery shops, 57
  income allocation patterns, 47,48
  personal value survey, 51,52

Italy
    advertising in, 58, 59
    as collectivist culture, 76
    consumer expenditures, 47
    consumers' lifestyles, 53
    consumption patterns, 47,48,49
    grocery shops, 57
    personal value survey, 51,52

James, Henry, 31
James, William, 98
Japan
    advertising in, 77
    as collectivist culture, 74,75-77
    Disneyland in, 26,28
    innovations diffusion rate in, 71
    intimacy in, 76-77
Japanese firms, attitudes towards customers, 77
Judaism, right-left symbolism of, 193,195,202
Judeo-Christian culture, right-left symbolism of, 192,193, 194,196
Jung, Carl, 188,198

Korea, innovations diffusion rate in, 71

Language, as Euromarketing barrier, 54
Leisure activities, value measures for, 170
Lifestyle
    effect on consumer behavior, 13,15
    effect on consumer decision process, 44,45-46,51,53,54
Lifestyle Four-C classification system, 51,53,54
Localism, 28,29
Luxembourg
    advertising in, 59
    consumer expenditures, 47
    consumption per capita, 49

*Mademoiselle*, sexually-explicit advertising in, 19,215, 219,222-223,224,226n.
Madonna (media personality), 25
Magazines, sexually-explicit advertising in, 7-8,19, 211-228
    comparison with television advertising, 222,224
    consumers' message comprehension in, 212
    cross-gender physical contact measures of, 215,217-218, 220,225
    dress/undress measures of, 215, 217-218,219,220,221, 224-225
    "gratuitous," 224
    habituation effect in, 223
    longitudinal changes in, 213,215, 218,221,222,223-224
    sex/gender roles in, 212,214,215
    women as sex objects in, 8, 213-214,225
Marketing
    of branded goods, 2
    Euromarketing, 3,17
    globalization of, 17,40,41
    versus adaptation, 20
    regiocentric, in Eastern Europe, 5,6,18,146
Marlboro Man, 29
Marxist theory, of culture, 11-12
McDonald's, 2,24,25,30. *See also* Ronald McDonald
Media personalities, globalized hyperreality and, 25,29,31
Media usage, value measures for, 170

Mexico, "Gringolandia" tourist towns of, 32
Michelin Man, 24,25
Mickey Mouse, 24,25,26,29
Microsoft Word, thesaurus of, 189
Models, in sexually-explicit advertising, 213
Moscow, McDonald's restaurant in, 25
Motorscooters, "regendering" of, 33
*Ms*, sexually-explicit advertising in, 213
Multinational corporations, marketing strategies of, 40

Native-American culture, right-left symbolism of, 189,190,192, 193,194,195,196
Neo-nationalism, 27,28
Netherlands
 advertising in, 58,59
 consumer complaining behavior, 71,72,89
 consumer expenditures, 47
 consumers' lifestyles, 53
 consumption patterns, 47,48,49
 cultural integration within, 55-56
 grocery shops, 56,57,58
 personal value survey, 51,52
Newspapers, as advertising medium, 59
*Newsweek*, sexually-explicit advertising in, 213
North America, cultural entities of, 56
Norway, customer complaining behavior in, 71-72
Nudity, use in advertising, 212,217, 218,220,222,224


Pele, 25
Personal computers, German-U.S. ownership pattern comparison, 129-130
Personal factors, in consumer behavior, 13-14,15,20
*Petra*, sexually-explicit advertising in, 19,215-216,219,220, 222,224,226n.
Pharmaceuticals, European Union marketing regulations for, 60
Pharonic Village theme park, Cairo, Egypt, 30
*Playboy*, sexually-explicit advertising in, 213
Poland
 Catholicism in, 147,151,152,153
 Communism in, 151-152,153,155
 consumer demographics/personal values relationship in, 5-6,18,146-147,150-164
  age factors in, 155,159, 160,162-163
  educational factors in, 156, 159,160,161,162-163
  income level factors in, 156-157,159,160,161,162-163
  implications for marketing, 162-163
  instrumental values, 155,156, 157,159,160,161,163,164
  terminal values, 155,156,157, 159,161,163
 consumer expenditures, 153,154
 Gross Domestic Product, 152,153
 Gross National Product, 152,153
 as individualist society, 5-6, 147,155
 privatization in, 151-152
Polynesian Cultural Center, Oahu, 20
Portugal
 advertising in, 58,59
 consumer expenditures, 46,47
 consumer expenditures, 47
 consumption per capita, 49
 grocery shops, 56-57
 income allocation patterns, 46

Privatization, in Eastern Europe, 147,151-152
Product adaptation, lack of, 40-41
Product image, relationship to country image, 65
Product ownership, value measures for, 170

Radio, as advertising medium, 58,59
Rationalization, commodified, 32-33
"Real Thing, The" (James), 31
Religions, of Eastern Europe, 147,151,153
Retail industry, of European Union countries, 56-58
Right-left symbolism, 188-207
   art associations of, 192
   beliefs and behaviors associated with, 193-194,195-196
   cultural associations of, 192,194, 201,204,205-206
   dark/light associations of, 189-190,191
   exceptions to, 196
   gender associations of, 190,192, 193,194,196,200-201, 203-204
   implications for international advertising, 201-207
   nature associations of, 194,204
   origins of, 197-201
   quality-of-life associations of, 189,191
   relationship to brain lateralization, 198, 200-201,204
   relationship to left-handedness, 197,199-200,206
   relationship to right-handedness, 197-199,206
   supernatural associations of, 190, 191-192,193-194,195
*Roget's Thesaurus*, 189
Romania
   as collectivist society, 5-6,147,151,153,155,162
   consumer demographics/personal values relationship in, 5-6, 18,146-147,150-151
   age factors in, 155,159-160,162
   educational factors in, 156, 159,160-161,162
   implications for marketing, 162-163
   income level factors in, 156, 157,160,161,162
   instrumental values, 155,156, 157,160-161,163
   terminal values, 155,156, 157,159-160,161,163
   consumer expenditures, 153,154
   ethnic groups, 28
   foreign cigarette brands use in, 25-26
   national religion, 147,151
   resistance to globalization in, 28
Ronald McDonald, 24,25,26, 29,30,31,32,33
Russians, 146-147

Santa Claus, 25
Self, components of, 98
Self-concept, 171-172
   in collectivist cultures, 73,74, 75,99
   definition of, 98
   in individualist cultures, 72-73, 74-75,98-99
   self-consciousness scale for, 4-5, 17,99-101
Self-consciousness
   components of, 100
   Japanese-American comparison, 101-120
   confirmatory analysis use in, 104-105,106-108,117
Self-consciousness scale, 4-5, 17,99-101
Self-esteem, 98

Self-image, 171-172
Self-schemas, 98
Serbs, 146-147
Shopping malls, 27,29-30,32
Slovaks, 146-147
Soap operas, 26,28
Social anxiety, 100
Social factors
    in consumer behavior, 13-14,
        15,20
    in consumer decision process,
        44,45
    in information technology
        acceptance, 130,
        135-136,138
Spain
    advertising in, 58,59
    consumer expenditures, 47
    consumers' lifestyles, 53
    consumption per capita, 49
    grocery shops, 57
    personal value survey, 51,52
Standardization, customization
    versus, 40-41
Superstructure, cultural, 12
Swastika, 195
Symbols, universal. *See* Right-left
    symbolism

Taylorism, 33
Telecommunications, deregulation
    of, 126
Telephone-based technologies,
    consumer attitudes toward,
    German-U.S. comparison of,
    128-129,134,135,137, 139
Television
    advertising on, 58,59,61
        sexually-explicit, 222,224
    cable, 128,129
    ownership patterns of,
        German-U.S. comparison,
        128,129
    satellite, 61,126
    viewing patterns, German-U.S.
        comparison of, 128,129
Television-based technologies,
    consumer attitudes towards,
    German-U.S. comparison
    of, 128,135,137
Television characters, effect on
    social construct of reality,
    26-27
Television programs, American,
    foreign perceptions of, 28
Thailand, customer complaining
    behavior in, 71-72
Theme parks, hyperreality of,
    29,30,32
*Throne of the Third Heaven of the*
    *Nations' Millennium*
    *General Assembly*
    (sculpture), 203
Tokyo, Disneyland in, 26,28
Tourism, value measures for, 170
Trademark agencies, 60
Transnational consumer goods and
    services corporations, as
    change agents, 2,25
Trinidad, American television
    programs in, 26,28
Turkey, consumer complaining
    behavior in, 71

Uncle Scrooge (cartoon chracter), 26
United Kingdom
    advertising in, 58,59
    consumer complaining behavior, 71
    consumer expenditures, 47
    consumers' lifestyles, 53
    consumption patterns, 47,48,49
    grocery shops, 57
    personal value survey, 51,52
United States
    cultural differences within, 56
    innovations diffusion rate in, 71
Urban areas, individualist nature of, 79

Values, 6,18,169-185
  characteristics of, 149
  in consumer decision process, 44,45,46,48,51,52
  consumer prioritization of, 6, 170-171,172-184
    of deficit values, 177,178
    product involvement correlation in, 173-174, 175,178-181,182,183
    of "real" versus "ideal" values, 175, 176-181, 182-183
    of surplus values, 177,178
  cultural context of, 146
  cultural learning effects on, 150
  definition of, 148,170,171
  measurement scales for, 148,149,172-173,174
  personal learning effects on, 150
  regional differences in, 56
  relationship to consumer demographics, 5-6, 18,146-164
    age factors in, 155, 159-160,162-163
    educational factors in, 156, 159,160-161,162-163
    income level factors in, 156-157,159,160,161, 162-163
    instrumental values, 155,156, 157,159,160,161,163,164
    terminal values, 155,156,157, 159-160,161,163
    urban versus rural differences in, 164
  social learning effects on, 150
  verbalization of, 170-171
VAT (value-added tax), 60
VCRs, German-U.S. ownership pattern comparison, 128,129,130
Venezuela, consumer complaining behavior in, 71-72

Victoria's Secret, 213
*Vogue*, sexually-explicit advertising in, 19,215-216,219, 220,222-223,224,226n.

*Webster's New World Dictionary*, 189,207
West Germany. *See* Germany
Women, as sexual objects, in advertising, 8,213-214, 222,225
"Young and the Restless, The" (television program), 26
Yugoslovia, national religion of, 147

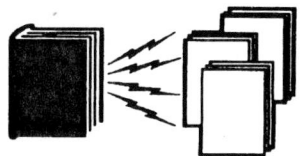

# Haworth
# DOCUMENT DELIVERY SERVICE

This valuable service provides a single-article order form for any article from a Haworth journal.

- *Time Saving:* No running around from library to library to find a specific article.
- *Cost Effective:* All costs are kept down to a minimum.
- *Fast Delivery:* Choose from several options, including same-day FAX.
- *No Copyright Hassles:* You will be supplied by the original publisher.
- *Easy Payment:* Choose from several easy payment methods.

---

*Open Accounts Welcome for . . .*
- Library Interlibrary Loan Departments
- Library Network/Consortia Wishing to Provide Single-Article Services
- Indexing/Abstracting Services with Single Article Provision Services
- Document Provision Brokers and Freelance Information Service Providers

---

**MAIL or *FAX* THIS ENTIRE ORDER FORM TO:**

Haworth Document Delivery Service
The Haworth Press, Inc.
10 Alice Street
Binghamton, NY 13904-1580

**or FAX:** 1-800-895-0582
**or CALL:** 1-800-342-9678
9am-5pm EST

---

PLEASE SEND ME PHOTOCOPIES OF THE FOLLOWING SINGLE ARTICLES:
1) Journal Title: _____
   Vol/Issue/Year: _____ Starting & Ending Pages: _____
   Article Title: _____

2) Journal Title: _____
   Vol/Issue/Year: _____ Starting & Ending Pages: _____
   Article Title: _____

3) Journal Title: _____
   Vol/Issue/Year: _____ Starting & Ending Pages: _____
   Article Title: _____

4) Journal Title: _____
   Vol/Issue/Year: _____ Starting & Ending Pages: _____
   Article Title: _____

(See other side for Costs and Payment Information)

**COSTS:** Please figure your cost to order quality copies of an article.
1. Set-up charge per article: $8.00
   ($8.00 × number of separate articles) _____
2. Photocopying charge for each article:
   1-10 pages: $1.00 _____

   11-19 pages: $3.00 _____

   20-29 pages: $5.00 _____

   30+ pages: $2.00/10 pages _____
3. Flexicover (optional): $2.00/article _____
4. Postage & Handling: US: $1.00 for the first article/
   $.50 each additional article _____

   Federal Express: $25.00 _____

   Outside US: $2.00 for first article/
   $.50 each additional article _____
5. Same-day FAX service: $.35 per page _____

                          **GRAND TOTAL:** _____

---

**METHOD OF PAYMENT:** (please check one)
❏ Check enclosed   ❏ Please ship and bill. PO # _____
            (sorry we can ship and bill to bookstores only! All others must pre-pay)
❏ Charge to my credit card:   ❏ Visa;   ❏ MasterCard;   ❏ Discover;
                              ❏ American Express;

Account Number: _____  Expiration date: _____

Signature: **X**_____

Name: _____  Institution: _____

Address: _____

_____

City: _____  State: _____  Zip: _____

Phone Number: _____  FAX Number: _____

---

**MAIL or *FAX* THIS ENTIRE ORDER FORM TO:**

| Haworth Document Delivery Service | **or FAX:** 1-800-895-0582 |
| The Haworth Press, Inc. | **or CALL:** 1-800-342-9678 |
| 10 Alice Street | 9am-5pm EST |
| Binghamton, NY 13904-1580 | |